The South Asian Military Law Systems

The South Asian Military Law Systems

Wing Commander
(Dr) **U C Jha** (Retd)

KNOWLEDGE WORLD
KW Publishers Pvt Ltd
New Delhi

KNOWLEDGE WORLD
KW Publishers Pvt Ltd
NEW DELHI: 4676/21, First Floor, Ansari Road, Daryaganj, New Delhi 110002
Email: mail@kwpub.in/knowledgeworld@vsnl.net Tel.: +91.11.23263498 / 43528107
MUMBAI: 15 Jay Kay Industrial Estate, Linking Road Extn., Santacruz (W), Mumbai 400054
email: mumbai@kwpub.in Tel.: +91.22.26614110 / 26613505

www.kwpub.in

ISBN 978-93-80502-43-4

Published by Kalpana Shukla, KW Publishers Pvt Ltd
4676/21, First Floor, Ansari Road, Daryaganj, New Delhi 110002

Printed at Aegean Offset Press, NOIDA

To My Parents

Ganga Dhar Jha
Kanti Devi

Contents

Preface

The armed forces play an important role in nation-building and national security. They may assist the civil power, but their principal object is to fight and win wars. It is for this reason that disciplinary procedures to support the command authority in war have been an enduring and universally recognised requirement for military forces. In South Asia, since the inception of armed forces, military personnel have always been subject to a strict disciplinary code. These countries, which were subject to British rule for a large chunk of their history, adopted the military laws made for mercenaries by the colonial masters after becoming independent. These laws were harsh and largely based on the whims of the British commander rather than on prescribed laws.

Morgenthau H.J. (1973), in *Politics among Nations* has rightly stated the domestic role of the military in the nation-building and foreign policy process: "What gives the factor of geography, natural resources, and industrial capacity their actual importance for the power of a nation is military preparedness……it requires a military establishment capable of supporting the foreign policies pursued. Such ability derives from a number of factors of which the most significant are…..technological innovations, leadership, and the quantity and quality of the armed forces".

The armed forces in the South Asia, in the last 60-years or so, have performed a variety of functions. While the military in India has remained apolitical, in Pakistan and Bangladesh it has played a major role in the governance of the state. In Sri Lanka the armed forces have been involved in internal security tasks for the last 25 years, while in democratic Nepal the role and governance of the army is yet to be defined. The armed forces in all these countries have been modernised, and have been playing a major role in the United Nations Peacekeeping Missions, but their legal system remains largely unchanged. One reason could be the insulation of the armed forces from the rest of society. It has prevented the civil society from acknowledging the basic rights of military personnel. Another reason is the reluctance on the part of the military hierarchy to bring about any change. Thus there is a need for a more authentic projection of the military, its traditions and style of working. There is also a need to redefine the rights and duties of military personnel, since the military can no longer be looked upon as an instrument of colonial power.

The establishment of the rule of law[1] is a basic prerequisite for the governance of any organisation, be it military, civil or judicial. This presupposes the existence of a set of rules drawn up in advance to govern the powers of institutions and the government. In the absence of such rules, arbitrariness prevails, and there is widespread violation of human rights. The rule of law is the basis for any liberal political system, which is characterised by a system of checks and balances and which recognises individual rights protected by an independent judiciary.

The rule of law must apply to institutions, all organs of society and every citizen. The primary meaning of the rule of law is that the ruler and the ruled must be subject to law and no one is above the law and hence, everyone is accountable under the law. The modern concept of the rule of law is fairly wide and serves as an ideal for any government. This concept was developed by the International Commission of Jurists during the Delhi Declaration, 1959: "The rule of law implies that the functions of the government in a free society should be so exercised as to create conditions in which the dignity of man as an individual is upheld. This dignity requires not only the recognition of certain civil or political rights but also the creation of certain political, social, economical, educational and cultural conditions which are essential to the full development of his personality".

Human rights and the rule of law are linked historically and functionally. Both concepts emerged, albeit at different times, as a response to the threat of the State's abuse of power, in order to defend the citizen's rights and security. As for the functional interdependence of the two, the fundamental human rights encoded in international covenants, such as the International Covenant on Civil and Political Rights (ICCPR), can be protected only if institutions based upon the rule of law function effectively. For example, to guarantee the rights to life and to freedom from arbitrary arrest, degrading punishment and torture, a State requires an independent judiciary, a disciplined police force and an efficient prison system. The procedural requirements encoded in the ICCPR, like the right to a fair trial, the presumption of innocence and the non-applicability of retroactive laws, echo the principles of legality and can be fulfilled only in a rule-of-law regime. In the South Asian countries, an outdated and obscure conception of military discipline that is antagonistic to the rule of law and to human rights persists because the society, including the judiciary, the executive and political leaders, prefers to remain un-informed.

1. There are seven principal meanings of the term rule of law: (1) law and order; (2) fixed rules; (3) elimination of discretion; (4) due process of law or fairness; (5) natural law or observance of the principles of natural justice; (6) preference for judges and ordinary courts of law to executive authorities and administrative tribunals; and (7) judicial review of administrative actions.

This book discusses the military legal systems of five South Asian countries: Bangladesh, India, Nepal, Pakistan and Sri Lanka. Though the military Acts of India, Sri Lanka and Bangladesh are available on the Internet, subordinate legislations and the jurisprudence of these countries are difficult to trace. The Army Act of Nepal is available in Nepalese and it is possible that a few errors might have been introduced in translation. In the case of Pakistan, the Internet has been the main source of information. The difficulty in gaining access to such information brings one to the conclusion that all too often the regulations that make it possible to invoke the confidentiality of military information are diverted from their original purpose and used to impede the course of justice. Confidentiality is certainly justifiable when it is necessary to protect information that may be of interest to foreign intelligence services. It should, however, be dispensed with where measures involving the deprivation of liberty are concerned; under no circumstances should such measures be kept secret.

This study does not try to examine all the aspects of the military law systems of the South Asian countries, but focuses on the practices and procedures followed in military courts to try members of the military or civilians. The term 'military law' is also applied to 'administrative' matters such as removal, discharge, censure, redress of grievance, pay and pensions, health and safety, accommodation and so on. Some of these provisions are statutory but others are purely administrative in nature.

The book has been divided into 11 chapters. Chapter I is introductory and discusses the constitutional position of the armed forces in the South Asian countries. Chapter II covers the militaries in South Asia and the introductory aspects of their legal systems. The provisions of arrest and award of minor punishments has been covered in Chapter III, whereas Chapter IV deals with military offences and prescribed punishments under the military law system. Chapter V covers the kinds of tribunals, their powers and jurisdictions, and the role of various court functionaries. A comparison with the military justice systems followed in the USA, Israel, China, Russia, Canada and South Africa has also been undertaken. The next chapter is devoted to the process of confirmation and revision of punishment awarded by military tribunals and the system of appeals available to a military accused who has been tried by a military tribunal. Chapter VII discusses the right to a fair trial, and the extent to which it is afforded to a military accused in the South Asian countries. The armed forces in the South Asian countries have been employed on a regular basis in internal security duties. Chapter VIII contains a critical analysis of the legal system under which the armed forces operate while deployed in internal conflicts. The international human rights law has grown in the last five decades and the South Asian countries have signed and ratified a large number of international treaties. Chapter IX discusses the impact of international human rights laws on the armed forces in the South Asian countries. Chapter X covers the implementation of the IHL treaties in these countries. The last chapter makes certain recommendations that require to be implemented in the South Asian countries.

This book is the result of the research done for a fellowship awarded by the Centre for the Study of Law and Governance, Jawaharlal Nehru University, New Delhi in 2008-09. I am grateful to my guide Professor Niraja Gopal Jayal for her valuable suggestions. I would like to thank Ms Medha and Ms Chandana for editorial assistance, and my wife Ratna and son Aditya for letting me work in peace.

U C Jha

1
Introduction

The South Asian region[1] is one of the most dynamic regions of the world. It cradled a civilization that predated those of Egypt and Europe and has provided ground for intermixing of races, cultures and religions down the ages. Conventionally, it has been understood to include India, Pakistan, Bangladesh, Sri Lanka, Nepal, Bhutan and the Maldives. Though the South Asian Association for Regional Cooperation (SAARC), the only significant international institution of the region, binds these States loosely, they are bound intimately by the ties of a shared past.

Nearly population: 1.55 billion people inhabit India, Pakistan, Bangladesh, Sri Lanka and Nepal. Every independent nation in this area has internal and external feuds that often erupt into border conflicts and sometimes even into declared wars. Portuguese, Spanish, and British imperialist holdings controlled large areas of these countries from about 1750 until 1945, after which independence rushed into this area. Yet, many vestiges of Western rule remained however. All these nations have constitutions and some form of elected representation.[2]

India is the largest country of this region with an estimated population of 1173 million.[3] It has a democratic form of government ever since it gained independence from Britain in 1947. Pakistan has a population of around 177 million.[4] It borders India, China, the former Soviet Union, Afghanistan, and Iran. It was created out of the Muslim-majority parts of British India in 1947, and is an Islamic republic with universal adult suffrage. Initially, there were two parts of Pakistan, East and West, separated by about 1000 miles of Indian territory. In 1971, East Pakistan became Bangladesh as a result of an ethnic revolt supported by the Indian Army. Bangladesh, with a population of 158 million,[5] has a democratic government, though as in Pakistan, the military remains the most important element in the society.

Sri Lanka is an island off the southwestern coast of India. It has a population of about 21.5 million.[6] It was formerly called Ceylon, and got independence form the British in 1948. It has been strongly democratic and has had internal trouble with ethnic Tamils, who constituted about 25 per cent of the population. Nepal has common frontiers with the China and India and has a population of about 28.9 million.[7] Its constitutional monarchy system of government was replaced by the democratic system in 2006, after Maoist insurgents staged a war against the government. Bhutan is landlocked nation in the Himalayan Mountains, with its capital at Thimphu. It has an area of 47,000 square kilometers. Bhutan entered a new era of democracy starting, with its first elections in 2008. The Republic of Maldives is an island nation consisting of a group of atolls in the Indian Ocean. The Maldives' 26 atolls encompass a territory featuring 1,192 islets, roughly two hundred of which are inhabited by local communities. The Maldives is the smallest Asian country in terms of population. All the South Asian countries have volunteer armed forces.

Armed Forces: Constitutional Positions

The supremacy of the Constitution is well recognised in a democracy. The Constitution is the basic law and the founding document of both the State, and its system of government. In countries with a written constitution, the document is normally regarded as the source of all power assumed by the State, and since it is the source of that power it also defines and limits it (Oliver, 2003: 5).[8] In a democratic set-up the Constitution derives the powers related to the armed forces between the executives and the legislatures, and the sole function of the armed forces is to fight and win wars (Finer, 1962:7).[9] In all the five South Asian countries, a written constitution provides the basis for the legitimacy of state institutions, and the armed forces are a key state institution, one that protects citizens, territorial integrity, the system of government, and essential services. The constitutions guarantee that every person (limited to citizens in some cases) shall be entitled to certain fundamental rights without any discrimination. These rights are enforceable in a court of law.

Aristotle in his *Politics* has regarded the warrior class as an essential element of the State. He says: "They [the warrior class] are as necessary as any of the others, if the country is not to be the slave of every invader. The State depends for its existence as an independent entity upon its ability both to preserve order within its territories and to protect its citizens against external attack." Kautilya in his *Arthashastra*, has laid a great emphasis on the King's duty towards the armed forces.

Today, the defence machinery of a State is one of the pillars of political organisation. The stability of a State is inextricably linked with the strength and weakness of the armed forces and their importance in the political structure. In the organisation of a modern State, defence is a recognised term which occurs in almost every written constitution and conveys a well-known and distinctly defined sphere of governmental function and activity. Civilian control over the armed forces is one of the basic tenets of a democratic system. The essential components of strong democratic control have two dimensions; first, the institutionalised control of the activities of the armed forces by the civilian government agencies in combination with the military hierarchy; and second, the professionalisation of armed forces. Civilian control is achieved by politicians and bureaucrats determining defence policies and approving military activities through an institutionalised defence bureaucracy. The prime reason for civilian control of the military is to allow the *de jure* authority to maintain control over the *de facto* power afforded by weaponry and military competence.

The civil-military relations in the South Asian countries have been diverse and complex. In a democratic system (like India, Nepal and Sri Lanka), a professional and apolitical military acknowledges the civilian authority and executes the orders of a democratically elected government. In a military regime (like in Pakistan till 2008), the control and loyalty of the military as an institution remained problematic. Yet another type, in the military supported democracy (like Bangladesh in 2007 and 08), there was always a fear that it may turn into a military regime. In all these countries, the expanding role of the military in the internal security has increased the friction between the civilian democracy and the military at the local levels.

Military intervention in politics has been an important feature of the developing world. In South Asia, Pakistan and Bangladesh have faced many such military interventions as a result of the inability of the elected leaders to steer the State through a politically stable path in the initial years. The decline of democratic structures, such as political parties, pressure groups, parliament, judiciary, and the executive and the virtual death of political processes like constitutionalism and political processes led to strengthening of the military as an institution. It was regarded as the only alternative, the only organised force that could walk into the political vacuum created by the repeated failure of civilian governments.

India

The Indian Army of the British Empire, which was created as a mercenary force, went through a lot of changes after the first war of independence of 1857. The changes were to do with the command and control of the armed forces. They reflected the idea of keeping the armed forces under civilian control as a constitutional principle, which was developed and perfected by Britain over a span of about three centuries. Thus, post 1857, civilian supremacy was established in every detail of military administration in India. However, Lord Kitchner, the Commander-in-Chief in 1905, raised strong objections to the prevalent system of dual command and control of the army. The reforms suggested by him gave the

Commander-in-Chief direct access to the Governor General without an intervening Member of Council.

In 1946, the Commander-in-Chief in India was the administrative and executive head of the Royal Indian Navy, the Army and the Air Force in India Command. As War Member he was the defence advisor of the Governor General. The War Department had a secretary to the Government of India, perhaps an equivalent to the present-day defence secretary. His constitutional right was limited to access to the Governor General and to the right to call any paper on the subject assigned to his department.

After independence, the Navy and the Air Force were given independent status equal to the Army. The ostensible reason for this division was to foster a 'balanced' growth among the three services. The unofficial reason was to reduce the risk of challenge to civilian authority from a numerically dominant army. The Ministry of Defence was created under the charge of a cabinet minister, and each service was placed under its own Commander-in-Chief. In 1955, the Commanders-in-Chief were renamed the Chief of the Army Staff, the Chief of the Naval Staff and the Chief of the Air Staff. [10] The supreme command of the defence forces of the Union came to be vested in the President and the principle of parliamentary control over the armed forces was firmly established.[11] The three service chiefs are responsible to the Defence Minister, and are collectively the professional military advisors to the government.[12]

The Constitution of India defines the term 'defence' in the Union Legislative List in the following words: "Defence of India and every part thereof including preparation for defence and all such acts as may be conclusive in times of war to its prosecution and after its termination to effective demobilisation" and places this wide and important sphere of activity within the exclusive competence of the Union Parliament. The Constitution in Article 355 prescribes that "It shall be the duty of the Union to protect every State against external aggression and internal disturbance." This important function is performed by the President of India with the assistance of the defence forces of which he is the 'supreme commander' in accordance with Article 53 (2) of the Constitution.

In classical theory of military professionalism, Samuel Huntington argues that a professional military is "politically sterile and neutral"—concentrating on military strategic matters and leaving political decisions (affairs of governance) to civilian authorities. He also holds "Autonomy leads to professionalism, which leads to political neutrality and voluntary subordination, which leads to secure civilian control."[13] This allows the desirable condition of "civilian control" over the armed forces.[14] The Indian armed forces have always upheld the principle of civilian supremacy,[15] which has been achieved by the following devices:

- The President is the supreme commander of the defence forces and has to act on the advice of the Council of Ministers.
- The responsibility for national defence rests with the Cabinet, headed by the Prime Minister.
- The Parliament controls not only the Prime Minister, but also exercises financial control. It votes money from year to year thereby sanctioning the maintenance of the armed forces.
- The Chiefs of the Staff Committee (headed by one of the service chiefs in rotation), implements the orders of the government during the peace and war.
- The Parliamentary Committee of Defence, consisting of about 30 members across the party line, is empowered to examine various issues affecting the armed forces independently and submit reports to the Parliament. The Ministry of Defence is, however, not bound by the recommendations of the committee.

This makes the Indian armed forces unique among the militaries in the developing world. They have never launched a military coup, for example, or ever attempted to usurp civilian power---even when their relative pay, power and influence in civil society declined sharply after independence in 1947 or when faulty politico-strategic decisions and political interference in the conduct of military affairs led to major military setbacks.[16] The armed forces have remained neutral for the 63 years of the country's independence. During the period of political failures in Punjab, Jammu and Kashmir and the North-East, the armed forces have helped the government in fighting insurgency, but remained apolitical. Even frequent calls to aid civil authorities in maintaining law and order and coping with natural calamities have not distracted them from their primary professional responsibility.[17]

Pakistan

For most of its existence, Pakistan has been under direct military rule or governments dominated by the military. Pakistani military leaders claim that their primary mission is combat, or the external defence of the state, but the military's perception of professionalism also includes internal missions and roles.[18] Although the norms of military subordination to civil authorities are formally embodied in the constitution framed in 1973, Pakistan's military leaders have chosen to ignore these constitutional curbs on their functioning. Indeed, successive military rulers have claimed constitutional authority for their political roles and missions.[19] Since the armed forces have emerged as the only organised and disciplinary entity in the state and thus the sole guarantor of Pakistan's survival, the military justifies its internal role on the grounds of the threat posed to the Pakistani's security and stability by inept civilian governments. The Pakistan armed forces have also tried to maintain an Islamic identity since the beginning.[20] With each successive intervention, the Pakistani armed forces have assumed new non-militay missions, with all their attendant political and economic benefits.

Pakistan's constitutional history had begun before it was a state. A Constituent Assembly met on 11 August 1947, before Pakistan came into being, and served as the federal parliament of Pakistan while it framed the new constitution. Jinnah was elected the first President of the assembly and became Pakistan's governor-general (the title for head of a state that replaced the position of viceroy), snubbing Britain's Lord Mountbatten, who had wanted to be governor-general of both new countries—India and Pakistan.[21]

Pakistan's Constitution provides that the Federal Government shall have control and command of the armed forces and that the control of the armed forces shall remain with the President, who is entrusted with the power to raise and maintain the military, naval and air forces of Pakistan, and the reserves of such forces; and to grant commissions in such forces. The President in consultation with the Prime Minister appoints the Chairman of the Joint Chiefs of Staff Committee and chiefs of the Army, Navy and Air Force.[22] Under Article 244 of the Constitution, every member of the armed forces is required to take oath to uphold the Constitution and refrain from engaging in any political activity whatsoever.[23]

In theory there is no confusion regarding the functions of the armed forces, as contained in Article 245 of the 1973 Constitution: "The armed forces under the directions of the Federal Government are to defend Pakistan against external aggression or threat of war, and also act in aid of civil power when called upon to do so. The validity of the direction of the Federal Government cannot be questioned in any court. The high courts are excluded from the jurisdiction under Article 199 in relation to an area in which the armed forces act in aid of civil power." However, the military has directly ruled the country for more than half of its 62 years of independent existence.

Even during the periods of democratic rule, the Pakistani armed forces have refused to accept the authority of civilian institutions and organisations such as parliament and defence ministries. According to Samina (2001; 154-55), in the military's perception, it alone is professionally equipped to formulate and implement institutional policy on a whole range of issues. These include strategic planning, force structure, budget, armes procurement, recruitment, promotions and postings, military training, and professional education. Civilians, it claims, are not professionally competent to understand the requirements of military doctrine, force posture, or training, and civilian intervention in issues such as promotions adversely affect the military's internal cohesion, undermining its professional competence as a combat force.

Any civilian threat to the military's internal autonomy has been dealt with swiftly. After the restoration of democracy in 1988, for instance, military chiefs removed three elected governments and finally conducted a coup in 1999 since successive prime ministers were percieved as threats to the military's institutional interests. The military's actions have been justified on the grounds of national security—including the threat posed by the civilian leadership to the cohesion of the militaty institutions.[24] In his first address after the October 1999 coup, Army Chief General Pervez Musharraf accused the Nawaz Sharif government of attempting to "interfere with the armed forces—the last remaining valuable institution" and to "policitise the army, destabilise it, and to create dissension within its rank." [25] Repeated military interventions have denied the civilian leadership any exposure to defence issues, thus reinforcing the military's charge that civilians lack the professional competence to deal with national security affairs. When questioned about his regime's inability to meet its stated targets at the end of its first year, General Musharraf, claimed: "The malaise is so profound, the cancer is so deep-rooted, that all areas of governance, all areas of economy, all institutions need to be addressed.....I have an agenda and my agenda is Pakistan. I would like to fulfil that agenda."[26]

In Pakistan, "Only a stable civil government enjoying popular support and legitimacy can restrain the military in its professional domain and deal with it from a position of strength."[27] This is, perhaps, becoming less and less likely as the vicious circle becomes stronger and as the militay sinks deeper roots into civilian institutions and the economy.[28] Pakistan is likely to remain a state in the possession of uniformed bureaucracy even when civilian governments are perched. Regardless of what may be desirable, the army will continue to set the limits on what is possible in Pakistan. Stephen P. Cohen (2004) has succinctly defined the Pakistan Army's multi-dimensional role: "There are armies that guard their nation's borders, there are those that are concerned with protecting their own position in society, and there are those that defend a cause or an idea. The Pakistan Army does all three." [29] The army lacks the capability to fix Pakistan's problems, but it is unwilling to give other state institutions and the political system the opportunity to learn and grow, its tolerance for the mistakes of others is very low, yet its own performance, when in power, has usually dug the hole deeper. According to Mahmud (2000), Pakistan is a victim of ... "an army conquering its own country".[30]

The Pakistan army's relationship with the political process, according to Cohen (2004; 124), can be characterised as a five-step dance. First, the army warns what it regards as incompetent or foolish civilians. Second, a crisis leads to army's intervention, which is followed by the third step: attempt to "straighten out" Pakistan often by introducing major constitutional changes. Fourth, the army, faced with growing civilian discontent, "allows" civilians back into office, and fifth, the army reasserts itself behind a façade of civilian government, and the cycle repeats itself.[31]

Currently, Pakistan is passing through a major judicial crisis. Its judiciary, lawyer community and civil society are together asserting the need to establish the rule of law instead of rule of power.[32] The Supreme Court of Pakistan on 16 December 2009, declared the National Reconciliation Ordinance (NRO) null and void and ordered that criminal and civil cases withdrawn under this controversial law be restored and proceedings reinstituted against the accused. The NRO was decreed by the former President General Pervez Musharraf in 2007, giving immunity to the present President Zardari and several other important political personalities.[33]

In Pakistan, the 18th Constitutional Amendment has initiated a reversal of the mangling of the original 1973 constitution by military dictators Zia ul Haq and Pervez Musharraf. Besides repealing of 17th amendment by which the former President Musharraf had transferred decisive powers to the presidency, it has done away with the Concurrent List to give more provincial autonomy. An important part of reforms is the amendment to Article 6 that will now explicitly see any attempt to abrogate, subvert, suspend or hold in abeyance the Constitution, an act of high treason. For a nation which has witnessed number of military coups, the importance of this amendment cannot be understated. In Pakistan three new fundamental rights have been introduced: The Right to Fair Trial (Article 10A), the Right to Information (Article 19A), and the Right to (free and compulsory) Education for all children in the five-to-16 age-group (Article 25A). The North-West Frontier Province (NWPF) has been rechristened Khyber-Pukhtoonkhwa to confirm recognition of the Pathan identity in the region.[34] The Amendment has also put in place institutional mechanisms for making key appointments. The newly created judicial commission will have seven members with the judiciary having higher representation and the chair. Decisions made by this commission will be sent to the eight-member Parliamentary committee that will oversee all crucial appointments. The 18th Amendment to the Pakistani Constitution will make future army takeovers more difficult by delegitimising the doctrine of necessity. It is only time which would tell us whether the institutions in Pakistan have become stronger or the Army still owns the state.

Bangladesh

Europeans began to set up trading posts in the area of Bangladesh in the 16th century. Eventually the British came to dominate the region, which became part of British India. In 1947, West Pakistan and East Bengal (both Muslim-dominated) separated from India and jointly became the new country of Pakistan. East Bengal became East Pakistan in 1955, but the awkward arrangement of a two-part country with its territorial units separated by 1000 miles left the Bengalis marginalised and dissatisfied. East Pakistan seceded from its union with West Pakistan in 1971, and was renamed Bangladesh.

Sheikh Mujibur Rahman returned to a newly independent Bangladesh from a Pakistani jail on January 10, 1972 to assume leadership of the provisional government. He entered office with overwhelming public sympathy and support for the role he had played in helping Bangladesh gain independence. Two days after his return, Mujib relinquished the office of President to become Prime Minister. Under the new constitution, adopted in November 1972, the President appointed the Prime Minister, but only with the approval of the parliament. Basic civil and political rights were guaranteed by the constitution.[35]

At the end of the war of freedom, the army was split between two hostile groups, "freedom fighters" and "repatriates". Freedom fighters had fought with the separatist armed forces against West Pakistanis, while repatriates had been interned in Pakistan. The ranks of the freedom fighters were also split between those who had not served in the pre-war professional army and those who had deserted the Pakistan Army to join the separatist force. Mujib favoured the former over the latter in promotions and plum postings. He distrusted and discriminated against the repatriates in the matters of promotions and postings.[36]

As the Mujib government came under increasing political and economic pressure, he declared emergency in December 1974, citing the national security powers of Article 2 of the Constitution. It abridged civil rights and drastically curtailed the judiciary's authority to check and review executive actions. It gave him the power to order arrests, reduce the independence of the judiciary, and limit the freedom of the press. In January 1975, Mujib used his leverage and influence with his party to amend the constitution and further increase his personal power. The amendment created a presidential system and made him President for five years. It gave him full executive power and authorised the formation of a single party to which all government employees were required to belong. Other parties were banned. The courts were enjoined to quit enforcing the fundamental rights enumerated in the constitution. Bangladesh had been transformed from a democracy into a personal dictatorship by the man who led its independence movement. On August 15, 1975, a group of middle-level army officers, mostly majors, assassinated Mujib and killed several members of his family, including his wife and young son.[37]

The assassination was followed by severe instability and brought a second military coup less than three months later, on November 3, 1975, by a radical faction of the Army. A third coup, by the traditional, professional core of the Army, came four days later. The professional army restored stability and selected former Chief Justice Abu Sadat Muhammed Sayem as President and as concurrent Chief Martial Law Administrator (CMLA). Sayem appointed General Ziaur Rahman as deputy martial law administrator. Zia reversed Mujib's policy and utilised talented civil servants and others, irrespective of their past loyalties. This improved the efficiency of the senior administration. Zia used his power as CMLA to issue a series of proclamations which modified the constitution and changed the course taken by Bangladesh. Zia's take over in April 1977 after Sayem resigned citing health reasons was a reflection of his power over the military and his immense popularity with the public. He called for a referendum on whether he should continue in office.[38] He also survived an unsuccessful coup in 1977.[39]

Zia won the next presidential elections held in June 1978, and became the legitimate freely elected President of Bangladesh. In order to further civilianise the government, Zia resigned as Chief of the Army Staff. He also pledged to withdraw martial law after the elections and make the new parliament sovereign. The opposition, however, demanded that martial law be rescinded before the elections. The elections for the new parliament were finally held in February 1979. A fully democratic structure was restored when Zia proposed and his Parliament passed the fifth amendment to the constitution, which removed all martial law actions. Martial law was abolished in April 1979, three-and-half years after it had been introduced. Zia'a era ended in May 1981, as it had started, in blood.[40]

Under the Bangladesh Constitution of 1972, the President is the commander-in-chief of the armed forces. Parliament is constitutionally responsible for working with the President and the service chiefs in ensuring the nation's defence. In practice, however, members of Parliament have never played a significant role in the defence planning or budgeting. The services are divided into the army, navy, and air force. In theory, the three service chiefs are coequals in the national command structure; in practice, the army dominates the defence establishment because of its imposing size and its historic role in monitoring or commandeering the political process.

Following the British pattern, the ministry of defence is technically responsible for overseeing the military. Though the ministry's bureaucracy is predominantly civilian, the military exerts substantial influence over its operations. After seizing power in March 1982, President Ershad followed the practice of his military predecessors by reserving the minister of defence portfolio for himself. Through the appointment of military retirees and serving officers to the ministry of defence, the military indirectly controls the ministry.

Historically, command-and-control arrangements at the national level have been dominated by the army chief of staff. In the past, coup leaders such as General Zia and General Ershad consolidated control over the country by assuming the powers of the army chief of staff, the president, and the extra-constitutional position of chief martial law administrator. During periods of direct military rule, the navy and air force chiefs of staff served as deputy chief martial law administrators, subordinate to the chief of the army staff. Bangladesh has had two lengthy military-led governments in its 38 years of independence, but the army has stayed out of politics since the end of General Ershad's government in 1990.

Like the Pakistan Army, the Bangladesh Army also perceives itself as the only force holding Bangladesh together. It has a poor opinion of the country's fractious polity and its competence in governance. In its perceived mission of holding the country together and putting an end to misgovernance, the army has carried out military coups, counter-coups and even assassinations of military presidents. The army continues to hold the opinion that it should have a constitutional role and larger say in the country's foreign policy.[41]

Nepal

Nepal has existed as a kingdom in the Kathmandu Valley for more than 1,500 years. Modern Nepal began its evolution with the founding of the House of Gorkha by Dravya Shah in 1559. In the early nineteenth century, Gorkha power came into conflict with the British East India Company. The resulting Anglo-Nepalese War (1814-16) was devastating for Nepal. The Treaty of Sugauli reduced the kingdom to the boundaries it has since occupied, less than 900 kilometers from east to west.

The next stage of Nepalese politics was the period of hereditary Rana rule or the dictatorship of successive Rana prime ministers beginning with Jang Bahadur Kunwar in 1846. The Nepal Army was utilised by the British in the suppression of the 1857 mutiny. It killed about 5,000 mutineers and helped to capture more than 500. In return, an agreement was signed between the British and Nepal governments whereby the plain between the Mahakali and Rapti rivers, which Nepal had lost in the 1816 Sugauli Treaty, were returned by the British.[42]

During the period of Rana rule, which lasted until the end of 1950, Nepal was governed by a landed aristocracy; parliamentary government existed only in name. This period was characterised by stability, but political and economic development were inhibited because the Ranas isolated the country and exercised total control over internal affairs. Although during this period, Nepal was a constitutional monarchy with universal suffrage for those of 18 years of age and above, political parties were not formed until the mid-twentieth century and were later banned.

In 1951, the Nepalese monarch ended the century-old system of rule by hereditary premiers and instituted a cabinet system of government. Reforms in 1990 established a multi-party democracy within the framework of a constitutional monarchy. An insurgency led by Maoist extremists broke out in 1996. The ensuing ten-year civil war between insurgents and government forces led to the dissolution of the cabinet and parliament, and the assumption of absolute power by the king. Several weeks of mass protests in April 2006 were followed by several months of peace negotiations between the Maoists and government officials. These culminated in a peace accord in November 2006 and the promulgation of an interim constitution.

Following a nationwide election in April 2008, the newly formed Constituent Assembly declared Nepal a federal democratic republic and abolished the monarchy at its first meeting the following month. The Constituent Assembly elected the country's first president in July 2008 and the interim constitution was adopted on 15 January 2007. The Maoists, who received a plurality of votes in the Constituent Assembly election, formed a coalition government in August 2008. In April 2008, a Constituent Assembly was elected to draft and promulgate a new constitution by May 2010, extended further till May 2011. Maoist chairman Pushpa Kamal Dahal "Prachanda" had assumed the charge of Prime Minister in a coalition government. The Prime Minister took a unilateral decision to sack the Chief of the Army Staff,[43] but the President reversed the decision[44] and consequently the Prime Minister resigned.

During the time of constitutional monarchy in Nepal, though the monarch wore the military uniform and ranks, he was not a trained soldier. The palace had an institution called the Principal Military Secretariat, through which the security forces were managed. The Ministry of Defence was very small and managed by non-professionals. Invariably, the Prime Minister himself headed it. After the 'janandolan' or people's movement of 1989, the National Security Council (NSC) was introduced. The president of this body was the Prime Minister and its members were the defence, home and finance ministers. The army, armed police, Nepal police and national investigation department officials filled the NSC secretariat.[45]

The Interim Constitution of Nepal describes the management of the Nepal Army. Article 144.1 states: "There shall be a 'Nepal Army' in Nepal as an institution." The Commander-in-Chief of the Army shall be appointed by the Council of Ministers.[46] The Council of Ministers, in accordance with the law, shall control, mobilise and manage the Nepal Army. The Council of Ministers shall, with the consent of the political parties and by seeking the advice of the concerned committee of Parliament, formulate an extensive work plan for the democratisation of the army and implement it.[47] While formulating and implementing the action plan, and determining the strength of the Nepal Army, its democratic structure and national and inclusive character shall be developed. Training shall be imparted to the army in accordance with the norms and values of democracy and human rights.[48]

Nepal is changing from a kingdom to a republic.[49] The traditional relations of the Army with the monarch have to be replaced with a new relationship with the elected and legitimate people's representative. The constitution has clearly spelt out that the Nepal Army has to be inclusive and democratic. This implies the exercise of civilian control over the army. The Chief of the Army Staff is appointed by the Council of Ministers and he remains accountable to Parliament through the cabinet. National security strategy and military strategy should be complementing the 'grand strategy', which is made by the civilian authorities. The Council of Ministers is responsible for the control, mobilisation and arming of the army.[50]

The integration of the People's Liberation Army (PLA), the military wing of the Communist Party of Nepal–Maoist (CPN-M), into Nepal Army (NA) was a major demand of the former rebel group before entering into agreement in November 2006. The initial government led by the Maoists accorded due importance to integration of PLA into NA and formed the Army Integration Special Committee (AISC), headed by the Prime Minister. Military integration of rebels is often cited as an effective strategy for peace-building in post-conflict situations.[51] However, despite the formation of the AISC, there is an uncertainty about the future of the peace process, mainly due to a lack of consensus over the issue.

Sri Lanka

The first Sinhalese arrived in Sri Lanka late in the 6th century B.C., probably from northern India. Buddhism was introduced in about the mid-third century B.C., and a great civilization developed in the cities of Anuradhapura (a kingdom from circa 200 B.C. to circa A.D. 1000) and Polonnaruwa (from about 1070 to 1200). In the 14th century, a south Indian dynasty established a Tamil kingdom in northern Sri Lanka.

During the colonial era, parts of Sri Lanka came under the control of three colonial European powers, namely, the Portuguese in the 16th century, the Dutch in the 17th century and the British in the 18th century. Yet, until the entire island was ceded to the British in 1815, regional kingdoms maintained most of their independent defence forces and were able to successfully repulse repeated thrusts by the European armies. However, the British, unlike their earlier counterparts, were not primarily restricted to maritime power, and thus had the capability to bring the entire island under their control and integrate the locals into the British defence forces.

In colonial Ceylon, there was no regular large armed force, except for the Ceylon Defence Force, which consisted of regulars from the British Army stationed for service in Ceylon, together with a local volunteer force that was trained and called upon for duty only when necessary. In 1915, following Sinhala-Muslim clashes and an anti-colonial agitation, martial law was declared. Prominent Sinhala leaders of the anti-British nationalist movement were court martialled and sentenced to death. These sentences were commuted to life imprisonment once martial law was revoked when the Colonial Office in London reviewed the colonial government's handling of violence.[52]

The country, still known as Ceylon, became independent in 1948; its name was changed to Sri Lanka in 1972. Emergency was clamped down in 1958 in response to Sinhala-Tamil communal violence, and this meant that the army was called upon to play a major role. Army units were mobilised and were under orders to 'shoot and shoot to kill'. This was the first time in independent Sri Lanka that military officers were gazetted as coordinating officers of the provinces, superseding the civilian government agents of the province.[53] Sri Lanka has not been governed by a military regime, though it has experienced an unsuccessful military coup in 1962.[54] It has deployed the military to maintain law and order during labour and communal unrest.[55] Tensions between the Sinhalese majority and Tamil separatists erupted into war in 1983. Tens of thousands died in the ethnic conflict. After two decades of fighting, the government and Liberation Tigers of Tamil Eelam (LTTE) formalized a cease-fire in February 2002, with Norway brokering peace negotiations.[56] Violence between the LTTE and government forces intensified in 2006 and the government regained control of the Eastern Province in 2007. In January 2008, the government officially withdrew from the cease-fire, and by May 2009, the LTTE was completely wiped out from the island. In the internal war against the LTTE, 6,261 members of the security forces died from the time of the start of military operations in August 2006, while 29,551 were injured, with 2,556 of them left disabled. It has been alleged that more than 20,000 innocent Tamil civilians were killed in the conflict.[57]

The President of the Republic is the head of the state, the head of the executive and of the government, and the Commander-in-Chief of the Armed Forces.[58] The President is empowered to appoint the heads of the Army, the Navy, the Air Force and the police force.[59] The Sri Lankan Constitution restricts the fundamental rights of armed forces personnel. Article 15 (8) of the Constitution provides: "The exercise and operation of the fundamental rights declared and recognised by Articles 12 (1), 13 and 14 shall, in their application to the members of the Armed Forces, Police Force and other Forces charged with the maintenance of public order, be subject to such restrictions as may be prescribed by law in the interests of the proper discharge of their duties and the maintenance of discipline among them."[60]

The Sri Lanka Army is the oldest and largest of the three armed services of Sri Lanka, the others being the Air Force and the Navy. The Sri Lankan Army Act was enacted by Parliament on the 10 October 1949, which is recognised as the day that the Ceylon Army was raised. The Army was to comprise a regular and a volunteer force. There were no formations and all units functioned directly under the army headquarters. Temporary field headquarters were formed at the time of a requirement, as was done during the 1958 communal riots. The first field formation was raised in 1963, to prevent illicit immigration from south India. This headquarters, known as Task Force Anti-Illicit Immigration (TFAII), was disbanded in 1981.

In May 1972, when Ceylon became the Republic of Sri Lanka, all army units were renamed accordingly. The army is responsible for overseeing land-based military and humanitarian operations. The Commander-in-Chief of the Sri Lankan armed forces is the President of the country. He provides operational direction to the Joint Operations Council and oversees other aspects of the three services through the Ministry of Defence, which is responsible for all security forces (armed forces and police). In the Sri Lankan Warrant of Precedence, the Chief of Defence Staff is placed below the Attorney General and permanent secretaries of ministries. Members of Parliament and the judges of the Supreme Court are placed above the Attorney General. The commanders of the three services, along with the Inspector General of Police, are placed just below the Chief of Defence Staff.[61]

The CDS will hold the rank of General in case of an officer of the Army, Admiral in the case of an officer of the Navy, and Air Chief Marshal in the case of an officer of the Air Force. The CDS will function to (a) assist in providing for strategic direction of the armed forces; (b) develop a doctrine for the joint employment of the armed forces; (c) facilitate the preparation of strategic plans for the armed forces; (d) co-ordinate matters in respect of the functions relating to intelligence as between the armed forces; (e) undertake assessments to determine the capabilities of the armed forces in comparison with those of their potential adversaries; (f) facilitate the preparation of operational plans for the armed forces and will co-ordinate the implementation of the same as between the armed forces; (g) prepare and review contingency plans relating to the armed forces; (h) tender advice on national security issues; and (i) facilitate the formulation of policies for the joint training and peace-keeping operations by the armed forces. The CDS will also be the chairman of the committee of the chief of defence staff which will comprise of the commanders of the Army, Navy and the Air Force.

Bhutan

The Constitution of Bhutan adopted on 18 July 2008 declares Bhutan a sovereign kingdom where the sovereign power belongs to the people of Bhutan. Article 2 of the Constitution states that the country would be governed by a democratic constitutional monarchy. The Constitution also provides that it shall be the fundamental duty of Bhutanese citizens to preserve, protect and defend the sovereignty, territorial integrity, security and unity of Bhutan and render national service when called upon to do so by Parliament.[62]

Article 28 of the Constitution, dealing with defence, makes the following provisions:

- The Druk Gyalpo shall be the Supreme Commander in Chief of the Armed Forces and the Militia.
- The Royal Body Guards shall be responsible for the security of the Druk Gyalpo while the Royal Bhutan Army shall serve as a professional standing army and both forces shall form the core of Bhutan's defence against security threats.
- The Royal Bhutan Police shall, as a trained uniform force under the Ministry of Home Affairs, be primarily responsible for maintaining law and order and prevention of crime, and shall also be considered an important part of the nation's security force.
- Parliament may, by law, require compulsory militia service for adult citizens to strengthen the defence of the country.
- The State shall be responsible for the maintenance of the Armed Forces to safeguard the security of the country and the well-being of the nation.
- Bhutan shall not use military force against a foreign State except in self-defence or for the purpose of maintaining its security, territorial integrity and sovereignty.

The Royal Bhutan Army (RBA) was organised as a regular military force in the 1950s with the encouragement of India and in response to China's takeover of Tibet. Following the establishment of a national militia in 1958, the government announced a new conscription system the same year and plans for a standing army of 2,500 troops with modern equipment. Military training was given to all able-bodied men, and by 1963, the standing army was well established. A reorganisation in 1968 led to an increase in the army to 4,850 troops and a campaign aimed at recruiting 600 additional troops per year. In late 2003, the Bhutanese army successfully launched a large-scale operation to flush out anti-India insurgents who were operating training camps in southern Bhutan. The Royal Body Guards (RBG), an elite branch of the armed forces is responsible for the security of the King and the Royal family. The RBA has about 9,000 active duty personnel at present.

Maldives

The Republic of Maldives was never under direct British rule. The Maldivian Sultan had an agreement with the Governor of Ceylon in 1887 under which the Maldives were to enjoy the status of a protected state without actually becoming a protectorate. Thus, the British only controlled external affairs and had no jurisdiction in the internal matters of the islands (although it is said that attempts to interfere in internal affairs were made at times). The Maldives obtained full independence from the United Kingdom in July 1965.

A written constitution did not exist in the Maldives till 1932. Customs and traditions along with the *Shariah* formed the law. The sultans usually consulted a group of advisors or *bodun,* including ministers and the *Fandiyaaru* or Chief Justice. Islamic scholars usually exercised much influence in government affairs but were quite often replaced when the sultans were at odds with them. The hereditary system continued, though on many occasions, power shifted from one family to another as a result of internal uprisings or following the demise of kings. A constitution was introduced in 1932, after the emergence of an educated elite. In 1948, the existing agreement between the Maldives and the British were renewed. In 1953, the Maldives changed from a monarchy to a republic, but after the failure of the First Republic, it reverted to a Sultanate until 1968.

The present legal system of the islands is an admixture of Islamic law and English common law, with the latter being more influential in some areas, such as commercial law. In the sphere of personal law, the basis is the *sharia*, adapted to the modern judicial system. Much of what is known about the legal history of the Maldives is of an anecdotal nature and is drawn from the works of travellers who visited the islands at different times.

The Maldives National Defence Force (MNDF) is a combined security force responsible for defending the security and sovereignty of the nation. It is responsible for all internal and external security needs of the country, including the protection of the Exclusive Economic Zone (EEZ).[63] The MNDF also carries out all major disaster relief operations and handles national emergencies. It functions directly under the command, direction and guidance of the Ministry of Defence and National Security. The inception of the service was by a royal prerogative, but today it functions under an act of the parliament and as stipulated by the constitution. The sovereign head of the country assumes the office of the Commander-in-Chief.[64]

In this analysis, the military legal systems of Bangladesh, India, Nepal, Pakistan and Sri Lanka have been considered.

Notes

1. South Asian region encompasses the states of Afghanistan, Bangladesh, Bhutan, India, the Maldives, Nepal, Pakistan and Sri Lanka. These countries together comprise 23 percent of the world's population. Indians, Bangladeshis and the Pakistanis alone account for 21 percent of all human beings alive today and 95 percent of all South Asians. Its biggest country, India, is the world's largest democracy and is the globe's second most populous state with 1173 million people. The South Asian region is characterised by preponderant position of India in every sphere--military, economy and territorial. In South Asia every domestic problem becomes an inter-state problem and most efforts at bilateral or regional cooperation get embroiled in domestic politics. Chibber Bharati, 'Political and Military Dimensions of Regional Security: A Study of ASEAN and SAARC', *World Affairs*, Vol. 13 No. 2, (Sep 09) p. 18-38.
2. Sturgill Claude C. 1994. *The Military History of the Third World Since 1945*, London: Greenwood Press, p.35.
3. https://www.cia.gov/library/publications/the-world-factbook/geos/in.html
4. Pakistan population 177 million (July 2010 estimated). https://www.cia.gov/library/publications/the-world-factbook/print/pk.html
5. Bangladesh Population: 158 million (July 2010 estimated) https://www.cia.gov/library/publications/the-world-factbook/print/bg.html
6. Sri Lanka population: 21.5 million (July 2010 estimated) https://www.cia.gov/library/publications/the-world-factbook/geos/ce.html
7. Nepal Population: 28,9 million (July 2010 estimated) https://www.cia.gov/library/publications/the-world-factbook/print/np.html
8. Oliver, Dawn. 2003. *Constitutional Reforms in the UK*. New York: Oxford University Press.
9. Finer, S.E. 1962. *The Man on Horseback: The Role of Military in Politics*, London: Pall Mall Press.
10. According to Cohen (1971) a major blow to the autonomy and influence of the military—especially to the only substantial service, the army--was struck on Independence Day, August 15, 1947, when the position of Commander-in Chief in India was abolished. India had always had a Commander-in-Chief, and he had hitherto been the single source of military advice for the Indian Government. The navy and air chiefs were his subordinates. After this date the three service chiefs were collectively the professional advisors to the government. The ostensible reasons for this drastic reduction in the relative influence of the chief of the army were: to promote "balanced" growth among the three services, to provide better advice on technical navy and air force matters, and to follow all "modern" armed forces, which have each of the three services under an independent chief. There were also good unofficial reasons for this step. The only challenge to civilian authority could come from the numerically dominant army, reducing the authority to the point where he was not even first among equals made it easier to balance off the army with the other two services. Cohen, Stephen P. 1971. *The Indian Army: Its Contribution to the Development of a Nation*, University of California Press, p. 171-172.
11. However, in India, no one, not even the greatest political leaders, has been quite clear about the role or significance of the armed forces in modern society. Jawaharlal Nehru, independent India's first Prime Minister wanted the armed forces to work for

peace. For Nehru--the military remained barbaric and mercenary. Mahatma Gandhi demanded (Cohen; *The Indian Army*: 1971) that the army "plough the land, dig wells, cleans latrines and do other constructive work to turn the people's hatred of them into love."

12. The issue of appointment of a Chief of the Defence Staff (CDS) in India has been pending with the government since 2001. Both the Kargil Review Committee and the subsequent Group of Ministers report in 2001 on reforming the national security system had stressed the need for a CDS to provide single-point military advice to the government and manage the country's nuclear arsenal. 36th Report of the Parliamentary Standing Committee on Defence, presented to Lok Sabha on 24. 2. 2009.
13. Samuel Huntington. 1957. *The Soldier and the State*. The Belknap Press of Harvard University.
14. It was believed in certain fractions that the post-independence, civilian leaders were distrustful of the military, and this resulted in intrusive monitoring of the armed forces by the civilian bureaucracy. As early as 1952, an office manual of the Ministry of Defence put forth that 'three wings of the armed forces report, not directly to political authority but the civilian bureaucracy.' Nalapat M D. 1999. 'Bhagawat Felled by Bureaucratic Act', *Times of India*, January 6, 1999. p.10.
15. In accordance with democratic principles, control over defence is exercised by the Cabinet Committee on Security, of which the Prime Minister is the Chairman. In effect, the supreme responsibility of commanding the armed forces rests with the Prime Minister. This is true of all democratic countries, whether monarchial like England, Canada or Australia, or republican like France and India. It is either the King or the President who is the Supreme Commander-in-Chief of the armed forces, but it is the Prime Minister who wields effective authority over them.
16. Banerjee, Major General Dipankar, 2001. 'India: Military Professionalism of a First-World Army', in Alagappa Muthiah (ed) *Military Professionalism in Asia*, USA: East-West Centre, p. 19.
17. Though the Indian Army primarily focuses on external threats, in the period 1982-89, the army was deployed in 'aid to civil power' 721 times. Rosen Stephen P. 1996. *Societies and Military Power: India and Its Armies*, Ithaca: Cornell University Press, p. 263
18. During the 63 years of Pakistan's independent existence, the military has directly ruled the country for half the period, and for the remaining half, it held an indirect dominating sway over it. As a result, normal democratic evolution of Pakistan suffered enormously, and, today, the political structure and authority of the State stands weakened. Masood Talat, 'Civil-Military Relations', in John Wilson (ed) *Pakistan: The Struggle Within*, Delhi: Pearson Longman, 2009, p.145. Also see Chawla Shalini, 2009. *Pakistan's Military and Its Strategy*, New Delhi: KW Publishers. The author comments: "The Pakistani Army has developed a reputation as the sole guardian of not only the military but also the political and social interests of Pakistan....and has progressively led the country into the mire of maladministration.", p. 1-2.
19. Ahmed Samina. 2001. 'Pakistan: Professionalism of an Interventionist Military', in Alagappa Muthiah (ed) *Military Professionalism in Asia*, USA: East-West Centre, p. 151.
20. 786: these three numbers represent the numerological equivalent of the opening

sentences of the Quran, *Bismillah ir-Rehman* (In the name of Allah, the Merciful and Beneficent), the words that all Muslims intone before the start of anything worthwhile in their lives. 786 became the identification number for the offices of the British northern command in India in Rawalpindi after independence. This numerical code was emblazoned on all gate posts and vehicles, as a reminder that this was the army of a Muslim country. But the Islamic identity was only in name....senior echelon were still British officers who had opted to stay on, and they were in turn succeeded by their native clones. Nawaz Shuja. 2008. *Cross Swords: Pakistan, Its Army, and the Wars Within*, Karachi: Oxford University Press, p. xxxi.

21. Zafar S.M. 2001, 'Constitutional Development', in *Pakistan: Founder's Aspirations and Today's Realities*, Hafeez Malik (ed.), Oxford University Press, p. 31-32.
22. Article 243, Constitution of Pakistan.
23. Article 244, Constitution of Pakistan. The form set out in the Third Schedule of the Constitution.
24. Supporting Gen Zia-ul-Haq'a decision to impose martial law after the 1977 coup, former Army Chief General Muhammad Musa declared: "There is no political ambition, but the army gets infected by its environment, by the chaos, by the instability. All the politicians.... are third rate, they are useless." Musa telephoned Zia after the coup and told him: "You have saved the country—well done, and you've saved the army." Quoted in Cohen Stephen P. 1998, *The Pakistan Army*, Canada: OUP, p. 127.
25. Amir Mir, "The Army Strikes Back" *Newsline*, October 1999, p. 32-33.
26. Hasan Ali Shahzeb, "You Cannot Expect Miracles in 11 Months," *Newsline*, October 2000, p. 22.
27. Hasan-Askari Rizvi. 2000. *Military, State, and Society in Pakistan*, London: Macmillan, p.3.
28. Hasan-Askari Rizvi, "Dimensions of the Military Role," *Daily Times of Pakistan*, April 5, 2005, accessed at http://www.dailytimes.com.pk.
29. Cohen, Stephen P. (2004) *The Idea of Pakistan*, Washington, DC: Brooking Institute, p.105.
30. Khalid Mahmud, 'Governance and National Security: Pakistan—a case study' in Banerjee Dipankar (ed.), *Security Studies in South Asia: Change and Challenges*, [Regional Centre for Strategic Studies, Colombo], New Delhi: Manohar Publishers, p.132.
31. Cohen, Stephen P. (2004) *The Idea of Pakistan*, Washington, DC: Brooking Institute, p.124.
32. Mahmood Talat. 2009. 'Civil Military Relations' in Wilson John (ed.), *Pakistan: The Struggle Within*, Delhi: Pearson Longman.
33. *THE HINDU*, New Delhi, 17 December 2009.
34. Gazdar Haris, Democracy in Pakistan: A Chasm, *Economic and Political Weekly*, Vol. XLV, No. 22, May 29, 2010, p. 10.
35. The Constitution of Bangladesh made superior judiciary independent. Articles 95 and 96 prescribed how judges were to be appointed and removed. Article 22 required that the state ensure the separation of the judiciary from its executive organs.
36. For example, Mujib refused to name General Ziaur Rahman, a very successful professional soldier before the war and a freedom fighter, as Chief of the Army Staff. Ziaur Rahman was a national hero and had been a key officer in the separatist forces.

He was the first to announce the formation of a provisional government of Bangladesh from a radio station in Chittagaon in March 1971. Milan William B. 2009. *Bangladesh and Pakistan: Flirting with Failures in South Asia*, London: Foundation Books, p. 35

37. The mid-level military officers felt aggrieved by Mujib's action towards army, especially his creation of the National Security Force, and his elevation of that force to a status superior to army. They also objected to his interference in police and military affairs. Milan William B. 2009. *Bangladesh and Pakistan: Flirting with Failures in South Asia*, London: Foundation Books, p. 38. Bangladesh executed the five convicted killers of President Mujibur Rahman at Dhaka central jail on 28 January 2010. *THE HINDU*, 28 January 2010, p.1.
38. According to official statistics, 98.9 per cent voted in his support. After referendum victory, Zia chose a civilian as Vice President, his number two—Abdul Sattar, a highly respected East Pakistan jurist, who had been appointed as Justice of the Supreme Court in united Pakistan in 1968. Zia entrusted Sattar the task of building a political party as an alternative to the Awami League.
39. In October 1977, a large number of air force personnel mutinied at the Dhaka air base. They were joined by some enlisted men from other services. They attacked Zia.s residence, but could not kill him due to the presence of alert guards. The rebel killed a number of air force officers at the airport. The mutiny was quickly, and bloodily, put down by the army. As a fall out of mutiny, air force chief was dismissed from both his command and his post as food minister, and sent abroad. The military intelligence chief and his civilian counterparts were also dismissed. Three senior army officers who were in the line for position of the army chief were sent to other assignments.
40. On May 29, 1981, Zia came to Chittagaon to sort out a dispute between two factions of his political party. In the morning of May 30, 1981 the circuit house where he was staying was stormed by a team of army officers, following a plan worked out and authorised by Major General Muhammed Manzur, commander of 24th Division. Zia was shot down by Lt Col Motiur Rahman, ending his era, as it had started, in blood. Under the directions of Major General Ershad, a repatriate, who has replaced Zia, as Chief of the Army Staff when Zia gave up the position, General Manzur and his accomplishes were tracked down and either killed on the spot or tried and hanged as traitor.
41. The military regime in Bangladesh also attempted to distort the historical facts. On 21 June 2009, the Dhaka High Court ruled that it was Sheikh Mujibur Rahman, and not Ziaur Rahman, who proclaimed Bangladesh's independence from Pakistan in 1971. A two-judge bench of justices ABM Khairul Haque and Mamotaz Uddin Ahmed also ordered the cancellation of Bangladesh Liberation War Documents (Bangladesher Swadhinata Juddho Dalilpatra) that presented Ziaur Rahman, then a Major in the Pakistan army, as the "declarer of independence". The High Court verdict was given on a PIL by freedom fighter MA Salam. The High Court directed the government to include true history in textbooks at all level. http://www.bdnews24.com/details.php?cid=2&id=87839&hb=4
42. http://www.nepalarmy.mil.np/history.php
43. The Chief of the Nepalese Army, General Rukmangud Katawal was believed to be close to the palace, particularly since he had been adopted by the ousted King Gyanendra's father Mahendra. During the Jan Andolan, Katawal was accused of being stridently

against the Maoists. Katawal had stoutly resisted the induction of the Maoist People's Liberation Army (PLA) into the army, and brought matters to a head when the army refused to participate in the National Games because the Maoist Army personnel were also part of it. Katawal had also started recruitment of 3,000 soldiers and refused to retire eight generals despite being asked by the government to do so. All this has pitted him strongly against the Maoist leadership.http://timesofindia.indiatimes.com/World/Maoists-move-to-sack-Nepal-army-chief-alarms-India/articleshow/4427748.cms

44. The Nepal President termed the prime minister's decision as "unconstitutional", and ordered the army chief to stay in his job after the Maoist government tried to sack him in a power struggle between the prime minister and the military.
45. The interim Constitution, Article 145.1 states: There shall be a National Defence Council in order to recommend to the Council of Ministers for mobilisation, operation and use of the Nepal Army comprised of the following chairman and the members: a. Prime Minister as the Chairmen; b. Defence Minster and Home Ministers as Member; and d. three other ministers as Members as nominated by the PM. The Article further provides that the senior most member of the Council of Ministers shall be the member of the NDC in case the PM holds the portfolio of the Defence Minister. The NDC, if it deems necessary, could invite other persons at the meeting of the Council. The secretary of the Ministry of Defence shall work as the secretary of the NDC. Except in case of mobilisation of the NA for reasons of natural calamities, the decisions made by the Council of Ministers of the Government of Nepal for the mobilisation of the Army shall have to be presented to the special committee prescribed by the parliament within a month of decision, and be approved accordingly.
46. Article 144.2.
47. Article 144.3.
48. Article 144.4.
49. A United Nations Mission to Nepal (UNMIN) with a limited political mandate and characterised as "a focused mission of limited duration" was established in Nepal in early 2007. UNMIN's mandate is confined to "monitoring arms and armed personnel" of both sides, providing technical support for the planning, preparation, and conduct of elections, and assisting in the monitoring of ceasefire arrangements. UN Security Council Resolution 1740, January 23, 2007.
50. Sharma Lt Gen (Retd) Bala Nanda, *Civil-Military Relation in Nepal* <www.telegraphnepal.com/news_det.php?news_id=5359> visited 15 May 2009.
51. Nayak Nihar, PLA Integration into the Nepal Army: Challenges and Prospects, *Strategic Analysis*, Vol. 33 No. 5, September 2009, 730-744.
52. Mel Neloufer De. 2007. *Militarising Sri Lanka*, New Delhi: Sage, p. 59-60.
53. Sri Lanka Army Committee 1999, p.102.
54. In 1962, an unsuccessful coup was planned by several senior military and police officers that failed. The plot was due to be carried out in the night of 27 January 1962; however, before the coup could be launched the key leaders were rounded up and arrested. Due to the confusion that followed in the investigation and lengthy legal procedure, the full extent of the coup remains unclear.
55. Mel Neloufer de. 2007. *Militarising Sri Lanka*, New Delhi: Sage, p. 23.
56. For several decades Sri Lanka has experienced a series of internal armed conflicts between successive governments and forces of the LTTE fighting for an independent

Tamil homeland in the northeast of the country. During this time both sides have committed gross violations of human rights and humanitarian law, including massacres, extra-judicial killings, and enforced disappearances. However, the Sri Lankan legal system has rarely succeeded in holding perpetrators accountable for these violations. On the contrary, the complex and confusing emergency and anti-terrorism laws that have been put into place have frequently served to exacerbate rather than resolve the crisis by infringing on the rights of ordinary citizens, including human rights defenders, lawyers and journalists. *International Commission of Jurists Report*, March 2009.

57. http://www.hindu.com/2009/05/23/stories/2009052356421300.htm See: Matthes Bruce. 2010. The Limits of International Engagement in Human Rights Situations: the Case of Sri Lanka, *Pacific Affairs*, Volume 82, No. 4, Winter 2009/2010, p. 577-596: The killing of LTTE leader Velupillai Prabhakaran on 17 May 2009, brought to an end of civil war in Sri Lanka. The civil war came at a huge cost of life (estimated 70,000 victims). The war has also seen a serious diminishment of civil and human rights everywhere in Sri Lanka. Even in Colombo and other southern locations far from the war zone, there has been an exponential rise in extra-judicial killings, illegal arrests, unlawful detentions, abductions and assassinations of innocent people—some perpetrated by the LTTE, others associated with the armed forces and police.
58. Article 30 (1), Constitution of Sri Lanka.
59. Article 54, Constitution of Sri Lanka. After the Seventeenth Amendment to Constitution in 2001, Article 61 E now provides that the President shall appoint the Heads of the Army, the Navy and the Air Force.
60. Article 15 (8), Constitution of Sri Lanka.
61. The Sri Lankan parliament on 26 June 2009, passed the Chief of Defence Staff (CDS) Bill. The CDS will function under the direction, supervision and control of the secretary to the defence ministry. The CDS Act No. 35 of 2009 states that the CDS will be appointed by the President, initially for a term of two years. Soon after winning the internal war against LTTE, President Mahinda Rajapkasa had promoted the commanders of the three forces to the next rank in recognition of their service to the nation. Accordingly, army commander was promoted to the rank of General, the navy commander to Admiral and the air force commander to Air Chief Marshal ranks. The Sri Lankan government designated the serving Army Chief, Sarath Fonseka as the new CDS effective from 15 July 2009. *THE HINDU*, July 13, 2009, p.10. Fonseka took voluntary retirement from service and was a candidate for Presidential election in January 2010. He lost the election and was arrested three days later as the government charged him with attempting to overthrow the President. *THE HINDU*, February 02, 2010.
62. Article 8, the Constitution of Bhutan.
63. Article 236 and 237, The Constitution of the Republic of Maldives, 2008.
64. All the judges of the High Court, the highest court in the country, and the lower courts are appointed and can be dismissed by the President. The 1995 presidential decree gives power to a five-member advisory council appointed by the President to review the high court's decisions. The High Court serves as court of appeal, and ultimate appeal lies with the President. Therefore, there is no independence of judiciary in Maldives. The lack of proportionality between crime and punishment is a serious problem. The primary reasons for this are politically motivated trial and lack of proper knowledge and training among the judges on English common law and *Sharia* law. In Maldives a

multi-party democracy was ushered in towards the end of the year 2008. Articles 240 and 242 of the Constitution further provide: “The security services shall be organised as two separate services (military and police), and shall operate independently of each other. Each security service shall be under the responsibility of a Minister, who shall be answerable for its operations to the President and to the People’s Majlis.

2

Militaries and their Legal Systems

The armed forces of a nation are created to safeguard its boundaries against external aggression and maintain its integrity and sovereignty. In the South Asian context, the activities of the armed forces could be divided into three: (a) combat activities like attacks, raids and direct activity, (b) governance of the country, [1] and (c) non-combat activities. The non-combat activities could be further sub-divided into three: (i) domestic assistance to the civil authorities such as assistance during natural calamities and riot, and assistance in the maintenance of law and order; (ii) assistance in refugee control and unconventional warfare, security assistance (combating terrorism, counter-insurgency), psychological operations and show of force; and (iii) international assistance and peacekeeping operations.

Amongst the South Asian countries, India has a large army, consisting of 1,100,000 personnel. Its navy and air force have a strength of 55,000 and 120,000 personnel, respectively. The paramilitary forces in India have over 1,300,000 personnel. In addition, the strength of the Indian reserve force is over 1,155,000. Bangladesh has an active army of 126,000 personnel, while the navy has 16,000 and the air force has 14,500 personnel. In addition, it also has 63,000 paramilitary personnel. Nepal has an army of 69,000 personnel. It has an army-air wing which consists of 650 personnel and flies several aircraft within the 11th Brigade.[2] Nepal's paramilitary forces have strength of more than 62,000. Nepal Maoist Political leadership is attempting to integrate its 23,500 strong Peoples Liberation Army into the Nepalese National Army. Pakistan maintains an army of 550,000, navy of 22,000 and air force of 45,000 personnel. Its paramilitary forces have about 304,000 personnel. Sri Lanka has 117,900 personnel in the army, 18,000 in the air force and about 15,000 in the navy. [3] The strength of the Sri Lankan paramilitary forces is about 62,000. Induction in the armed forces is voluntary in the South Asian countries.[4]

Though women have been working in the armed forces of the South Asian countries as medical and nursing officers since the 1940s, the armed forces have been sceptical of their ability to perform the role of a soldier. Today, women are working in virtually all the non-combat branches in the armed forces but their exclusion from combat makes women officers feel that they are being discriminated against. The career profile of women does not compare favourably with that of men in the armed forces.[5] The aim of the armed forces has been to use women to fill the existing gaps in the cadre on a short-term basis, with no thought of planning a viable career for women. The general apprehension among military hierarchy is that the women members of the armed forces may be captured during an international armed conflict and taken prisoner of war (POW). The third Geneva Convention of 1949, however, elaborately directs States to take particular measures where women combatants become POW.

Despite remarkable efforts by the United Nations and other regional organisations, respect for human rights of women has failed to attain universal status, especially in case of South Asia. There is a great deal of difference between the treaty text and its interpretation and implementation.[6] Though all the South Asian countries are signatories to the UN Convention on the Elimination of All Forms of Discrimination against Women (CEDAW), there is a lack of understanding as well as mechanism to redress discrimination against the women employed in the armed forces.[7] In the existing environment, women members also remain at risk from sexual predation of men soldiers. In a recent case in the Indian Army, an officer of the rank of major general was dismissed for making sexual advances towards a junior women officer. The armed forces need to put in place a procedure to protect women soldiers from this type of activity. The existing grievances redress system need to be suitably modified, to ensure that women soldiers do not hesitate in making a formal complaint.

Today, roughly 40 per cent of the soldiers deployed around the world in the United Nations peacekeeping missions belong to South Asian countries.[8]

The Military Legal Systems

Armed forces the world over are governed by a special code to ensure the highest standard of discipline among the members. Almost all democracies have provided an independent legal system for the armed forces to ensure troop discipline. Speedy trials and predictable decisions aid the military in its effort to maintain order and uniformity. In addition to enhancing discipline, order, uniformity, efficiency and obedience, the military court addresses certain offences unique to the military.[9] Military law consists of Acts and Rules, departmental regulations, the orders issued by senior military commanders and the inherent authority of military commanders. Military law includes criminal jurisdiction exercised by the courts-martial and the administrative jurisdiction exercised by commanders with respect to non-judicial punishment.

The British military justice system is the progenitor of the military legal systems of the South Asian countries. The British Parliament in the Militia Act of 1671 had declared that the 'supreme government the militia and of all forces by sea and land' was the undoubted rights of the King, but it did not permit the King to keep a standing Army. But the Bill of Rights, 1688 succeeded in wrestling control over the creation of a standing Army from Crown and placed it in the hands of Parliament. The Bill of Rights therefore declared that 'the raising or keeping a standing Army within the Kingdom in time of peace, unless it be with the consent of Parliament, is against law'. However, in attempting to control the power of the King, Parliament had made the country vulnerable to invasion. A standing Army was therefore established by the Parliament, but its existence was limited to fixed period. The Mutiny Act 1689 not only recited the terms of the Bill of Rights but it also provided a basic disciplinary code for its members and it set a pattern which continued until 1981.

During their rule, the British trained and organised three separate defence forces. The army was the first to be raised on a regular basis in 1754 under the British Crown Act (27 Geo. II Ch. 9), followed by the navy in 1830 and the air force, which was the last to be established, in 1932. During World War II, these forces had been highly organised and were being governed under three separate but similar laws, *viz.* the Indian Army Act, 1911, the Indian Navy Discipline Act, 1934, and the Indian Air Force Act, 1932.

To preserve the continuity of the legal system, it was provided under the Indian Independence Act that the existing laws of British India, including the services' laws, were to continue to operate in the new countries until superseded by subsequent legislation. Prior to 15 August 1947, the British Army Act applied to all British and Indian officers, who were holding the King's commission in His Majesty's Land Forces. Other Indian personnel of the Indian army (including Indian commissioned officers) were governed by the Indian Army Act of 1911. This Act was not sufficiently comprehensive. Wherever it was silent, the provisions of the corresponding British Act were invoked. From 15 August 1947, the British Army Act became inapplicable and King Commissioned Indian Officers (KCIOs) were made subject to the Indian Army Act by an Ordinance promulgated on 23 January 1948 (Ordinance No. II of 1948) but effective from 15 August 1947, which amended the Indian Army Act to provide that the expression 'Indian Commissioned Officer' would also include a person of Indian nationality holding His Majesty's commission in His Majesty's Land Forces. This amendment was later incorporated in the Indian Army (Amendment) Act, 1948 (Act No. XLIII of 1948) so that the KCIOs remained subject to the Indian Army Act 1911 until the Act itself was revised to cover all commissioned officers of the army.[10]

In India, the laws operated for some time and those with respect to the army and the air force were later replaced by the Army Act, 1950, and the Air Force Act, 1950, respectively. The Indian Navy Act was passed in 1957.[11] In essence, these laws were replicas of the British-Indian laws and only a few cosmetic changes were made in them.

In Pakistan, the three services' laws continued to operate until they were repealed by the present laws, viz., the Pakistan Army Act of 1952, the Pakistan Navy Ordinance of 1961 and the Pakistan Air Force Act of 1953. These laws, though greatly improved in language and form, are in substance the same as their respective predecessors and continue to retain their inter-se similarity. Pakistan has been following subordinate legislations: (a) Pakistan Air Force Act and Rules in the Manual of Pakistan Air Force Law (MPAFL); (b) Pakistan Army Act and Rules in the Manual of Pakistan Army Law (MPAL); and (c) Pakistan Navy Ordinance and Rules in the Manual of Pakistan Naval Law (MPNL). The nomenclature and composition of military courts vary slightly according to the service, but the courts procedures, type of offences, scale of punishments, jurisdictional authority, appeal, review and procedure for commutation and suspension of sentences are almost identical for all the services. The amendment of the Pakistani Army Act in November 2007 awarded powers to military courts to try civilians on charges of terrorism, anti-national activities, sedition, attacks on Army personnel and attacks on the President.

Bangladesh has not carried out any significant change in the Pakistan Army Act, 1952, adapted after Independence in 1972.[12] The Bangladesh Army (Sena Bahini) is governed by the Act of 1952, the Air Force (Biman Bahini) by the Act of 1953 and the Navy (Nou Bahini) by the Ordinance of 1961. The service laws have been amended on a few occasions, though no substantial changes have been made in them. In essence, the military legal systems of India, Pakistan and Bangladesh are identical. The Sri Lankan armed forces are governed by the Army Act, 1949, the Air Force Act, 1949, and the Navy Act, 1950.[13] The democratic government in Nepal has passed the Nepalese Army Act, 2006.[14] These legal systems regulate the rights and discipline of the armed forces personnel in the South Asian countries.

However, the fundamental rights of armed forces personnel have been restricted by the constitutions of the South Asian countries. In India, a reading of Article 33 suggests that Parliament can make a law abrogating or restricting the fundamental rights of members of the armed forces, or the forces charged with the maintenance of public order only for two reasons. The first is, "for ensuring the proper discharge of their duties" and the second is, "for the maintenance of discipline among them". Section 21 of the Indian Army Act, 1950, states that army personnel cannot (i) be associated in any way with any trade union, or any society, institution or association, or any class of societies, institutions or associations; (ii) attend or address any meeting or to take part in any demonstration organised by any body of persons for any political or other purposes; and (iii) communicate with the press or to publish or cause to be published any book, letter or document.

Similarly, the Constitution of the Islamic Republic of Pakistan, 1973, Part II deals with Fundamental Rights and Principles of Policy.[15] Article 8 (3) under Part II expressly exempts from its operation laws relating to the armed forces. Article 45 of the Bangladesh Constitution declares: "Nothing in this Part (Part III dealing with fundamental rights) shall apply to any provision of a disciplinary law relating to members of a disciplined force, being a provision limited to the purpose of ensuring the proper discharge of their duties or the maintenance of discipline in that force." The Constitution of Sri Lanka, in Article 15 (8), [16] echoes the language of the Article 33 of the Indian Constitution. The interim Constitution of Nepal, 2007, makes no such restrictions on the fundamental rights of military personnel. However, Section 19 of the Nepal Army Act, 2006, lays restrictions on the activities of persons subject to the Act. These restrictions are similar to those laid down in Section 21 of the Indian Army Act.[17]

Jurisdiction

Persons subject to military law fall into two categories---those who are permanently subject and those whose subjection is only temporary. In the former category are commissioned officers, junior commissioned officers (JCO), warrant officers and other ranks (below the rank of JCO), who join the military on a regular basis and remain permanently subject to respective military law until "duly retired, discharged, released, removed, dismissed or cashiered from the service". These individuals form the bulk of the armed forces. Into the second category fall reservists, persons seconded (transferred) from the other services and civilians who become temporarily subject to military law under certain contingencies.

Civilians Employed or Accompanying the Armed Forces

In the interest of discipline, it is considered necessary that civilians, who are employed in the armed forces, should be amenable to respective service Act. The army acts and the air force acts of India, Bangladesh and Pakistan provide that the persons[18] not otherwise subject to military law, on active service become subject to the military law. The term "active service" means the time during which the military or a part of it is "engaged in operations against an enemy." The question of whether the subjection of civilians to military law is valid has been raised in India. The Supreme Court, in *OKA Nair v Union of India* held that civilians become subject to the Army

Act, Air Force Act or the Navy Act only when specified conditions of the respective Act become operative, and these persons on active service, in camp, although non-combatant, are an integral part of the armed forces.[19]

Extension of Jurisdiction over Ex-servicemen

Normally, officers and other ranks cease to be subject to the military Acts when they are "duly retired, discharged, released, removed or dismissed from the service" either upon completion of their normal tenure of service, or as a result of administrative action, or as a result of a sentence by court martial. The services Acts remain applicable for three years after release or retirement from service, and during this period, the person may be taken into custody, tried and punished for offences as if he continues to be subject to the respective Act's provisions. However, trial for the offence must commence within three years of his ceasing to be subject, except where he is accused of desertion on active service, fraudulent enrolment or mutiny, for which there is no time limit.[20]

Prisoners of War

Article 82 of the Geneva Convention Relative to the Treatment of Prisoners of War of August 12, 1949, subjects a prisoner of war (POW) to the same laws, regulations, and orders as those followed by service personnel of the capturing nation. Article 84 provides that a POW shall be tried only by a military court, unless the existing laws of the detaining power expressly permits the civil courts to try a member of the armed forces of the detaining power in respect of the particular offence alleged to have been committed by the POW. After 1971 Indo-Pak War, few Pakistani POW were tried by courts martial in India. During World War II, 48 special and 119 general court martial were convened against Axis POW (227 Germans and 49 Italian) held in the United States.[21]

Civilians not Related to the Military Service

Under the Pakistani military Acts, civilians who were accused of spying and other related offences, or who were accused of an offence under the Official Secrets Act, 1923, could be tried by a military court. Sections 2 and 71 of Pakistan military Acts were amended by Defence Services Laws Amendment Ordinance 1967. The Acts were amended retrospectively. In Pakistan, few civilians accused of spying and other related offences were tried by a general court martial and sentenced to various terms of imprisonment. The case was challenged in the Provincial High Court. The court upheld the trial on the grounds, inter alia: "(a) the amendments did not amount to *ex post facto* legislation as they neither created a new offence nor provided a new punishment, but merely created a new forum of trial, namely court martial; (b) the amendments involved only changes in procedural law and "no person can have a vested right in the course of procedure and it is an elementary principle that alteration in a procedure is always retrospective unless there can be some good reason against it or by necessary intendment the procedural law is stated to be prospective; and (c) the case involved no violation of the fundamental rights of 'protection against retrospective punishment.'"[22]

The intention behind the above legislation was to deter people from compromising the security of the services, for which the ordinary civil law was found ineffective.[23] In 2007, the Pakistan military Acts were amended retrospectively to try civilians under the military law for of offences related to the defence and security of the country, including the Pakistan Penal Code.[24] During the martial law regimes in Bangladesh and Pakistan, military courts were established for the trial of civilians. The armed forces in India, Nepal and Sri Lanka had no such powers.

Fundamental Rights and Grievance Redress System

In the South Asian countries, the fundamental rights of armed forces personnel are restricted to ensure the proper discharge of duties and maintenance of discipline among them. They are generally denied the right to be members of trade unions or associations, to attend political meetings and to communicate with the press. The States have, however, bestowed on them the right to make complaints seeking the redress of their grievances.[25]

It is provided that an officer or any person below the officer rank (PBOR) who deems himself wronged by any superior may complain to the commanding officer (CO) for the redress of his grievance. When the officer complained against is the officer to whom the complaint should be preferred, the aggrieved person may complain to the officer who is next in superiority to such officer. The complaints must be confined to a statement of facts. A joint complaint is not allowed as it amounts to 'mutiny'. It is also an offence against service discipline to make a complaint which is untrue to the knowledge of the complainant. On receipt of the application, the CO is to investigate the case and, if possible, redress the grievance. If the CO is not in a position to redress the grievance, the application, together with a report from the CO, is to be forwarded to the next higher formation in the chain of command. The channels through which complaints must be preferred are specified. The application is to be continued to be forwarded to the next higher authority until it reaches the services headquarters. The applicant is to be informed of the fact that his application has been forwarded to the next higher authority. The final authority for the redress of grievance rests with the government, except in case of Sri Lanka, where it is with the President.[26]

The grievance redress system, however, has the following shortcomings.

- During the processing of a complaint, the complainant is not informed about the comments of the section commander/commanding officer (CO) and intermediate authorities on his grievance application.[27]
- Undue delays in the processing and disposal of complaints, which is often justified under the pretext that the military chain of command is engaged in making investigations, is another source of problem. There have been cases where final decisions on the grievances relating to promotions have been delayed until the complainant retires. The delay in the finalisation of a complaint often frustrates the complainant, leading to dissatisfaction and demoralisation.
- All levels of the military hierarchy are entitled to seek legal advice on a complaint. However, the aggrieved person is not provided any legal help for preferring his complaint. The persons objected to may participate in disposing of the objection. If the grievance is against the CO or higher military authorities, the affected individual or his family may also face social seclusion and harassment.[28]
- The decision on an application is not required to be a "reasoned" order and it could be conveyed in a brief sentence, such as: "Your application has been rejected by the competent authority as being devoid of merit." Stereotype rejection orders reinforce the doubt that complaints are treated arbitrarily and against the principles of natural justice. [29]

  The need of a reasoned decision could be justified on the grounds: (i) In case the individual affected by the decision desires to go for appeal, he must have the opportunity to study the reasons on which the original judgement was based, so as to be able to present his counter-arguments in appeal; (ii) The need to give reasons for a legal decision is closely linked to the character of law. A judgement which does not give reasons may not be, but certainly appears to be arbitrary; and (iii) For reasons of transparency, a judgement must assure that appropriate care has been given to determining the result, and that outcome is not the result of improper motives.
- In the Indian Army, if a complainant has made an accusation, he/she is required to render a certificate, "I undertake that any false statement or false accusation made by me in this complaint will render me liable for disciplinary action." In cases of the use of abusive language, misbehaviour and sexual harassment, which may take place in private, it may not be possible for a victim to support his/her accusation with any documentary proof or witness. Then the victim would be liable to disciplinary action based on the certificate rendered with his/her petition. This 'coercive' provision often deters the victim from seeking redress and makes the statutory right meaningless.

- The service regulations of the South Asian countries state that the grievance applications are to be processed expeditiously; however, the time-frame for processing is different in the case of each service. The regulations do not provide any time-frame for the Army Headquarters or the Central Government to give its final decision in the matter.[30]

In contrast to the South Asian countries, in the United States, the military persons have the right to complain and request redress of grievances against (i) mistreatment by a superior; (ii) failure to act on a request (such as a request for medical attention or a request for hardship discharge); (iii) unlawfully restricting a military person's rights; (iv) justice rights; (v) unlawful discrimination or sexual harassment; (vi) damage to, or improper seizure of, personal property.

There are several formal methods for requesting redress of grievances, including (i) complaints through the chain of command; (ii) correspondence with a Member of Congress, (iii) an Inspector General (IG) complaint for instances of fraud, waste, and abuse, (iv) an Equal Opportunity complaint for instances of discrimination or sexual harassment, (v) article 138 Uniform Code of Military Justice (UCMJ) complaint, for instances of specific abuse, discriminatory practices of a superior officer, or where the command is not following regulations; (vi) article 139, UCMJ complaint, where personal property is taken or destroyed, (vii) petition the Board for correction of military records to change adverse entries. Complaints made to Members of Congress and the Inspector General, including Equal Opportunity complaints, are "protected communications" under the Whistleblower Protection Act. The complainant is protected to some extent from adverse actions deemed to be taken in "reprisal" for their complaint.

A complainant who desires to submit a grievance may consult a military lawyer for advice and assistance in drafting. If the commander refuses to redress the grievance, the soldier may submit the complaint, along with the commander's response, to the next superior officer, who is mandated to forward the complaint to the General Court martial Convening Authority (GCMCA). The superior officer may attach additional documentary evidence and comment on witnesses or evidence, but may not comment on the merits of the complaint. The GCMCA is to examine the complaint. Specific findings are to be made as to whether the act or omission complained of was in violation of law or regulation; beyond the legitimate authority of the respondent; arbitrary, capricious, or an abuse of discretion; or materially unfair. The GCMCA is required to notify the complainant of the action taken on the complaint.

Canada was the first country to establish a grievance redress system that includes an external review, separate and independent from the chain of command in the Canadian Forces. The Canadian Forces Grievance Board (CFGB) was created under the National Defence Act in 2000. Canada's military personnel are entitled to file grievances on almost any matter affecting them, including financial benefits, personnel evaluation reports, postings, medical issues, harassment or release from the Canadian Forces (CF). The complainant is required to first submit the grievance to his or her CO. If he is satisfied with the CO's decision, the grievance process ends there. If the complainant is not satisfied, the CO is to forward the grievance to the Grievance Board. The CFGB is mandated to review all military grievances, and submits its findings and recommendations to the Chief of Defence Staff, and also to the complainant. The CFGB consists of civilians and former military personnel who, alone or in panel, are responsible for reviewing grievances. The Board has quasi-judicial powers and can summon witnesses and compel them to give oral or written evidence. The Board can hold a public hearing to benefit the participants and serve public interest.

In the UK, a person in service, or one who has ceased to be subject to service law, but thinks himself wronged in any matter relating to his service, may make a complaint under Section 334 of the Armed Forces Act 2006. The Armed Forces (Redress of Individual Grievances) Regulations, 2007 provides three modes for redress: (i) a complaint may be lodged with the service complaint commissioner (civilian), (ii) a grievance application can be forwarded to the CO, and (iii) where a complaint has been considered by a Service Board, an officer has the right that a report on his service complaint be referred to the Sovereign.

Roskill (1964) in *The Art of Leadership* has assigned the duties of a commander towards his subordinates.[31] He writes: It is my belief that the Commanders should encourage their juniors to come to them with their ideas and their problems, and even with their grievances and complaints. If grievances are bottled up, discipline will suffer—probably through irresponsible talk among junior officers already condemned. Merely to be given an opportunity to state a grievance goes a long way towards eliminating it; since no responsible man will nurse a grievance after he has been brought face to face with the cause of it. Nor should the senior officer hesitate to admit error, or even to make an apology, if he feels there is justice in a complaint against himself.

As the armed forces constitute the most powerful weapon of the executive, their internal management and other functional systems are required to be efficient, modern and in tune with the times. In the South Asian countries, the unscrupulous processing of a grievance petition damages the effectiveness of statutory right of the military personnel. The military profession can maintain its dignity and professionalism only if the human rights of soldiers are respected.

Notes

1. The military governance of the country is exhibited by Bangladesh and Pakistan.
2. It was established in 1979, as part of the Army. The main objective of this flying element is transport, flying paratroopers and assistance in case of an emergency (e.g. natural disasters). Apart from the 11th Brigade the country has established a VIP Flight. All aircraft are stationed at Kathmandu-Tribhuvan. There are 36 airfields, scattered around the country to support military operations. Many of them are configured only for short take-off and landing operations. http://www.scramble.nl/np.html
3. During the last three years, strength of the Sri Lankan armed forces swelled to over 200,000. The strength of the army is expected to increase further from 200,000 to 300,000. THE HINDU, 13 July, 2009, p. 10. <http://www.dailymirror.lk/DM_BLOG/Sections/frmNewsDetailView.aspx?ARTID=51607>
4. The Military Balance 2009, London: Routledge.
5. In India, the Ministry of Defence in a reply to Unstarred Question (No 908, answered on March 07, 2007) has informed the Rajya Sabha that a study undertaken by the Chief of the Staff Committee has recommended exclusion of women officers in the combat roles where chances of physical contact with the enemy are high.
6. Dhaliwal S. 'Human Rights of Women in South Asia: Promotion and Protection Under SAARC', *Kashmir University Law Review 2008*, Vol. XV, No. XV, p. 31-44.
7. The Government of India has approved grant of permanent commission to women officers in Judge Advocate General Department of the Army, Army Education Corps and their corresponding Branch/Cadre in Navy and Air Force, Accounts Branch in the Air Forces and Naval Constructor of the Navy. Reply to Starred Question no. 434 in Parliament. Answered on 03.8.2009.
8. SA Countries: Troop Contribution in UN Peacekeeping Missions as on 31 January 2010.

S. No	Country	Police	Mil Observers	Troops	Total
1.	Bangladesh	1,603	80	8,913	10,596
2.	India	737	78	7,944	8,759
3.	Nepal	888	62	4,212	5,162
4.	Pakistan	926	114	9,786	10,826
5.	Sri Lanka	77	13	959	1,049
	TOTAL	4,231	347	31,814	36,392
	Total in UN	-	-	-	99,943

http://www.un.org/Depts/dpko/dpko/contributors/2010/jan10_1.pdf

9. Besides offences at the time of war, other military offences triable by courts-martial are mutiny, desertion, absence without leave, use of insubordinate language, disobedience, insubordination, ill-treatment of a subordinate and violation of good order and discipline.
10. Venkateswaran A.L. 1967. *Defence Organisation in India*, Publication Division, Ministry of Information and Broadcasting, Govt. of India, p. 254.
11. The Naval Discipline Act in existence at that time differed from the laws relating to the Army and the Air Force in many respects. In the UK, a special committee had been set up to examine the question of revision of the British Naval Codes, and the Government

of India awaited the committee's report. The Navy Act, 1957, was finally passed by Parliament on 27 December, 1957, and came into effect from 1 January, 1958.

12. Adapted by the Bangladesh (Adaptation of Existing Laws) Order 1972.
13. Recently the military law professionals from the US Pacific Command hosted a military law exchange programme with the Sri Lankan Defence Ministry to exchange ideas on ways to improve transparency, accountability and human rights in military justice system. http://www.dailynews.lk/2007/08/25/sec10.asp.
14. Section 22 of the Nepalese Army Act, 2006 has been considered as objectionable provision. The International Commission of Jurists, a Geneva based NGO, has urged for amendment to Section 22 of the Act, as it provides for amnesty (statutory bar, or blanket immunity, from legal proceedings in any court, for acts carried out by a member of the Nepal Army in the "course of discharging his duties" that result in the death of, or loss to any person), for crimes under international law such as crimes against humanity, war crimes, and gross human rights violations in general such as extrajudicial killings, enforced disappearances and torture. http://www.icj.org/news.php3?id_article=4201&lang=en
15. Articles 7 to 40, the Constitution of Pakistan, 1973.
16. Article 15 (8) of the Sri Lankan Constitution: ...the exercise and operation of the fundamental rights shall in their application to the members of the armed forces..... be subject to such restrictions as maybe prescribed by law in the interest of the proper discharge of their duties and the maintenance of discipline among them.
17. 19. Prohibition on the establishment, conduct and participation in an organisation and institution: (1) Any person who falls under the jurisdiction of this Act shall be prohibited to act as follows: (a) To establish, operate, become a member, assist a union, institution or organisation, or participate in a programme organised by such union, institution or organisation. (b) To participate in a meeting or deliver a speech, or participate in a demonstration organised for political or similar objectives by any individual or group. (c) To print any poster, pamphlet or other similar document.

    (2) Not withstanding anything provided by Subsection (1) (a) any person who falls under the jurisdiction of this Act shall not, unless with permission from the Nepal Government and subject to this Act, be prejudiced from helping any religious, social, cultural, and entertaining union, institution or organisation, or shall not be deemed to prejudice participation in programmes organised by such union, institution or organisation.
18. Section 2(i) of the Indian Army Act states: "persons not otherwise subject to military law who, on active service, in camps, on the march, or at any frontier post specified by the Central Government by notification in this behalf, are employed by, or are in the service of, or are followers of, or accompany any portion of, the regular Army" shall be subject to the Army Act. Similar provisions exist in the Pakistan and Bangladesh military Acts.
19. *OKA Nair v Union of India* AIR 1976 SC 1179.
20. Section 122, Indian Army Act; Section 91, Pakistan and Bangladesh Army Acts; and Section 56, Sri Lankan Army Act.
21. In the US current domestic authority to exercise military jurisdiction over enemy POW is contained in Article 2 (a) (9) of the Uniform Code of Military Justice.
22. *Raza Khan and others v. Government of Pakistan*, PLD 1967 Peshawar, (Pakistan) 118.

23. Anwar Sqn Ldr Sheikh Mohammed. 1973. 'The Administration of Justice in the Pakistan Air Force', 61 *Military Law Review*, p. 41-88.
24. In 2007, President, General Pervez Musharraf promulgated Pakistan Army (Amendment) Ordinance, 2007 to amend the Pakistan Army Act 1952. It came into force retrospectively from January 1, 2003. It amended section 2 of the Army Act, 1952 and gave wide powers to the military courts to try any offence, "if committed in relation to defence or security of Pakistan or any part thereof or Armed Forces of Pakistan, punishable under the Explosive Substances Act, 1908 (VI of 1908), Prejudicial conduct under the Security of Pakistan Act, 1952 (XXXV of 1952), the Pakistan Arms Ordinance, 1965, the Prevention of Anti-national Activities Act, 1974 (VII of 1974) or Anti-terrorism Act, 1997 (XVII of 1997), sections 109, 117, 120B, 121, 121A, 122, 123, 123A, 124, 124A, 148, 302, 353 and 505 of the Pakistan Penal Code, or attempt to commit any of the said offences."
25. Section 167 and 168 Bangladesh and Pakistan Army Acts, Sections 132 and 133 Sri Lankan Army Act, Section 26 and 27 Indian Army Act, and Section 27, Nepal Army Act.
26. On receipt of the application, the section commander or commanding officer (CO) is to investigate the case and, if possible, redress the grievance. If the CO is not in a position to redress the grievance, the application, together with a report from the CO, is to be forwarded to the next higher formation in the chain of command. The channels through which complaints must be preferred are specified in regulations. The application is to be continued to be forwarded to the next higher authority until it reaches the final authority. The applicant is to be informed of the fact that his application has been forwarded to the next higher authority.
27. In the case of *Maj Gen Arun Roye* (2008), CWN 528, the Calcutta High Court opined: "...non-furnishing of comments of the intermediate authorities to the complainant who lodged the statutory complaint is tantamount to violation of the principles of natural justice." The Court held, "This is because the comments that are furnished by the intermediate authorities to the Central Government are essential to the complainant, so as to enable that person to know what has been commented against him/her by the said military authority while forwarding the complaint to the Government."
28. There have been allegations that those lodging complaints against their military superiors have been transferred to far-flung places, causing harassment to them and their family members.
29. The Supreme Court of India has recently held that failure to give reasons amounts to denial of justice. It held, "reasons are live links between the minds of the decision taker to the controversy in question and the decision or conclusion arrived at. Reasons substitute subjectivity with objectivity." *Arunima Baruah v. Union of India* (2007) 6 SCC 1201.
30. For example, in the case of the Indian Army, when the complaint does not contain any accusation requiring investigation, it must reach the Army headquarters within 135 days. If the complainant has made an accusation requiring investigation, the complaint should reach the headquarters within 180 to 195 days. If the final decision on the statutory complaint, regardless of whether it contains an accusation against any superior officer, is not taken within a period of 12 months or 9 months, respectively, from the

date of submission of the complaint, the complainant has a right to represent directly to the Army Headquarters or the Central Government. Paragraph 364, Regulations for the Indian Army.

31. Roskill, Capt S.W. 1964. *The Art of Leadership*, London: Collins, p. 136.

3

Arrests and Summary Punishments

The military laws in the South Asian countries provide that a military person, who is charged with an offence, may be taken into military custody by the superior officer or by the military police. A junior officer may order into military custody a senior officer who, being a person subject to military law, is engaged in a quarrel, affray or disorder.[1] For arrest no warrant is required. Basically military custody includes two types of arrests---the "open arrest" and the "closed arrest". The restraint imposed under each type is according to the usages of the service and the regulations. Under closed arrest, a person is usually confined to a room or barracks and remains under the escort of a person of equal rank. Under open arrest, he remains under a moral restraint not to go beyond a certain area, usually the camp.

Under an amendment to the Pakistan's services Acts, the scope of "close arrest" has been enlarged to include "detention in a civil prison".[2] Such type of detention can be ordered only by the commanding officer and is limited to 15 days at a time. The provision is meant to be used only in those rare cases, like riot or mutiny, when the arrest and the segregation of a large number of offenders becomes necessary and when adequate facilities do not exist at a base.

Arbitrariness in Arrest and Detention

Article 9(1) of the ICCPR provides: "Everyone has the right to liberty and security of person. No one shall be subjected to arbitrary arrest or detention. No one shall be deprived of his liberty except on such grounds and in accordance with such procedure as are established by law." As to the principle of legality, the Human Rights Committee has held that "it is violated if an individual is arrested or detained on grounds which are not clearly established in domestic legislation"; in other words, the grounds for arrest and detention must be "established by law". In a case where a person was arrested without a warrant, which was issued more than three days later, contrary to the domestic law that lays down that a warrant must be issued within 72 hours after arrest, the Committee concluded that article 9(1) had been violated because the author had been "deprived of his liberty in violation of a procedure as established by law".[3]

With regard to the meaning of the words "arbitrary arrest" in article 9(1), the Committee has explained that "'arbitrariness' is not to be equated with 'against the law', but must be interpreted more broadly to include elements of inappropriateness, injustice, lack of predictability and due process of law. ....This means that remand in custody pursuant to lawful arrest must not only be lawful but reasonable in the circumstances. Remand in custody must further be necessary in all the circumstances, for example, to prevent flight, interference with evidence or the recurrence of crime".[4] In other words, remand in custody pursuant to lawful arrest must not only be "lawful" but also "reasonable" and "necessary" in all the circumstances for the aforementioned purposes.

Article 9(2) of the ICCPR provides that "anyone who is arrested shall be informed, at the time of arrest, of the reasons for his arrest and shall be promptly informed of any charges against him". The Human Rights Committee has explained that "one of the most important reasons for the requirement of 'prompt' information on a criminal charge is to enable a detained individual to request a prompt decision on the lawfulness of his or her detention by a competent judicial authority".[5] It concluded that article 9(2) of the Covenant had been violated in a case where the complainant had not been informed upon arrest of the charges against him and was only informed seven days after he had been detained.[6]

The system of bail does not exist in the military Acts in the South Asian countries. Once a serviceman has been placed under arrest, the proper authority to release him from arrest is the commanding officer of the accused or other superior military authority. A commanding officer is under a legal duty to commence investigation of the charge within 48 hours after the arrest is reported to him. If it is impracticable to do so, he is required to explain the reasons in writing to the court martial convening authority/superior authority and to follow it up with periodic reports in case the detention becomes prolonged. An accused awaiting trial is not supposed to be under arrest unless he is charged with a serious offence, or is undermining discipline.

It is not necessary that every person charged with an offence, must be put under close arrest. If the offence is not serious it may be investigated and disposed of without placing the offender under arrest. Unless there is a very serious reason, which is spelt out in the order of the competent authority placing the accused under arrest during the trial, the accused should not be placed under arrest. The arrest is governed by the following factors (i) that the offender may not abscond and is available to stand trial; (ii) that the offender may not do harm to himself; (iii) that the offender may not temper with he prosecution evidence or witnesses; and (iv) that the offence involved is serious or the ends of discipline require an immediate arrest to set an example, to be deterrent to others.[7]

The above provisions have been reinforced by making unnecessary detention without trial or failure to bring the case of an arrested person before the proper authority for investigation an offence punishable by two years imprisonment. [8] In Pakistan, if a military person is unnecessarily detained, he can apply to the civil court and demand that he be dealt with according to law or that he be set at liberty.[9] Such provisions are not available in the military manuals of other countries. In India, a military accused was held in pre-trial custody beyond three months without the approval of the Central Government. The Supreme Court found that the action on part of the military authorities was illegal and violated rule 27 (3) of the Army Rules. The Apex Court awarded Rs 30,000 as compensation for illegal pre-trial custody.[10]

The European Court of Human Rights has held that the British Armed Forces Act and Queen's Regulations for the Army violated the European Convention on Human Rights by allowing a soldier's commanding officer to decide whether to retain a soldier accused of a crime in pretrial confinement.[11] Article 5 (3) of the European Convention on Human Rights provides: "Everyone arrested or detained in accordance with the provisions of paragraph 1(e) of this Article shall be brought promptly before a judge or other officer authorised by law to exercise judicial power and shall be entitled to trial within a reasonable time or to release pending trial. Release may be conditioned by guarantees to appear for trial." *In Boyle v. United Kingdom*, the appellant's main complaint was that his commanding officer could not constitute a suitable judge or other officer because he was part of the prosecution machinery, because his power to decide on close arrest conflicted with his responsibility for discipline within his command and because he lacked the necessary qualifications or experience. The European Court, relying on its decision in *Hood v. United Kingdom*,[12] held that because the commanding officer exercised a prosecutorial role in the system, he lacked the independence and impartiality necessary to be considered a "judicial power".

Action against a Military Offender

In the system of military law, a commander occupies an important position. Unlike a superior in a civilian government organisation, a military commander exercises discretion in deciding whether an offence should be charged and how an offender should be punished. One of the most difficult decisions facing a commander concerns the manner in which to dispose of the case. An administrative or disciplinary action may be taken against a service person who fails to meet or uphold the service's standard of conduct. The fundamental purpose of administrative or disciplinary processes is to foster and promote discipline and the type of behaviour required for the maintenance of operational effectiveness. The commander has a number of options for the resolution of disciplinary problems. He may: (i) choose to take no action;[13] (ii) initiate administrative action against a military offender; [14] (iii) dispose of the offence summarily with a minor punishment; or (iv) dispose of the case with the help of a court martial.

The commanding officer of the accused is responsible for initiating necessary action against the accused. During the hearing of a charge, a commanding officer may dismiss the charge, if in his opinion the evidence does not show that an offence under the military law has been committed. In case he desires to proceed with the charge the options available to him are (i) dispose of the case of persons below the rank of junior commissioned officer by warding suitable punishment; (ii) refer the case to the proper superior military authority; (iii) adjourn the case for the purpose of having the evidence reduced to writing (summary of evidence).[15]

Summary of Evidence

In case the military accused is an officer, JCO or a warrant officer it is necessary that the commanding officer orders for recording of a summary of evidence. A summary of evidence will also be necessary in case of other ranks, if the commanding officer desires that the accused be tried by a court martial.

A summary of evidence is a record of evidence for the prosecution and the defence, made by the commanding officer or by another officer on his orders, in relation to a charge against a military person, to enable the commanding officer to determine whether or not, a prima facie case exists on the alleged charge, and whether the charge be proceeded with or dismissed. The summary of evidence can be recorded by the commanding officer himself or by an officer detailed by him for the purpose. The officer detailed to record the summary of evidence may or may not be under the command of officer, who ordered its recording. The summary of evidence is not recorded on oath or affirmation and the accused is not authorised to be represented by a counsel.

Summary of evidence is recorded in writing in the presence and hearing of the accused. The accused shall be at liberty to cross-examine prosecution witnesses. After the evidence of all prosecution witnesses has been recorded in a summary of evidence, the accused is cautioned in the presence of an independent witness: "Do you wish to make a statement? You are not obliged to say anything unless you wish to say anything but whatever you will say will be taken down in writing and given in evidence." Any statement made by the accused is taken down in verbatim. In case accused makes a statement or refuses the signature of the accused and independent witness is obtained.[16] The accused may produce any witness in his defence, and their evidence is also recorded in the same manner as of other witnesses. After completion of a summary of evidence, the commanding officer has following options: (i) he can remand the accused for trial by a court martial, or (ii) he can refer the case to proper superior military authority, or (iii) if he thinks it desirable, re-hear the case and either dismiss the charge or dispose it if summarily. The procedure for summary or minor punishments is as follows.

Summary Punishment

The basic philosophy behind summary punishments[17] under military law is that a court martial is not an appropriate means of preserving the discipline and effectiveness of the service in all the cases. Commanders, therefore, must have the authority to act swiftly, effectively and inexpensively in minor cases. In such cases a elaborate rules of trial procedure give way to a rather summary procedure which, nonetheless, should be fair in order to be effective. Summary punishments do not apply to officers of the rank of Major (equivalent in the Air Force and Navy) and above,[18] who can be punished by only a court martial. An accused is not entitled to any legal help during a summary trial.

The officers, junior commissioned officers (JCO) and warrant officers can be punished by certain commanders and higher staff officers, who have been delegated this power by the respective chief of the staff. Persons below the rank of JCO can be summarily punished by all the commanding officers and other officers on whom the power is delegated, subject to the limitations of their rank and power to award the punishment. Theoretically, any offence can be disposed of summarily.[19] However, to prevent the abuse of power at the lower levels, military laws list a number of serious offences which cannot be punished summarily by a commander without prior sanction in writing of the superior/convening authority.[20]

Trial of persons below the rank of Junior Commissioned officer

The procedure before the commanding officer is quite different from the magistrate's court. The accused is not entitled to legal representation, he does not plead to the charge, laws of evidence need not apply and the proceedings are not open to the public. Where a commanding officer, after hearing the case, considers that the accused is guilty, he may impose a penalty that involves a loss of liberty, field punishment,[21] loss of pay or promotions. The maximum punishments that can be adjudged are: (1) severe reprimand to a Havildar/Sergeant; (2) relinquishment of substantive rank to a Naik/Corporal; and (3) detention up to 28 days, confinement up to 14 days, or field punishment up to 28 days (on active service only), to a person below the rank of Naik/Corporal. Additionally, six other punishments including a fine and penal deductions of up to 14 days pay are provided in the services Acts which may be awarded in lieu of, or in conjunction with, the above punishments.[22] Under the Indian Navy Act, a commanding officer's power to award summary punishment is higher. He may award imprisonment for a period not exceeding three months; or detention for a period not exceeding three months; or dismissal from the Naval service; in addition to the punishments which can be awarded under the Indian Army or Air Force Act.

Trial of Officers and Junior Commissioned Officers (JCO)

In the case of trial of officers, JCOs and warrant officers (WOs), where the commanding officer or superior officer wishes to award punishment affecting the future service prospects of the accused, the latter has the right to elect trial by court martial.[23] In the other cases, a military accused has no such right. The procedure in the case of officers, JCOs and WOs is slightly different. Unless the charge is dismissed the commanding officer, may order a summary of evidence and forward the case to the proper authority authorised to deal with the case. If the accused has not, by prior consent in writing, dispensed with the attendance of witnesses, the case is formally heard by the proper authority much the same way as in other cases. The witnesses are examined under oath and a brief record of their evidence is made.

The Sri Lankan Army Act, however, provides that in cases of summary trials an accused may demand that the evidence against him to be taken under oath. Section 44 of the Sri Lankan Army Act states: "where a commanding officer has power to deal with a case summarily, the accused may demand that the evidence against him shall be taken on oath or affirmation, and if the accused so demands the same oath or affirmation as that required to be taken by witnesses before a court martial shall be administered by the commanding officer to each witness in such case."

Officers, JCOs and WOs can be given one or more of the following punishments: (1) forfeiture of service or seniority not exceeding 12 months; (2) stoppages of pay and allowances to recover loss and damage; (3) forfeiture of pay and allowances (for negligent flying or negligent handling of aircraft); and (4) severe reprimand or reprimand. In the case of either of the first two punishments, the accused, before the imposition, is given the option to elect trial by court martial.

In the South Asian countries, there are no summary appeal courts and the military accused do not have a right to appeal against the commander's decision to the next higher commander. However, there is a provision under which an authority (superior in command to the officer who awarded the punishment) may review the proceedings of the summary trial and cancel, vary or remit the punishment, if it is illegal, unjust or excessive in his opinion. He may also make other directions as may be appropriate in the circumstances of the case.[24]

In the South Asian countries an accused virtually has no legal rights during his summary trials. Under the UK's military justice system a pamphlet containing a list of rights is issued to every soldier who is arrested for or charged with an offence under the Armed Forces Act, 2006. The guide explains the procedure that would be followed in case of arrest, the rights during custody, the right to communication (at least one telephone call at public expense to a legal advisor), help of an assisting officer, the right to free legal assistance, and the right to be produced before a judicial officer, in case he remains in custody beyond 96 hours.

Arrest and Summary Punishments in the UK

The British military legal system confers powers of arrest on officers, warrant officers and non-commissioned officers to arrest those persons subject to military law who commit or are reasonable suspected of having committed, an offence under the Armed Forces Act, 2006. Such powers are usually exercised by officers of Provost Branch and warrant officers and non-commissioned officers of the Royal Air Force/Military Police who exercise this authority on behalf on the Provost Marshal. The power of arrest and the power to retain a person in arrest is not an unfettered power. The Armed Forces Discipline Act 2000 has made few changes to ensure that the powers of arrest and custody within all three services complied with Article 5 of the ECHR.[25]

The European Court of Human Rights in a pre-2000 case held that the British Armed Forces Act and Queen's Regulations for the Army violated Article 5 (3) of the ECHR by allowing a soldier's commanding officer to decide whether to retain a soldier accused of a crime in pretrial confinement. The Court awarded a compensation of EUR 3,096 in accordance with Article 44 (2) of the ECHR.[26]

In broad terms custody is divided into pre-charge custody and post-charge custody. In the case of pre-charge custody, continued arrest will only be authorised when it is necessary to secure or preserve evidence relating to offence for which a service person is under arrest or to obtain such evidence by questioning him. The custody in such cases, up to 48 hours, is authorised by the commanding officer, which will be reached in 12-hours long stages. After each 12-hours period of custody a review will be necessary to extend the period. This ensues that the period of custody is no longer than absolutely necessary to further the investigation. In case it is necessary to extend the period of custody beyond 48 hours, the suspect's commanding officer must apply to a judicial officer, usually a judge advocate or an experienced lawyer appointed by the Judge Advocate General. The judicial officer can authorise continued custody up to 96 hours from the time of initial arrest. The suspect has the right to legal representation during the hearing.

The British Armed Forces Act, 2006, lists the offences which can be dealt with at a summary hearing[27] and provides that a commanding officer can award detention up to a period of 30 days.[28] In the UK, a Summary Appeal Court was established on 2 October 2000, for hearing appeals against findings recorded and punishments awarded by commanding officers and appropriate superior authorities while dealing summarily with the charges. The court consists of a judge advocate and two officers. Any person in respect of whom a charge has been dealt summarily may appeal to the Summary Appeal Court against the finding or punishment or both. The Court has the power to rehear the charge, confirm the findings, quash the findings and punishment, or vary the punishment. On appeal against the punishment alone, the Court may confirm the punishment awarded or substitute any other punishment that would have been within the powers of the commanding officer or appropriate superior authority to award. However, the punishment awarded by the court shall not be more severe than the original punishment awarded.[29]

Arrest and Summary Punishments in the US

In the United States, the Congress shortly after World War II, created the Uniform Code of Military Justice (UCMJ)[30] to provide a uniform and fair system of criminal justice for all branches of the armed forces of the United States. The UCMJ was needed because of the two reasons; first the outcry of the citizen soldiers, who had been subjected to the antiquated Articles of War; and the second to put an end to some services' primitive approach to military justice. In the new Code, all criminal offences were defined, and the procedural rights of service-members were guaranteed by law. The President was given the authority to promulgate rules to implement the Code by developing a Manual for Courts-Martial (MCM). Over the years, both the Code and the Manual have been modified, but the essential structure has remained the same, except for the expansion of the role and the independence of the military judges and military defence counsel. The purpose of non-judicial punishments (NJP), contained in Article 15 of the UCMJ is the same as that of summary punishment under the South Asian military legal systems.

The UCMJ provides for the imposition of disciplinary measures by a commander that are not considered criminal proceedings. This is referred to as "non-judicial punishment," or "captain's mast." Unlike a court martial, where a finding of guilty would be a criminal conviction, a guilty finding under Article 15 does not create a criminal record for the service-member. Some services remove an NJP from a service-members' records upon a promotion, a specified period of time with no new offences, or other events. NJP is supposed to be limited to minor disciplinary infractions; however, there are instances when a commander resolved serious offences utilising NJP. This is usually done in the cases of officers or high-ranking enlisted members.

The procedures for imposing NJP are similar for all the services. However, the army and the air force require a standard of proof of "beyond a reasonable doubt" for a finding of guilt, while the navy and marines use only a "clear and convincing standard." As a practical matter, most commanders rarely understand the meaning of beyond a reasonable doubt. Except when "attached to or embarked on" a ship, a service-member has the right to reject non-judicial punishment and request a trial by court martial. This affords the service-member greater rights, but conversely exposes him or her to greater punishment if found guilty and counts as a federal criminal conviction.

If the case is referred to a summary court martial (SCM), where one officer is judge, jury, prosecutor and defence counsel, this proceeding can also be rejected by the service-member. There is no right to assigned counsel at a SCM, but civilian counsel can be used at the service-member's own expense. The conviction is reviewed locally and the only appeal is to the Judge Advocate General under Article 69 of the UCMJ.

The service-member has a right to see the evidence before the start of the proceedings. While a service-member in an NJP proceeding may not be represented by a military lawyer, he should be given the opportunity to meet a military defence lawyer before deciding to accept or reject NJP. The service-member can also have another service-member or a civilian lawyer as a representative or spokesperson at NJP. A service-member may present both evidence concerning the facts of the case and character and other evidence to "mitigate" (reduce) any punishment imposed after a guilty finding. The evidence can be documents or affidavits or live testimony of witnesses. After imposing punishment, the commander may suspend any portion or all of it. The punishments listed under Article 15 of the UCMJ may be imposed by a commanding officer on all ranks under his command.[31]

A service-member has an absolute right to appeal any imposition of NJP to the next higher command without fear that the punishment will be increased. A lawyer from the higher command's staff judge advocate's office normally reviews the appeal. It is then forwarded to the senior commander for decision. This commander may affirm the punishment, reduce it, or set it aside altogether. The lower commander cannot attempt to use the same evidence at another proceeding. Military appellate courts cannot review the findings imposed through non-judicial punishment. The service-member can, however, file a petition to the Board for Correction of Military Records (BCMR) of that service for further review.

A few dissimilarities exist between the US's and the South Asian systems. In the US, much of the Constitution's Bill of Rights designed to protect the individual from arbitrary and unfair prosecution has also been codified in the Uniform Code of Military Justice (UCMJ). For example, a service-member must be informed of the charges against him or her, and these charges must relate to a specific article in the UCMJ. The service-member must be told at the outset that he or she has a right to counsel and a right to remain silent when questioned (Article 31, UCMJ). This provision is broader than the well-known "*Miranda* rights" guaranteed by the Constitution. These two rights—the right to counsel and the right to remain silent—are probably the two most important legal rights of an accused service-member.

Notes

1. In the armed forces, a person who is charged with an offence may be taken into military custody. The provisions relating to arrest are as follows: (a) a military person may be ordered into military custody be any superior officer; (ii) an officer may order into military custody any officer, though he may be of a higher rank, engaged in a quarrel, affray or disorder; (iii) a provost martial, his deputies and assistants may arrest and detain any person subject to military laws; (iv) a police officer or magistrate may arrest within his jurisdiction a military person who is accused of an offence or who is a deserter, on a written request in that behalf of the commanding officer of such person; and (v) a police officer may arrest without warrant a person reasonably believed to be a military person and to be a deserter. Manual of Indian Military Law, Volume I, Chapter III, paragraph 1.
2. Pakistan (Services) Amendment Ordinance VII of 1972.
3. Communication No. 770/1997, *Gridin v. Russian Federation* (Views adopted on 20 July 2000), in UN doc. *GAOR*, A/55/40 (vol. II), p. 175, para. 8.1.
4. Communication No. 458/1991, *A. W. Mukong v. Cameroon* (Views adopted on 21 July 1994), in UN doc. *GAOR*, A/49/40 (vol. II), p. 181, para. 9.8.
5. Communication No. 248/1987, *G. Campbell v. Jamaica* (Views adopted on 30 March 1992), p. 246, para. 6.3.
6. Communication No. 597/1994, *P. Grant v. Jamaica* (Views adopted on 22 March 1996), in UN doc. *GAOR*, A/51/40 (vol. II), p. 212, para. 8.1.
7. Regulations for the Indian Army, paragraph 392 and the Manual of Indian Military Law, Vol. I Chapter III, para 1.
8. Section 50 of the Indian, Bangladesh and Pakistan Army Act; section 61, Nepal Army Act; and section 112, Sri Lankan Army Act.
9. Pakistan Air Force Act Rule 46.
10. *Bhuwneshwar Singh v. Union of India* (1993) 4 SCC 327.
11. *Boyle v. United Kingdom*, (Application No. 55434/00) (ECtHR Jan. 8, 2008).
12. *Hood v. United Kingdom* 29 EHRR 365 (1999).
13. The circumstances surrounding an event may warrant that no adverse action be taken. The preliminary inquiry might indicate that the accused is innocent, that the only evidence is inadmissible, or the commander may decide that other valid reasons exist for not prosecuting the alleged accused.
14. The Commander might decide that the best disposition for the offence and offender is to take administrative rather than punitive action.
15. Rule 22, Indian Army Rules.

16. Rule 23, Indian Army Rules.
17. Sections 80, 83, 84 and 85, Indian Army Act; section 23, Bangladesh and Pakistan Army Acts, section, 105 Nepal Army Act; and section 42, Sri Lankan Army Act.
18. Under the Indian and Sri Lankan Army Acts, minor punishments could be awarded to the officers up to the rank of Major. Section 84, Indian Army Act, 1950 and Section 42 Sri Lankan Army Act.
19. Paragraph 405, Regulations for the Indian Army states: "There is no offence which a commanding officer is compelled by law or rules to send before a court martial and each case should be considered on its merit, but a commanding officer should not, of course, dispose of summarily a case which he is debarred by Army Act, section 120 (2) from trying by summary court martial (SCM) without reference to a superior authority, or any other case which obviously deserves a more severe punishment than he is empowered to award summarily."
20. Bangladesh and Pakistan Army Acts, section 99; Pakistan Air Force Act, section 83. The Indian Army Act, section 120 (2) provides that a commanding officer should not dispose of summarily, offences which he cannot dispose of by a SCM. These are: (i) very serious offences punishable with death under section 34 of the Act; (ii) mutiny under section 37 of the Act; (iii) civil offences under section 69 of the Act; and (iv) offences against himself.
21. In India, field-punishment was abolished in 1992.
22. Under the Nepal Army Act, term 'battlefield punishment' is used in place of 'field punishment'. Indian Army Act, section 80; Bangladesh and Pakistan Army Acts, section 23; Nepal Army Act, section 104 and 105; Sri Lankan Army Act, section 42 and 43.
23. Indian Army Act, section 84 (a).
24. Section 87 of the Indian Army Act provides: If any punishment which has been awarded....appears to a superior military authority....to be illegal, unjust or excessive; such authority may cancel, vary or remit the punishment and make such other direction as may be appropriate in the circumstances of the case. Section 118, Nepal Army Act.
25. Article 5 (3) of the European Convention on Human Rights provides: "Everyone arrested or detained in accordance with the provisions of paragraph 1(e) of this Article shall be brought promptly before a judge or other officer authorised by law to exercise judicial power and shall be entitled to trial within a reasonable time or to release pending trial. Release may be conditioned by guarantees to appear for trial."
26. The applicant had joined the British Army in 1990. On November 1, 1999, while he was serving as a gunner with the 12th Regiment of the Royal Artillery and stationed in Germany, a woman alleged that she had been raped by the applicant. On 2 November the applicant was arrested, along with two other soldiers, by the service police. He was assisted by a lieutenant from Army Legal Services. On that date he also signed a certificate acknowledging that he had been informed of his right to have the assistance of an "accused advisor" during any summary hearing before his commanding officer (CO). On 5 November 1999 he was charged by his CO, under Section 70 of the Army Act 1955, with indecent assault contrary to section 14(1) of the Sexual Offences Act 1956. The CO referred the case to the Higher Authority and remanded the applicant in close arrest. On 16 November 1999 the applicant was transferred to the Military

Correctional Training Centre in the United Kingdom. The Court held that there has been a violation of Article 5(3) of the Convention in respect of the lack of independence and impartiality of the applicant's commanding officer deciding to keep him in the custody. The court relied on its earlier judgment in *Hood v. the United Kingdom* (1999), where it found that the commanding officer's concurrent responsibility for discipline and order in his command exhibits an additional reason for an accused reasonably to doubt that officer's impartiality when deciding on the necessity of the pre-trial detention of an accused in his command. As a result, the Court held that the CO was not sufficiently impartial to be considered "an officer authorised by law to exercise a judicial power". ECtHR in *Boyle v. United Kingdom,* application No. 55434/00, decision of January 8, 2008.

27. Section 53, Armed Forces Act, 2006.
28. However, in case a commanding officer has extended powers under section 133 of the Armed Forces Act, 2006, he can award detention up to 90 days.
29. Rowlison Simon P. 2002. The British System of Military Justice, Vol. 52, *The Air Force Law Review*, p. 17-51.
30. The UCMJ has two main parts, a procedural system for carrying out discipline and a series of punitive articles describing the offences for which a service-member can be punished. The criminal code covers the same type of criminal offences found in civilian life: murder, rape, robbery, etc. It also covers offences unique to the military: insubordination, failure to obey orders, unauthorised absence, desertion, etc. The UCMJ also provides for appeals from court martial convictions and for redress of grievances when the service-member believes he or she has been treated unfairly by the superior military authorities.
31. Under Article 15 of the UCMJ, the following punishments could be awarded (1) Upon officers: restriction to certain specified limits, with or without suspension from duty, for not more that 30 consecutive days; or arrest in quarters for not more than 30 consecutive days; or forfeiture of not more than one-half of one month's pay per month for two months; or restriction to certain specified limits, with or without suspension from duty, for not more than 60 consecutive days; or detention of not more than one-half of one month's pay per month for three months. (2) Upon other personnel: if imposed upon a person attached to or embarked in a vessel, confinement on bread and water or diminished rations for not more than three consecutive days; or correctional custody for not more than seven consecutive days; or forfeiture of not more than seven days' pay; or other lower punishments.

4

Offences and Punishments

The military legal systems of the South Asian countries regulate a broader spectrum of conduct than do the civilian criminal laws in these countries. For instance, in the civilian sphere, it is not a crime to report late for work, whereas, in the armed forces, a person can be prosecuted for being absent without leave and may be punished with up to three years of imprisonment. Similarly, military legal systems have provisions for punishing conduct that is not considered to constitute an offence elsewhere, such as using foul language or failing to behave as an officer.

The military Acts cover generally three types of offences. The first type of offence is 'military' in character and concerns, for example, acts related to enemy or insubordinate conduct. The second type of offence is essentially criminal in nature and relates to acts such as assault and the falsification of documents. Finally, the third type of offence is related to civilian criminal offences and concerns, specifically, acts such as assault and misappropriation. It would be difficult to examine all military offences;[1] however, certain provisions uniquely addressing military offences warrant a discussion.

Offences Relating to Misbehaviour before Enemy

The offences under this category are considered 'most serious' and the maximum punishment for them is death. In Nepal, since the death penalty has been abolished, an accused may be awarded the punishment of life imprisonment and confiscation of his entire share of ancestral property. The offences in this category may include acts such as: (i) shamefully abandoning or delivering to the enemy any garrison or post, which it was one's duty to defend, or compelling or inducing any commanding officer to commit such acts; (ii) intentionally using any means to compel or induce any person subject to military law to abstain from acting against the enemy, or to discourage such person from acting against the enemy; (iii) in the presence of the enemy, showing cowardice by shamefully casting away arms, ammunition or equipment; (iv) treacherously holding correspondence or communicating intelligence to the enemy; (v) directly or indirectly assisting the enemy with money, arms, ammunition, stores or supplies; (vi) treacherously or through cowardice sending a flag of truce to the enemy; (vii) in time of war or during any military operation, intentionally raising a false alarm; (vii) while in action, spreading reports calculated to create alarm or despondency; (ix) in time of action, leaving one's commanding officer or post without being regularly relieved or without leave; (x) having been made a prisoner of war, voluntarily serving with or aiding the enemy; (xi) knowingly harbouring or protecting an enemy; (x) being a sentry in time of war, sleeping on post or being intoxicated; or (xii) knowingly acting in a way that imperils the success of the military.

There are other categories of offences which also relate to misbehaviour before the enemy but are not punishable with death. A military person who is taken prisoner by the enemy owing to want of due precaution or through disobedience of orders, or who has been taken prisoner and fails to rejoin service when able to do so will be charged under this category of offences. Everyone connected with the armed forces needs to recognise the grave danger of assisting the enemy by gossip, whether verbal or written, as to plans, prospects, operations, etc. Therefore, a military person who, without due authority, holds correspondence with the enemy or sends a flag of truce to the enemy could be charged and the punishment may extend up to fourteen years of imprisonment.

For the purpose of these offences, the term 'enemy' includes all armed mutineers, armed rebels, armed rioters, pirates and any person in arms against whom it is the duty of any person subject to military law to act.

Offences on Active Service

The armed forces are on active service during military operations or before being deployed against an enemy. Military law provides that in such situations, a military person may be considered guilty of an offence if he (i) uses criminal force against a sentry; (ii) breaks into any house or other place in search of plunder; (iii) being a sentry, sleeps upon his post or is intoxicated; (iv) without orders from his superior officer, leaves his guard or post; or (v) intentionally or negligently raises a false alarm or spreads reports to create unnecessary alarm or despondency. The use of force against a sentry does not necessarily mean the use of physical force. Passing the sentry when warned by his superior officer not to do so, would amount to an offence.

Mutiny

The Indian rebellion of 1857 began as a mutiny of sepoys of the British East India Company's army on 10 May 1857.[2] Historically mutiny has been viewed as the gravest offence under the military codes. Mutiny implies collective insubordination, or a combination of two or more persons to resist, or to induce others to resist a lawful military authority. It is considered a serious offence in the militaries the world over, and a person could be held accused of the offence of mutiny, if he is present at any such mutiny and does not do his utmost to suppress the same. A military person who has knowledge of a mutiny or has reason to believe in the existence of any mutiny, any intention to mutiny or any such conspiracy, could also be held as an accused of the offence of mutiny, if he does not give information to his commanding or other superior officer. Collective petitions and representations, or the submission of a petition through the medium of any association in respect of military matters are forbidden on this ground.

Unauthorised Absence and Desertion

Absence without leave (AWL) is culpable. A military person who remains absent from duty or overstays the leave granted to him without sufficient cause would be committing an offence of AWL. In case a military person, who is on leave of absence and receives information from the proper authority that the corps or unit to which he belongs has been ordered on active service and yet fails to rejoin without delay, he would also be considered to have committed the offence of AWL. Similarly, the charge of AWL would be brought against any person who (i) without sufficient cause fails to appear at the parade or duty at the time fixed, or (ii) when on parade or on the line of march, without sufficient cause or without leave from his superior officer, quits the parade or line of march. Absence without leave does not include involuntary absence, e.g., due to illness or admission in a civil or military hospital. The offence relates to AWL and not merely absence. The leave of absence must first be granted, then notified to the applicant. A person who has applied for leave and departs from the unit before it is actually granted commits the offence of AWL, even though the leave has been granted but not notified to him.

When a military person remains absent from duty without authorisation for a period of 30 days, assembly of a court of inquiry is mandatory. The purpose of this inquiry is to ascertain the intention of the absentee from the available circumstances and declare him a deserter. Intention to desert may be inferred from a long absence, wearing of disguise, distance from the duty station and the manner of termination of absence. Desertion is distinguished from AWL, in the sense that desertion or attempt to desert the service implies an intention on the part of the accused either (i) never to return to the service, or (ii) to avoid some important military duty (commonly called constructive desertion), for example, in a forward area. A person charged with desertion may be found guilty of an attempt to desert or of AWL. A military person who harbours a deserter can be charged for aiding desertion. Similarly, a military person who, being cognisant of any desertion or attempt at desertion, does not inform his superior officer, or does not take any steps to apprehend the deserter can also be charged for aiding desertion.

Contempt towards Officers and Insubordination

In the armed forces, the officers have the right to command and the soldiers are bound to obey, as long as the command is lawful. Assaulting a superior officer or using criminal force or threatening language to a superior officer can be a grave offence. An assault is something less than the use of criminal force, the force being cut short before the blow actually falls. A military person, who shows a wilful defiance of authority, disobeying any lawful command given personally by his superior officer in the execution of his office, would be considered to have committed a serious offence in the armed forces. An individual accused of such offences is punished more severely if he commits the offence while on active service, than otherwise.

To be legally enforceable, an order must be a positive command or a communication delivered orally or in writing, or by a signal which tells the military person receiving the order what to do or not to do. The command must be specific to an individual, i.e., it must be capable of individual execution by the person to whom it is addressed, and justified by military as well as by civil law and usage. The disobedience must be wilful and deliberate. In the armed forces, the term 'superior officer', does not mean only a commissioned officer; it is a relative term and when used in relation to a person subject to military laws, includes a junior commissioned officer, warrant officer and non-commissioned officer, or its equivalent in all the three services. The expression 'superior officer' means not only a superior in rank, but also a senior in the same grade, where that seniority gives power of command according to the usages of the service.

A military person charged with an offence may be taken into custody by orders of a superior officer. An officer may order into military custody any officer, though he may be of a higher rank, if he has been engaged in a quarrel, affray or disorder. An officer who has been involved in a quarrel, affray, or disorder is bound to obey the order of arrest given by another officer; and if he refuses the order of arrest or uses criminal force or assaults such officer, he would be committing an offence under the military laws. Similarly, while in custody, if a military person uses criminal force, assaults any person, resists an escort, or disobeys any order, he would be committing an offence under the military law. The officers and staff of the military police, exercising power under the command of the provost-marshal, have special powers of apprehension and custody of military offenders. A military person who impedes the provost-marshal or any person lawfully acting on his behalf, or refuses to assist a provost-marshal or any person lawfully acting on his behalf would be breaching the military law and can be tried by a military court for such breaches.

Offences Relating to Enrolment

Persons below the officer rank are enrolled in the armed forces in the South Asian countries. When a person who wants to be enrolled appears before the prescribed enrolling officer (a designated commissioned), the conditions of service and other questions set forth in the prescribed form of enrolment are explained to him. The person is cautioned that if he gives a false answer to any question, he shall be liable to punishment under the military law. If subsequently it is discovered that the enrolled person has given a false answer to any question in the form of enrolment, he can be charged and punished accordingly. Similarly, if an individual enrols himself in the armed forces fraudulently, without obtaining a regular discharge from another corps or service, he can be tried for the offence of fraudulent enrolment.

Disgraceful, Unbecoming Conducts and Ill-treatment

Being members of a disciplined force, armed forces personnel are required to maintain certain standards of conduct and behaviour, whether on duty or otherwise. Any deviation in conduct is considered unlawful. Section 45 of the Indian Army Act provides:

> Any officer, junior commissioned officer or warrant officer who behaves in a manner unbecoming of his position and the character expected of him shall, on conviction by court martial, if he is an officer, be liable to be cashiered or to suffer such less punishment as is in this Act mentioned; and, if he is a junior commissioned officer or a warrant officer, be liable to be dismissed or to suffer such less punishment as is in this Act mentioned.

The behaviour expected of an officer would include readiness to do one's duty under all circumstances, with mental robustness and strength of will, compatible with the ethics of courageous fighting men of the armed forces. For behaviour to be blameworthy, it must be unbecoming both of the accused's position and the character expected of him as an officer or junior commissioned officer. It should offend the accepted rules of social behaviour and be unsuitable in terms of character from a moral point of view. In serious cases of unbecoming conduct, instead of taking disciplinary action against the offenders, the armed forces in India have preferred administrative dismissal or removal from service. Similarly an officer, junior commissioned officer, warrant officer or non-commissioned officer who uses criminal force against or ill treats his subordinate in rank or position would also be committing an offence under the military law.

A charge of "disgraceful conduct" could be brought against a military person if he acts in a cruel, indecent or unnatural manner; or malingers, or feigns or produces disease or infirmity in himself, or intentionally delays his cure or aggravates his disease or infirmity; or with an intention to render himself or any other person unfit for service, voluntarily causes hurt to himself or another person. Feigning disease means not merely that the person concerned reports himself sick when he is not sick, but that he does so when he knows that he is not sick, pretending to feel, symptoms which do not exist. Malingering goes further, in that it implies some act committed with the object of producing the appearance of disease or infirmity.

Making a false accusation against a comrade or making a statement affecting the character of another military person is an offence under the military legal system. Similarly, making a false report, declaration or certificate with the intention of defrauding or obtaining for oneself any allowance or other advantage or privilege is a serious military offence.

Offences Relating to Illegal Arrests and Confinements

A military person who is accused of committing an offence may be arrested. The superior officers have an absolute right to arrest a military offender. There are two different types of arrest: 'open' and 'closed'. Open arrest is similar to being on bail, subject to certain conditions and restrictions which may be ordered by the commanding officer, with the individual still having the liberty to move around. When the accused is under closed arrest, he is deprived of the freedom of movement and may be detained in a guard room or place of safe custody. Irregularities in connection with arrest and confinement are offences under military law. In the armed forces, it is the duty of the commanding officer to take care that a person under his command, when charged with an offence, is not detained in custody for more than 48 hours without the charge being investigated. In order to detain a person for more than 48 hours, sanction from the higher military authorities is required. A military commander who unnecessarily detains a person in arrest or confinement without bringing him to trial, or an officer who having the custody of an offender, fails to deliver him for trial could be held liable under military law.

Similarly, if a guard commander (i) releases any person committed to his charge without proper authority, or (ii) refuses to receive any prisoner or person so committed, or (iii) wilfully or without reasonable excuse allows any person committed to his charge to escape would be committing an offence. Duty is also imposed upon a military person under lawful custody. If he escapes or attempts to escape, he would commit an offence under military law. A prisoner is said to 'escape' when he unlawfully goes out of sight, beyond the control of the person in whose custody he is placed. The attempt to escape is itself a substantive offence.

Extortion, Corruption and Offences relating to Property

A military person who commits extortion or without proper authority exacts from any person money, provisions or service would be held liable under military law. In the armed forces, committing theft of government or private property, dishonest misappropriations, criminal breach of trust, or defraud are considered serious breaches of military discipline and are punishable offences. Stealing from a person subject to military law is regarded as a particularly disgraceful military offence, considering that in the daily routine of military life, persons must constantly leave exposed their arms, uniform and equipment, as well as their private property, such as money, trusting the honour of their comrades. In a number of cases, the pay of offenders has been withheld due to theft of property. A mere error or irregularity in accounts or a mistaken mis-application of property does not constitute an offence under the law. There must be an intention to defraud on the part of the accused, either for his own benefit or the benefit of some other person.

The government issues property like arms, ammunition, equipment and clothing to military persons for their use. If they lose, sell, pawn, destroy or run away with such property, they will be held liable under military law. Wilful destruction of military property or destruction of property belonging to any other military force or institution is a serious military offence in the South Asian countries. Military persons are also expected to take care of animals entrusted to their care. In case they are found guilty of killing, injuring or ill treating such animals, they would be prosecuted under military law.

Offences relating to Court Martial

Courts martial are *ad hoc* military courts in the South Asian military legal system. A court martial is, in fact, not a part of the judiciary in the South Asian countries and is not included among the courts established by the parliaments under the constitutions. The military law systems provide that a military person would be held liable if he commits the following offences in relation to a court martial:

- Being duly summoned or ordered to attend as a witness before a court martial, failing to attend wilfully or without reasonable excuse; or
- Refusing to take an oath or make an affirmation legally required by a court martial to be taken or made; or
- Refusing to produce or deliver any document in one's power or control legally required by a court martial to be produced or delivered by one; or

- Refusing when a witness to answer any question which one is by law bound to answer; or
- Being guilty of contempt of court martial by using insulting or threatening language, or by causing any interruption or disturbance in the proceedings of such court.

A military person can also be convicted for giving false evidence, i.e., if he has been duly sworn or affirmed before any court martial and makes any statement which is false, and which he either knows or believes to be false or does not believe to be true.

Good Order and Discipline

Observance of good order and discipline is expected from all military persons, be they on duty or otherwise. It is also the duty of all ranks in the armed forces to uphold the good reputation of the service. Section 63 of the Indian Army Act, which deals with "violation of good order and discipline", provides: "Any person subject to this Act who is guilty of any act or omission which, though not specified in this Act, is prejudicial to good order and military discipline shall, on conviction by court martial, be liable to suffer imprisonment for a term which may extend to seven years or such less punishment as is in this Act mentioned."

This provision can be traced back to the Articles issued by the Earl of Essex in 1642, which provided: "All other faults, disorders and offences, not mentioned in these Articles, shall be punished according to the general customs and laws of war."[3] Article 70 of the Indian Articles of War (Act V of 1869) provided: "All offences not punishable with death, all neglects to obey any garrison or other orders, all acts and omissions, of which any person subject to these Articles is accused, shall, though not specified in these Articles, if they be prejudicial to good order and military discipline, be taken cognizance of and punished according to the nature and degree of offence, act or omission by any court martial empowered to try the person guilty of such offence, act or omission."

In the United States, Article 133 of the Uniform Code of Military Justice proscribes officers from engaging in unbecoming conduct.[4] The US adopted this more from the British Articles of War of 1765. The British version provided: "Whatsoever commissioned officer shall be convicted before a general courts martial of behaving in a scandalous, infamous manner, such as is unbecoming the character of an officer and gentleman, shall be discharged from the service." In 1806, Congress revised the language by omitting the terms "scandalous" and "infamous," leaving the provision to read: "Any commissioned officer convicted before a general court martial of conduct unbecoming an officer and a gentleman, shall be dismissed [from] the service." Congress ultimately incorporated the provision into the UCMJ in 1951 and enacted it as Article 133. The current version of the article renders the provision applicable to officers, cadets and midshipmen, and authorises any punishment that a courts martial may direct, including, but not limited to, dismissal from the service. There are a number of activities that may comprise the conduct prohibited by the provisions of Article 133. These activities include making false official statements or reports to superior officers; insulting or defaming another officer in the presence of other military members; giving false testimony before a courts-martial or board; neglecting to discharge pecuniary obligations; cruelty toward or maltreatment of subordinates; getting drunk in the presence of military inferiors; commission of a felony or crime; and gross disrespect or defiance of civil authorities.

In the UK, Section 69 of the Army and the Air Force Acts of 1955 provided that "any person subject to military/air force law, who is guilty, whether of any act, or omission or otherwise, of conduct to the prejudice to good order and military discipline, shall on conviction by court martial, be liable to imprisonment for a term not exceeding two years or any less punishment provided by this Act." To be held guilty under Section 69, the prosecution must prove that the accused did the acts alleged in the particulars of the charge, that the conduct was improper in the sense of being contrary to accepted military standards and the conduct was likely to be prejudicial to both good order and military discipline.

The Court Martial Appeal Court, in *R v. Dodman* (unreported case decided on March 13, 1998) has held that whilst an offence under section 69 requires proof of the basic *mens rea* to do the act alleged in the charge, it does not involve blameworthiness, in the sense of providing that the accused knew, or ought to have known, that the act was blameworthy. It was accordingly, not a defence that the accused did not realise that his conduct was prejudicial to good order and military discipline. In the UK, section 69 has been used to cover a wide variety of conduct including social conduct outside the military environment, which is alleged to be potentially prejudicial to good order and military discipline in circumstances in which it may be far from obvious to the accused that he has offended against the military code. In the new, tri-service Armed Forces Act, 2006 the offence appears at Section 19, which provides:

Conduct prejudicial to good order and discipline

- A person subject to service law commits an offence if he does an act that is prejudicial to good order and service discipline.
- In this section "act" includes an omission and the reference to the doing of an act is to be read accordingly.

- A person guilty of an offence under this section is liable to any punishment mentioned in the Table in section 164, but any sentence of imprisonment imposed in respect of the offence must not exceed two years.

An 'omission' to be punishable, must amount to neglect which is wilful or culpable. If wilful, i.e., deliberate, it is clearly blameworthy. If it is not wilful, it may or may not be blameworthy. Negligence has been defined by judicial pronouncements as 'the omission to do something which a reasonable man guided upon those considerations which ordinarily regulate the conduct of human affairs would do, or doing something which a prudent and reasonable man would not do'. In other words, it is 'doing some act which a person of ordinary care and skill would not do under the circumstances'. In India, the offences charged under this category include the improper use of words, use of abusive language on the telephone, use of unfair means in departmental examinations, negligent driving of service vehicles, violation of authorised channel and addressing of communication to higher military authorities, misuse of a service privilege, refusal to undergo a medical examination, unauthorised journey in service transport, removal of pages form service document to destroy evidence, and negligence in official duty.

The Sri Lankan Army Act makes a unique provision for offence relating to the use of traitorous words against the President. Section 124 of the Act states: "Every person subject to military law who uses traitorous or disloyal words regarding the President shall be guilty of a military offence and shall, on conviction by a court martial, be liable, if he is an officer, to be cashiered or to suffer any less severe punishment ......, and, if he is a soldier, to suffer simple or rigorous imprisonment for a term not exceeding three years or any less severe punishment...." This provision is similar to Article 88 of the US's Uniform Code of Military Justice, which states:

> **Art. 88. Contempt toward officials**
> Any commissioned officer who uses contemptuous words against the President, the Vice President, Congress, the Secretary of Defence, the Secretary of a military department, the Secretary of Homeland Security, or the Governor or legislature of any State, Commonwealth, or possession in which he is on duty or present shall be punished as a court martial may direct.

Civil Offences

Armed forces personnel accused of civil offences may also be tried by a military court.[5] The term 'civil offence' means an offence triable by a civilian 'criminal court'. Section 69 of the Indian Army Act provides:

> Subject to the provisions of section 70, any person subject to this Act who at any place in or beyond India commits any civil offence shall be deemed to be guilty of an offence against this Act and, if charged therewith under this section, shall be liable to be tried by a court martial and, on conviction, be punishable as follows, that is to say-
>
> - if the offence is one which would be punishable under any law in force in India with death or with transportation, he shall be liable to suffer any punishment, other than whipping, assigned for the offence, by the aforesaid law and such less punishment as is in this Act mentioned; and
> - in any other case, he shall be liable to suffer any punishment, other than whipping, assigned for the offence by the law in force in India, or imprisonment for a term which may extend to seven years, or such less punishment as is in this Act mentioned.

It thus follows that if a military person stationed in any country other than his own, commits an act or omission which is an offence under the civil law of that country but would not amount to a civil offence in his own country, he cannot be charged for committing a civil offence. In such cases, the military accused would be tried for act or omission prejudicial to good order and military discipline.

Inside the national territory, where a military person is accused of committing a civil offence and a competent civil court has been established, as a general rule, it is desirable to try him by a civil criminal court. The general rule is, however, subject to qualification. The line dividing the military from the civil offence may be narrow. The offence may have been committed within the military camp. The offender may be one of the body of a troop about to proceed on active service. There may be reasons making the prompt infliction of punishment expedient. In any such case, it may be desirable to try the offender by court martial. On the other hand, certain civil offences are not suitable for trial by court martial, like offences relating to civil property, where the co-accused is a civilian or where most witnesses are civilians. In such cases, it would be desirable to try the military offender in a civil court.

The military laws in the South Asian countries prohibit trial by court martial for three civil offences, viz., murder, culpable homicide not amounting to murder and rape against a person not subject to military, naval or air force laws, e.g., a civilian. However, if these civil offences are committed against a 'civilian' (a) while on active service, or (b) at any place outside India, or (c) at a frontier post specified by the Central Government by notification in this behalf, the accused military person could be tried by a court martial.[6] If a military person commits these three offences against a person subject to the military, naval or air force laws, he would be tried by a court martial.

In *Madan Lal v Union of India*,[7] the appellant was tried by general court martial on a charge of attempted rape. He was found guilty and sentenced to two years imprisonment and dismissal from service. His writ petition was dismissed by a Division Bench of Delhi High Court. In his appeal to Supreme Court, he contested that since under the Criminal Procedure Code (CrPC) the offence under Section 511 of the Indian Penal Code (IPC) could be tried by which the offence attempted is triable and the offence in question being Section 376 (punishment for rape) the same could have been tried only by a session court and not by the court martial.

The Supreme Court held that the question whether the court martial has jurisdiction to try a person, who commits an offence has to be adjudged from the provisions of Army Act itself and not with reference to the CrPC. A bare reading of Section 70 of the Army Act makes it clear that a person who commits '....a rape in relation to a person not subject to military, naval or air force law shall not be deemed guilty of an offence against this act and cannot be tried by a court martial'. However, in the instant case, the appellant was charged and tried for attempt to commit rape. The offence of rape has been defined under Section 375 of the IPC, and is different and distinct from attempt to commit rape. The Supreme Court dismissed the appeal and concluded that the court martial has jurisdiction under Section 70 of the Army Act to try the military offender for an offence of 'attempt to rape' in relation to a person not subject to military, naval or air force law.

In Sri Lanka, civil courts have absolute jurisdiction to try or punish any civil offence committed by any person subject to military law. However, if such a person is convicted of an offence and sentenced to punishment by a court martial and is afterwards tried for, and convicted of, the same offence by a civil court, then the civil court shall, in awarding punishment, have due regard to such punishment Imposed by the court martial as that person may have already been sentenced to.[8]

The Sri Lankan Army Act, in addition, deals with the issue of illegal gratification in connection with appointment or promotion. Section 130 of the Act states: "Every person subject to military law who gives or receives, or aids the giving or receiving of, any valuable consideration in respect of any appointment or promotion in or retirement from the army, or any employment therein, shall be guilty of a military offence and shall, on conviction by a court martial, be liable to be dismissed from the army." Section 64 (e) of the Indian Army Act provides: "any person subject to the Act who directly or indirectly....accepts....any gratification as a motive or reward for procuring the enrolment of any person.... shall on conviction by court martial suffer imprisonment which may be extended to seven years or such less punishment." In other countries, such offences may be dealt with under "violation of good order and discipline".

The Sri Lankan Army Act, in Chapter XV deals, with the offences which are not military offences.[9] These include unlawful recruitment; giving false answers during enlistment; falsely representing to be a deserter; inducing or assisting officers or soldiers to desert or absent themselves without leave; interference with military duties; illegal gratifications to persons not subject to military law for seeking appointments or promotions in the army; purchase of regimental necessaries, equipments and stores; unlawful possession of military certificates; unauthorised use of military decorations; failing to provide proper facilities to employees; misconduct of civilian witness at court martial; false evidence by civilian witness at court martial; and unauthorised training of a military nature. A person accused of these offences is tried in a civil court.

The Nepal Army Act, 2006 differs from the military laws of other South Asian countries in that it makes special provisions for offences relating to torture and disappearance. It provides that in cases of disappearance and allegations of torture, (and also corruption and theft), a special committee would investigate the matter.[10] The jurisdiction to try and proceed with such cases shall be vested with a Special Court formed under Section 119 (1) of the Act.

Punishments

In India, Bangladesh, Pakistan and Sri Lanka, the most severe penalty that can be imposed by a court martial is death. Nepal has abolished the death penalty from its military and criminal justice system.[11] Other punishments which may be inflicted in respect of offences committed by persons subject to the services Acts and convicted by courts martial, in descending order of severity, are: transportation for life or for any period not less than seven years; imprisonment, either rigorous or simple, for any period not exceeding 14 years; cashiering (disgraceful dismissal) in the case of officers; dismissal from the service; field punishment;[12] reduction to the ranks or to a lower rank or grade; forfeiture of seniority of rank; forfeiture of service for the purpose of increased pay, pension or any other prescribed purpose; reprimand; and forfeiture or stoppage of pay and allowances. Within the maximum punishment prescribed under a section of offence, the court martial has the discretion to apportion punishment according to the degree of guilt of the person convicted.[13]

The award of "field punishment" to personnel below the rank of **Non-Commissioned Officer** (NCO) in Bangladesh, Nepal, Pakistan and Sri Lanka is against the human rights norms.[14] An amendment to the military Acts in India in 1993 did away with this punishment. The Rules provide that during the punishment: "He (the military accused) may be kept in irons, that is to say, in fetters or handcuffs or both fetters and handcuffs, and may be secured so as to prevent his escape. When in irons, he may be attached for a period or periods not exceeding two hours in any one day to a fixed object, but must not be so attached during more than three out of any four consecutive days, not during more than 21 days in all." The explanations to the Rule further provide: "The offender must be attached so as to be standing firmly on his feet which, if tied, must not be more than 12 inches apart, and it must be possible for him to move each foot at least three inches. If he is tied round the body there must be no restriction of his breathing. If his arms or wrists are tied, there must be six inches of play between then and the fixed object. His arms must hang either by the side of his body or behind his back."

The Sri Lanka Army Act has additionally provided for the award of specific punishments in the case of serious civil offences. It provides: (1) where a person subject to military law is convicted by a court martial of the offence of treason, he shall be liable to suffer death; (2) where a person subject to military law is convicted by a court martial of the offence of murder, he shall be liable to suffer death; (3) where a person subject to military law is convicted by a court martial of the offence of culpable homicide not amounting to murder, he shall be liable to suffer simple or rigorous imprisonment for a term not exceeding 20 years; and (4) where a person subject to military law is convicted by a court martial of the offence of rape, he shall be liable to suffer simple or rigorous imprisonment for a term not exceeding 20 years.[15]

The power of punishment varies with the kind of court martial. A court martial has discretion in respect of the award of the punishment, based on the quantum of punishment provided in the concerned penal section of the Act. It can award maximum punishment laid down for the offence in each section or such less punishment as laid down in the Act. For example, section 34 of the Bangladesh Army Act provides: "**Neglect to obey orders--**Any person subject to this Act who neglects to obey any standing or routine or other orders shall, on conviction by court martial, be punished with rigorous imprisonment for a term which may extend to two years, or with such less punishment as is in this Act mentioned." In such a case a court martial in Bangladesh would have the power to award the maximum punishment of two years of imprisonment or lesser punishment as mentioned in section 60 (d) to (h) of the Army Act.[16]

A general court martial (GCM) is the highest court martial in military law. It has the power to try any person subject to the military Acts for any offence punishable therein and award a sentence up to death.[17] A district court martial (DCM) has the power to try any person subject to the Army Act other than an officer or a junior commissioned officer (JCO), for any offence made punishable therein; and to pass any sentence authorised by the Act, other than the sentences of death, transportation or imprisonment for a term exceeding two years.[18] In deciding whether an accused should be tried by a GCM or DCM, the convening officer must consider the following factors: (i) the nature of the offence; (ii) the prevalence of the particular offence which the accused been charged; (iii) the general state of discipline in his command; (iv) the character of the accused; and (v) the maximum punishment that can be imposed in the light of any sentence which the accused may be already serving.[19]

A summary/field general court martial (SGCM or FGCM) has the same power as a GCM. It can try any person subject to the Army Act for any offence punishable therein, and award any sentence authorised thereby. However, the sentence of death cannot be passed by a SGCM without the concurrence of all the members.[20] In Bangladesh, India, Nepal and Pakistan, a summary court martial (SCM) may try any person subject to the Army Act[21] under the command of the officer holding the court, except an officer, JCO or a warrant officer. A SCM may pass any sentence under the Army Act, except the sentence of death or imprisonment for a term exceeding one year in case the officer holding the trial is of or higher than the rank of Lieutenant Colonel, and three months, if the officer is below that rank.[22] A court martial has no jurisdiction to try war crimes or war criminals.[23]

The Nepal Army Act prescribes a peculiar punishment. A GCM may impose a penalty of life imprisonment and confiscation of entire share of the ancestral property of a military accused, if he is found guilty of the offences relating to the enemy, mutiny or desertion on active service.[24] In case of offence of the disobedience to a superior officer, a court martial can award the punishment of confiscation of the entire share of ancestral property of the accused. [25]

Although, the question of the choice and quantum of punishment is within the jurisdiction and discretion of the court martial, the sentence has to suit the offence and the offender. The Manual of Indian Military Law[26] provides that the court must always award such punishment as the members consider to be just and proper and must not presume that the convening authority, in sending the case for trial, took a more serious view of the facts. It further states that while awarding punishment, a court martial should take into consideration the following points:

- *Maintenance of Discipline*: The proper amount of punishment to be inflicted is the least amount by which discipline can effectively be maintained; occasionally the exigencies of discipline, apart from the circumstances of the case, may render a severe sentence necessary, but in all cases, the whole force should be in a position to realise that the punishment awarded to an individual is not more than necessary in the interest of the force itself and for the maintenance of discipline.

- *Degree of Criminality*: A non-commissioned officer should be dealt with more severely than a sepoy; where several offenders are found guilty of the same offence, it may be proper to award different amounts of punishment.
- *Premeditation*: An accused who has clearly made long preparation to commit some crime should be more severely punished than one who has acted on the spur of moment.
- *Provocation*: While provocation is no defence to a charge, the court will no doubt take this matter into consideration.
- *Previous Conviction*: A habitual offender deserves more punishment than an infrequent offender, and a first-time offender should be treated leniently if possible.
- *Prevalence of Offence*: Military offences must sometimes be considered in reference to circumstances other than those connected with the individual offender. When there is a general prevalence of offences or of an offence of a particular kind, setting an example may be necessary, and on that account a severe punishment may properly be awarded even if the offence is such as would otherwise have called for a more lenient punishment. In such a case, the punishment must be regarded more from the point of view of the effect which it will produce on the force to which the offender belongs than on the offender alone.

There is a major lacuna in the military legal systems of the South Asian countries. The military officers constituting a court may not be trained in law. They decide the questions of both guilt as well as punishment against an accused, and function under the command influence. A law-qualified military officer (judge advocate) is a must only in GCMs, but he does not take part in the deciding upon the guilt of the offender and the punishment to be awarded by the court martial. This often leads to the award of excessive or disproportionate punishments, which violates the human rights of a military accused.[27]

The offences and punishments contained in the South Asian military legal systems were based on the British military justice system. The UK has overhauled its military justice system and done away with independent service Acts and multiple ad hoc military tribunals.[28] The three services Acts have been abolished. It now has a court, known as the court martial. In the case of any proceeding, the court martial is to consist of a judge advocate and at least three, but not more than five, other persons, who should have held commission for at least three years. The number of members could increase up to seven in case the trial is for a serious offence. The composition of the court martial is not dependent upon the rank of the accused. A warrant officer is qualified for membership of a court martial in cases where the accused is below the officer rank.[29]

The range of sentences available to the court martial under the UK's Armed Forces Act, 2006 has also been streamlined. For serious offences relating to the enemy, military operations, desertion on active service and mutiny, an accused may be awarded life imprisonment; for offences like the use of violence against seniors and disobedience of a lawful command, the punishment could be up to 10 years' imprisonment; and the punishment for offences like absence without leave, the use of force against a sentry, malingering, and conduct prejudicial to good order and discipline could be imprisonment of up to two years.

Notes

1. The term "offence" has been defined as "an act or omission punishable under the services Acts and includes a civil offence". The offences contained in the military Acts could be divided into the following categories: (i) Offences in relation to the enemy and punishable with death; (ii) Offences in relation to the enemy and not punishable with death; (iii) Offences punishable more severely on active service than at other times; (iv) Mutiny, desertion and absence without leave; (v) Striking or threatening superior officers, disobedience to superior officers, and insubordination and obstructions; (vi) Fraudulent enrolment and false answers on enrolment; (vii) Unbecoming conduct, certain forms of disgraceful conduct, ill treating a subordinate and intoxication; (viii) Permitting escape of person in custody, irregularity in connection with arrest or confinement and escape from custody; (ix) Offences in respect of property, extortion and corruption, making away with equipment and injury to property; (x) False accusations, falsifying official documents and false declaration, signing in blank and failure to report; (xi) Offences relating to courts-martial and false evidence; (xii) Unlawful detention of pay; (xiii) Offences in relation to aircraft and flying; (xiv) Miscellaneous offences and violation of good order and discipline; (xv) Attempt to commit any of the above offences and abetment of these offences; and (xvi) Civil offences. See Sections 34 to 72 of the Indian Army and Air Force Acts, 1950 and Sections 34 to77 of the Indian Navy Act, 1957; Bangladesh and Pakistani Army Act, Sections 24-59; Sri Lanka Army Act, Sections 95-130; and Nepal Army Act, Sections 38-65.
2. David Saul. 2009. *The Bengal Army and the Outbreak of the Indian Mutiny*, New Delhi: Manohar.
3. Donagan Barbara. 2008. *War in England 1642-1649*, UK: Oxford University Press, p. 150-152.
4. **Art. 133. Conduct unbecoming an officer and a gentleman:** Any commissioned officer, cadet, or midshipman who is convicted of conduct unbecoming an officer and a gentleman shall be punished as a court martial may direct.
5. A criminal court and a court martial may each have jurisdiction in respect of same offence. Adjustment of jurisdiction is provided by Indian Army Act sections 125 and 126, which give the military authorities the right of deciding by which court the alleged offender is to be tried, subject, however, to the reservation that, when a criminal court considers that the proceedings ought to be instituted before itself, it may require

prescribed military authority to deliver the offender or postpone proceedings pending a reference to the Central Government. The decision of the Central Government is final.

6. Section 70 of the Indian Army Act, 1950.
7. *Madan Lal v Union of India*, Supreme Court Criminal Appeal No. 889 of 1996.
8. Section 77, Sri Lankan Army Act.
9. Sections 135-147, Sri Lankan Army Act.
10. The committee shall comprise of the following for conducting investigation: (a) Deputy Attorney General – chairperson, and (b) chief of legal section of the ministry of defence and representative of judge advocate not below the rank of lieutenant as members. Section 62 of the Army Act, 2006.
11. Section 101, Nepal Army Act.
12. In Bangladesh, Nepal, Pakistan and Sri Lanka.
13. Section 71, Indian Army Act, 1950; Section 60, Bangladesh and Pakistan Army Acts; and Section 133, Sri Lankan Army Act.
14. Article 7 of the ICCPR, article 5 of the African Charter, article 5(2) of the American Convention and article 3 of the European Convention all outlaw recourse to torture, cruel and/or inhuman or degrading treatment or punishment. This prohibition is valid at all times and allows for no limitations.
15. Section 131, Sri Lanka Army Act.
16. Bangladesh Army Act, Section 60. **Punishment.**--Punishments may be inflicted in respect of offences committed by persons subject to this Act and convicted by courts martial according to the scale following, that is to say: (a) death; (b) transportation for life or for any period not less than seven years; (c) rigorous imprisonment for any term not exceeding fourteen years; (d) dismissal from the service; (e) in the case of persons other than officers or junior commissioned officers, detention for a period not exceeding six months; (f) in the case of non-commissioned officers, reduction to the ranks or to a lower rank; (g) in the case of officers, junior commissioned officers and non-commissioned officers, forfeiture of seniority of rank; or, in the case of any of the aforesaid whose promotion depends upon length of service, forfeiture of all or any part of the service for the purpose of promotion; (h) forfeiture of service for the purposes of increased pay, or any other prescribed purpose; (i) in the case of officers, junior commissioned officers and non-commissioned officers, severe reprimand or reprimand; (j) forfeiture, fines and stoppages as follows, namely:- (i) in the case of a person sentenced to dismissal from the service, forfeiture of all arrears of pay and allowances and other public money due to him at the time of such dismissal; (ii) fine; (iii) stoppages of pay and allowances until any proved loss or damage occasioned by the offence of which he is convicted is made good; (iv) for an offence committed on active service, forfeiture of pay and allowances for a period commencing on the day of the sentence and not exceeding three months:

    Provided that,

    (1) a person shall not be sentenced to transportation or to be fined except in respect of an offence of which he is convicted under section 59 of this Act; and (2) where in respect of an offence under this Act there is specified a particular punishment or such less punishment as is in this Act mentioned, there may be awarded in respect of that offence instead of such particular punishment, but subject to the other provisions of this Act and regard being had to the nature and degree of the offence, any one punishment lower in the scale than the particular punishment.

17. Section 118, Indian Army Act, 1950.
18. Section 119, Indian Army Act, 1950.
19. Manual of Indian Military Law, Vol. I, Chapter IV, paragraph 24.
20. Section 132 (3), Indian Army Act, 1950.
21. SCM does not exist under the Sri Lankan Army Act.
22. Section 120, Army Act, 1950.
23. In the United States, these powers are exercised by a GCM under Article 18 of the Uniform Code of Military Justice.
24. Sections 38, 39 and 42 (1) (a), Nepal Army Act.
25. Section 101, Nepal Army Act.
26. Manual of Military Law, Volume I, Chapter IV, paragraph 84.
27. Dirk van Zyl Smit and Andrew Ashworth. 2004. 'Disproportionate Sentences as Human Rights Violations', *The Modern Law Review*, Vol. 67 (4), July 2004, p. 541-560.
28. Armed Forces Act 2006.
29. Sections 154 -156, Armed Forces Act, 2006.

5

Military Courts

If the commanding officer decides that the offence is serious enough to warrant trial by court martial, he may exercise the fourth option of preferring and forwarding charges. He may choose from four potential levels of court martial: summary, district, summary/field-general, or general. These courts-martial differ in the procedures, rights and possible punishments that can be awarded.

The courts-martial are *ad hoc* military courts which are specially set up for each trial brought before them. This means that they can sit wherever and whenever the convening authority directs, and so, fit in better with the operational requirements of the armed forces. The army Acts of India, Pakistan,[1] Bangladesh[2] and Nepal[3] have four kinds of courts-martial, viz., GCM, DCM, SGCM (FGCM),[4] and SCM. The Sri Lankan Army Act provides for only the GCM, DCM and FGCM, and not for the SCM.[5] A GCM may be convened by the Central Government, the Chief of the Army Staff (COAS) or an officer empowered in this behalf by warrant of the COAS. A DCM may be convened by an officer who has the power to convene a GCM or by any officer empowered in this behalf by warrant of any such officer. The senior most officer appointed to court martial acts as presiding officer under the Nepal Army Act,[6] the Indian Army[7] and the Air Force Acts;[8] whereas under the Bangladesh,[9] Pakistan,[10] and Sri Lankan Army Acts,[11] and the Indian Navy Act,[12] he is appointed by the convening authority.

The Nepal Army Act provides for the constitution of a special court[13] with original jurisdiction in cases relating to corruption, theft, torture and disappearance. Cases relating to these offences are to be first investigated by a committee comprising the deputy attorney general, who acts as chairman, the chief of legal section of the ministry of defence and a representative of the chief judge advocate not below the rank of lieutenant.[14] The special court has original jurisdiction to proceed and adjudicate the case further. An appeal against the decision of the special court may be preferred in the Supreme Court.[15]

The air forces of India, Bangladesh,[16] Pakistan[17] and Sir Lanka[18] have three kinds of courts-martial, i.e., the GCM, DCM and SGCM or FGCM. Under the

Indian Navy Act and Sri Lankan Navy Act,[19] there is one type of court martial, whereas the Bangladesh and Pakistan navies provide for GCM, DCM and SGCM. Under the Indian Navy Act, there is an additional disciplinary court which can be constituted during active service.[20] In India, a court martial convened under the services Acts is not a part of the judiciary and is not included among the courts which Parliament or the state legislature may ordain and establish under Article 246 or 247 of the Constitution. The same is the situation in other countries. These courts are not permanent, but created *ad hoc* for the trial of the military offenders (Clode, 1874: 58).[21]

A GCM consists of a president and four other serving officers who have held their commission for at least three years, while a DCM consists of a president and two officers of at least two years' standing. The services Acts of the South Asian countries do not require that the officers appointed to a court martial are legally qualified, experienced and competent to discharge judicial functions.[22] In case of Bangladesh, Pakistan and Sri Lanka, the president for a general, district or field general court martial are appointed by order of the authority convening the court.[23] However, In India[24] and Nepal[25] the senior most officer amongst the officers of a court martial assumed the functions of presiding officer.

A GCM is to be, and a DCM may be, assisted by a judge advocate from the staff of the Judge Advocate General. The judge advocate is a legally qualified officer, but unlike the US and the UK, in the South Asian countries he is a member of the military command structure. The convening officer appoints the prosecutor, who in serious cases is a legally qualified military officer and should invariably be in the chain of command. The accused is entitled to seek the services of a lawyer, provided that he pays the bill himself, or he may take the assistance of a legally qualified military officer, called the defending officer.[26] The defending officer may also be in the chain of command of the convening officer.

In the South Asian countries, the major difference between the military court and the civil legal system that in case of a military court an accused is tried by military officers, who are untrained in law. The officers constituting the court are from the chain of command of the convening authority, and thus could function under the command influence. Persons below the officer rank are not allowed to sit as members in the court, a practice which is being followed in the UK and the USA. Given that a court martial is also authorised to try civil offences, the lack of legal expertise within the court may affect the outcome of the case. The presence of a judge advocate in a court martial is not of any great significance since the judge advocate does not perform the functions either of an advocate or of a judge and functions under the command influence. He does not preside at a court martial trial, but sits beside the presiding officer in the capacity of the legal adviser to the court, prosecution and defence, and as the representative of the Judge Advocate General.[27]

Military Judiciary

In the South Asian countries, the Judge Advocate General (JAG) is the superintendent of the administration of military justice.[28] The Army, Air Force and Navy have their own JAGs who head the judiciary of their respective services. The judicial department has a selected cadre of officers qualified in law. The JAG department in Pakistan, Bangladesh, Nepal and Sri Lanka is small, when compared to that of India. It is divided into two cells, known as the 'pre-trial section' and 'post-trial section'. The JAG department renders pre-trial advice to the convening authorities, provides a judge advocate at GCM and at important DCM, and prepares reviews of all courts-martial proceedings. Neither the pre-trial advice nor the post-trial review is a requirement of law, but both have been made compulsory through administrative orders. The work of both the pre-trial and post-trial sections is supervised by the JAG who also renders legal opinions and deals with petitions arising out of court martial trials. The JAG department's other functions include representing the government in cases at the higher civil courts and providing legal training to officers.

The Sri Lanka Army Act provides that the powers and duties of the officer appointed to be the judge advocate at a court martial shall be as follows.[29]

- The judge advocate shall give advice on questions of law or procedure relating to the charge or trial to the prosecutor and to the accused. This advice may be given before or during the proceedings, however, advice during the proceedings shall be given with the prior permission of the court.
- The judge advocate shall invite the attention of the court to any irregularity in the proceedings. Whether or not he is consulted, he shall inform the court and the convening authority of any defect in the charge or in the constitution of the court.
- The judge advocate shall take all such action as may be necessary to ensure that the accused does not suffer any disadvantage in consequence of any incapacity to examine or cross-examine witnesses or to give evidence clearly, and may for that purpose, with the permission of the court, question any witness on any relevant matter.
- At the conclusion of the case, the judge advocate shall, unless both he and the court consider it unnecessary, sum up the evidence and advise the court upon the law relating to the case before the court.

The Indian Army Act is silent on the duties and responsibilities of a judge advocate, except that it states that every general court martial shall and every district or summary court martial may be attended by a judge advocate.[30] The Regulations for Indian Army further elaborate that the judge advocate general is the legal advisor to the chief of the army staff (COAS) in matters of military, martial and in international law.[31] In all cases where court martial proceedings are required to be confirmed by the COAS or central government, judge advocate general carries out judicial review of the court martial proceedings and makes recommendations. However, his recommendations are not binding on the COAS. The proceedings of a district court martial where the sentence is below dismissal or those of a summary general court martial may not be sent for advice of the deputy judge advocate general.[32] The reports by officers of judge advocate general department are confidential and are not communicated directly or indirectly to any authority lower than the authority to whom they are addressed. When proceedings are forwarded to lower formations or to units, such reports are removed.[33] The judge advocate general and his deputies are also empowered to issue commission for examination of witnesses.[34]

In most of the developed countries, the military judiciary is independent of the military chain of command. In the UK, the JAG is an independent judicial officer who is not accountable to the government. As the JAG and as a Circuit Judge, he holds judicial office and is independent of the executive. The judge advocates who sit as trial judge in court martial are also independent of the executive. The office of the JAG is an administrative office, staffed by civil servants. As part of the Department for Constitutional Affairs, it is answerable to ministers. The JAG monitors the workings of the military criminal justice system and renders advice on its efficiency and effectiveness. He may also act as the trial judge personally conducting some of the most serious, sensitive or controversial court martial trials. He advises reviewing authorities on reviews and petitions following every conviction and sentence. The JAG appoints judges to conduct Summary Appeal Courts and Standing Civilian Courts, and to rule upon applications for detention in custody.[35]

The JAG in the UK army and air force has always been a civilian judge. Following the decision of the European Court of Human Rights (ECtHR) in the case of *Grieves v. the United Kingdom* (2003), the responsibility for appointing judge advocates and judicial officers was shifted from the Chief Naval Judge Advocate to the Judge Advocate of Her Majesty's Fleet, who is a civilian and a circuit judge appointed by HM The Queen on the recommendation of the Lord Chancellor.

In the Canadian Forces JAG is by statute the legal advisor to the Government of Canada, the Minister and Deputy Minister of the Department of National Defence, the Canadian Forces and the Chief of Defence Staff on all issues related to military law. The Canadian Forces JAG is appointed by Cabinet and he is directly responsible to the Minister of Defence. The JAG is responsible for the superintendence and administration of the Canadian Forces military justice system, which includes an independent Director of Military Prosecution, an independent Director of Defence Counsel Services, and independent judges.[36]

In Australia, the appointment of the JAG is a statutory one, made by the Governor General. He or she must be a judge of a superior court. The JAG has certain reviewing and appointing functions under the Australian Defence Force Discipline Act and presents an annual report on military justice system to Parliament through the Minister of Defence. The JAG does not sit on military tribunals, nor does he give advice to the Department or the Minister of Defence. In Canada, the JAG is, by statute, the legal adviser to the Government of Canada, the Minister and Deputy Minister of the Department of National Defence, the Canadian Forces and Chief of Defence Staff on all issues relating to military law. The National Defence Act does not require the JAG to be an officer or other member of the Canadian Forces (CF).

The Israeli Military Justice Law (MJL) establishes a legal apparatus headed by the Military Advocate General (MAG). The MAG is an appointee of the Minister of Defence at the recommendation of the Chief of Staff (Section 177 of the MJL). The MAG and his staff operate in complete independence in the areas of their operation. The MAG is not subordinate to the Chief of Staff in respect of the exercise of his powers and is not under any command whatsoever de jure or de facto.

In the South African military justice system, the principle of judicial independence is ensured by security of tenure, of salary and of pension, as well as the institutional independence of military judges. The Military Discipline Supplementary Measures Act (MDSMA) dealing with the general duties of military judges and senior military judges states: "Every military judge and every senior military judge shall in the exercise of his or her judicial authority under this Act *(a)* be independent and subject only to the Constitution and the law; *(b)* apply the Constitution and the law impartially and without fear, favour or prejudice; and *(c)* conduct every trial and proceedings in a manner befitting a court of justice."

In the USA, the JAG is vested with various supervisory powers over the military justice system.[37] He is responsible for the review of the court martial, if there is an approved sentence of death, a punitive discharge or bad conduct discharge for enlisted personnel or dismissal for officers. The Uniform Code of Military Justice (UCMJ) has a unique feature to ensure that judicial officers are not subject to command influence. Article 37 (a) of the UCMJ states:

> No authority convening a general, special, or summary court martial, nor any other commanding officer, may censure, reprimand, or admonish the court or any member, military judge, or counsel thereof, with respect to the findings or sentence adjudged by the court, or with respect to any other exercises of its or his functions in the conduct of the proceedings. No person subject to this chapter may attempt to coerce or, by any unauthorised means, influence the action of a court martial or any other military tribunal or any member thereof, in reaching the findings or sentence in any case, or the action of any convening, approving, or reviewing authority with respect to his judicial acts.

Unlike the military justice systems of other democracies, the JAGs in the South Asian countries are organisationally and operationally subordinate to the convening authority, who controls their service career. The officers of the JAG department, therefore, may not be independent and thus in a position to give a fair and just opinion.[38]

Prosecutor

In courts-martial, the prosecuting officer is detailed by the convening officer or the commanding officer. Generally, he is the officer who records the summary of evidence. The Act expressly enjoins upon the prosecutor to assist the court in the administration of justice. He is required to act impartially, and to bring the whole of the transaction before the court and not take any unfair advantage of or suppress any evidence that is in favour of the accused. The court can stop him from referring to any matter not relevant to the charge and also restrain him from the use of violent language or object to the want of fairness or moderation on his part.[39] In difficult cases, the convening authority may select a specially qualified officer to act as prosecutor.[40] A civilian can also be allowed to appear on behalf of the prosecution at a general or district court martial, if the COAS or convening officer declares that it is expedient.[41] In Sri Lanka, the prosecution as well as the defence is entitled to be represented by counsel at all proceedings before a court martial.[42]

Defence

The accused is afforded a proper opportunity of preparing his defence and allowed free communication with his witnesses, and with anyone whom he may wish to consult. At least 48 hours before the trial, the accused is also asked to furnish the names of the witnesses whom he wishes to call in defence and for whose attendance "reasonable" steps are taken. If the accused fails to do so, the responsibility for the attendance of his witnesses shifts to him. Subject to the exigencies of service, the accused is provided with an officer of his choice, who is called the "defending officer", to represent him at the trial. The accused may, at his own expense, engage a civilian counsel, in which case he cannot as a matter of right also have a defending officer. A civilian counsel may be disallowed in case of expediency or in the interest of security.[43] The accused, in addition, may have any person subject to the Act as "friend of the accused" who, however, has no right of audience but can act as his advisor. The Nepal Army Act, however, provides that the accused, if requests, will be defended by a judge advocate assigned to him for that purpose.[44]

In practice, the system of providing a defending officer for the accused works like this: under each command headquarters, a list of law qualified officers is prepared and supplied to the accused, who selects any three officers, of which one may be detailed to defend him.[45] Officers of the JAG department are not included in the list of law qualified officers. Ultimately, the accused may have a defending officer who may not have any previous experience and may not depose a confidence in the accused. The accused's other alternative is to hire a civilian counsel worth the name, an option which may be beyond his means. In India, when an accused is tried by a court martial for an offence punishable with death and is unable to engage a counsel for his defence owing to lack of pecuniary resources, a counsel for his defence may be employed by the convening officer. The maximum amount payable to the counsel is Rs. 500 for each day.[46]

In the USA and the UK, the accused is afforded better opportunities for his defence. The JAG Corps represents the judicial arm of the US armed forces, and has autonomous departments in the Air Force, Army, Coast Guard, Marine Corps and Navy. These are charged with defence and prosecution in military law, as provided in the Uniform Code of Military Justice (UCMJ). In the US military justice system, it is the responsibility of the Judge Advocate General to certify the competence both of the trial counsel (prosecutor) and the defence counsel. In the USA, the trial counsel and defence counsel in a GCM must be certified judge advocates and be equal in other qualifications. The accused is also generally entitled to a qualified defence counsel at a special court martial, unless it is impossible on account of "physical conditions or military exigencies", for example, in "rare circumstances such as on isolated ship on high seas or in a unit in an inaccessible area, provided compelling reasons exist why trial must be held at that time and place". However, in any case when a qualified trial counsel has been detailed, the accused must have a similarly qualified defence counsel.[47]

In the UK, if an accused has been notified that he is to be tried by court martial, he should be afforded a proper opportunity to prepare his defence. The defending officer must be appointed by the commanding officer of the accused to assist him, unless the accused states in writing that he does not wish such an appointment to be made. The system ensures that the accused is provided with, or has access to, a great deal of information [48] that may not be automatically available to a person appearing before a civilian court.

Trial Procedure

The trial procedure of a GCM or DCM is identical in all the South Asian countries. In cases of serious offences, which are not disposed off summarily, the case is adjourned for recording a "summary of evidence" against the accused. A "summary of evidence" is a written statement of the evidence, similar to depositions taken at a magistrate's court. The accused is not entitled to be represented at the recording of the summary of evidence, but he can cross-examine all witnesses and is also allowed to call his witnesses. The convening officer, after receiving an application for trial by court martial from the commanding officer,[49] refers it to the judge advocate for pre-trial advice. The convening officer then appoints or details officers to form the court.

Once the court assembles, the accused is asked whether he objects to being tried by any officer sitting in the court.[50] The accused is also asked in respect of each charge whether he pleads "guilty" or "not guilty". He may object to a charge on the ground that it does not constitute an offence under the Act or is not in accordance with the Army Rules. The court, after hearing any submission which may be made by the prosecutor or by the accused, considers the objection in closed court and either disallows it and proceeds with the trial, or allows it and adjourns to report to the convening officer.

The accused may also offer a plea in bar of the trial.[51] If the facts stated by the accused are sufficient to support the plea, the court receives the evidence offered by the accused/his counsel and by the prosecutor in reference to the plea. If the plea in bar is proved, the court records its findings and notifies it to the convening officer and adjourns. If the findings in relation to the plea in bar are not confirmed, the court may be re-assembled by the convening officer and proceed since the plea had been found not proved.

When an accused pleads guilty to the charges or charge, it is recorded as a finding of the court.[52] A plea of "guilty" is not accepted in cases where the accused is liable, if convicted, to be sentenced to death, and where such plea is offered, a plea of "not guilty" is recorded and the trial proceeds accordingly.[53] After recording the plea of "guilty", the court receives any statement which the accused desires to make in reference to the charge. The summary of evidence is read in the court by the prosecutor and is annexed to the court proceedings. The accused can then make a statement in mitigation of punishment and may call witnesses to his character.

When the accused pleads "not guilty" to a charge(s), the same is recorded and the prosecutor begins his case by making an opening address stating the substance of the charge against the accused and the nature and general effect of the evidence which he proposes to adduce.[54] The prosecution witnesses are called, one by one. The witnesses, who are sworn or affirmed in accordance with the prescribed oath or affirmation, are examined by the prosecutor, may be cross-examined by the defence and may be re-examined by the prosecution. The court or judge advocate may also put a question to a witness if it considered relevant and necessary to elicit the truth.[55] After the evidence of the prosecution is over, the accused is asked whether he wishes to examine any witness in his defence. The defence witnesses are also subject to examination, cross-examination and re-examination. The accused may also make a statement orally or in writing, but no oath is administered to the accused.[56] The court or the judge advocate may question the accused, to seek an explanation for any fact appearing in his statement. The accused does not render himself liable to punishment for refusing to answer such questions, though the court is free to draw inferences from such refusals.

At the close of the case for the prosecution, the accused may offer a plea of "no case", implying that the evidence given on behalf of the prosecution in respect of the charge(s) has not established a prima facie case against him and he should not be called upon to make his defence to the charge(s). Where the accused takes such a plea, the prosecutor may address the court in answer thereto and the accused may reply.[57] If the court allows the plea, it records a finding of "not guilty" in respect of the charge(s). If it rejects the plea of "no case", it follows the procedure for taking down the statement of the accused and his evidence. The court may, on its own motion, after the close of the case for prosecution and after hearing the prosecutor find the accused "not guilty" of the charge(s), announce the finding in open court as subject to confirmation.[58]

After the examination of the witnesses, the prosecutor sums up the case and the accused or his counsel addresses the court in reply. This is followed by summing up by the judge-advocate in open court. He explains the charges, the provision of law on which they are based and the legal issues, and sums up the evidence on each of the issues of fact.[59]

The court is closed after the judge advocate's summing up for the consideration of the finding in the presence of the judge-advocate.[60] The finding is reached by a majority vote. A death sentence, however, cannot be passed by a GCM without the concurrence of at least two-thirds of the members of the court. No sentence of death can be passed by a SGCM/FGCM without the concurrence of all the members.[61] The finding on every charge is recorded as a finding of guilty or not guilty.[62] Under the Indian Army Act, it was not necessary till 1994, to give evidence on the basis of which the conclusion is arrived at. However, now the court is required to give a brief reasoned order, popularly known as a "speaking order" in support of its finding. [63]

In the South Asian countries, the members of a court martial may not be qualified in law. They discharge double functions of jury and judge and decide two distinct and separate matters. As jury, they consider whether according to the evidence, the accused is "guilty" or "not guilty" of charge(s). They also consider the sentence to be awarded for such offence. After deliberation on the finding is completed, the findings of the court are announced on each charge in open court, subject to confirmation.[64]

If the finding on the charge (s) is "guilty", then the court takes evidence of the records and the general character, age, service, rank, distinguished conduct of the accused, previous convictions by a court martial/criminal court, length of the time in custody and the military decorations or awards of the accused. Evidence on these matters is given by witnesses who have the relevant supporting documents in their custody and the accused may cross-examine such witnesses and may lead evidence in rebuttal. The accused is also entitled to address the court in mitigation of the punishment.[65]

The sentence is considered in closed court in the presence of the judge advocate.[66] The court awards a single sentence in respect of all the offences of which the accused is found guilty.[67] All the members of the court are required to vote in respect of the quantum of the sentence, which is entered in the proceedings and authenticated by the presiding officer and the judge advocate. If the court makes a recommendation for mercy, it must cite the reasons for its recommendation.[68] The sentence and any recommendation for mercy are announced in open court. The sentence is announced subject to confirmation.[69] The sentence has to suit the offence and the offender. It should not be vindictive, unduly harsh or disproportionate in a way that it amounts to conclusive proof of bias.[70] The proceedings are then forwarded to the convening authority for confirmation.

Summary/Field General Court martial

An exceptional kind of court martial is provided for under the military laws of the South Asian countries---the SGCM/FGCM which has no parallel in the American law. The FGCM existed in the British military system till 2006 but was rarely convened in the last 25 years. It is merely a 'summary' form of the GCM and can be convened when it is not possible without serious detriment to public service for the offence to be tried by one of the other types of court martial. In Pakistan, a FGCM consists of three officers with one year of service. It can try any person subject to the Act for any offence committed under the military Act and pass any sentence authorised thereby.[71] It can be convened during "active service", as well as during peacetime. In the latter situation, it can be convened only by officers empowered by the Central Government or Chief of Staff.[72]

The Bangladesh Army Act provides that besides the Central Government and the COAS, on active service, an officer commanding a portion of the Bangladesh Army, not below the rank of Brigadier General can convene a FGCM. However, the said officer must be of the opinion (which shall be recorded in writing) that it is not practicable with due regard to discipline and the exigencies of the service to try the alleged offender by a GCM.[73]

In India, the Act does not lay down minimum commissioned service as a condition precedent to the eligibility of an officer to sit as a member of a SGCM. It has the same power as a GCM and can try any individual subject to the Army Act and award the maximum punishment of death.[74] The Central Government or the Chief of the Army Staff can empower an officer to convene a SGCM at all times. Also, a SGCM can be convened by an officer commanding any detached portion of the regular Army on active service.[75] A SGCM is subject to exceptional rules under which the procedure is or can be of a more summary character than that of a GCM.[76] The court is not even required to frame a formal charge-sheet against the alleged accused. [77] The accused does not have a right to be represented by a counsel.[78]

Under the Sri Lankan Army Act, a FGCM can be convened only when in the opinion of the commanding officer; it is impracticable to convene a GCM. A FGCM consists of not less than three officers. However, if the officer convening a FGCM certifies that three officers are not available owing to the exigencies of the service, it may consist of only two officers. In such cases, the FGCM shall not have the power to inflict punishment severe than imprisonment or field punishment.[79]

The scheme of the SGCM/FGCM clearly suggests that such a type of court is essentially meant for combat situations. The Manual of Pakistan Military Law provides some guidance in this respect: "A court of this character is not suited to peace conditions, but it may sometimes be necessary to convene such a court at a remote station where a sufficient number of officers to constitute a general court martial are not available.[80] In India, the Air Force has not constituted any SGCM in the last 20 years. However, it has been constituted frequently in the Army.

Summary Court martial

A SCM is peculiar to the armies of the South Asian countries, except that of Sri Lanka. It may try any person subject to the Army Act and under the command of the officer holding the court, except an officer, JCO or warrant officer. A SCM may pass any sentence under the Army Act, except the sentence of death or imprisonment for a term exceeding one year in case the officer holding the trial is of or higher than the rank of Lieutenant Colonel, and three months, if such officer is below that rank.[81]

The provisions relating to the SCM were introduced only to discipline the Indian troops and were envisaged to facilitate the trial of native troops by British commanding officers. They were suitable for British military commanders who wanted to take swift action against Indian soldiers and were most frequently utilised for the trial of military offenders. They could award the punishment of one year's imprisonment and dismissal from service after a summary trial. Page 101 of the Manual of Indian Military Law (1935 Edition), states:

> The discipline of the Indian Army depends in a great measure on the summary court martial. When a soldier or other person amenable to the act has committed an offence which is ordinarily triable by court martial, a commanding officer, when determining by what court the accused is to be tried must bear in mind that the legislature, in conferring upon him the power of a summary court martial, intends that he shall exercise these powers.....It should, however, be remembered that even a comparatively slight punishment promptly inflicted is often more deterrent than a heavier one which follows long after the offence, and this is especially so with Indian troops.

The procedure to be followed at a SCM[82] is different in many ways to the procedure adopted by a GCM, DCM or FGCM. The jurisdiction of the SCM is co-extensive as to all offences and offenders with that of the superior court martial. In other words, a SCM is legally authorised to take cognizance of all military offences of soldiers (committed by Havildar and below), however grave, provided the same are not made punishable capitally or exclusively by a GCM.[83] Section 130 of the Indian Army Act, contains a provision that an accused can challenge his trial by the presiding officer/any member of the general, district or summary general court martial on the ground of bias or personal interest, however, no such right to challenge is available to an accused in a SCM. It can award punishment of dismissal with one-year imprisonment after a summary trial.

In a SCM, the commanding officer constituting the court looks at the case from the standpoint of policy, expediency and discipline, thus violating the basic norms of natural justice. The proceedings of a SCM are attended by two other persons, who may be officers or junior commissioned officers. They are not supposed to take any part in the proceedings and have no right to vote in determining either the findings or the sentence.

In India, the high courts and the Supreme Court have criticised the trials held under the SCM, as it is felt that the SCM awards excessive and harsh punishments and denies the procedural rights guaranteed under Article 14 of the Constitution. Other grounds for criticism are the lack of evidence and justice in such proceedings, as well as non-compliance with the Army Rules.

The Delhi High Court while deciding the case of *Lance Naik V.P. Singh v. Union of India,* along with six other petitions set aside conviction of seven Army personnel following a SCM. The SCMs against seven personnel were carried out by the commanding officers of another unit.[84] While disposing of the petitions, the High Court held: "A summary court martial can legitimately be convened when there is a grave and compelling cause for taking premature action which would be defeated if reference to a district and general court martial is made. Holding of summary court martial is an exception and not the rule."[85] While comparing the powers of the SCM in India with that in the USA, the court commented that the picture in India is a sad one, the law being a vestige of the colonial era. The Court further held:

> "Mindful of the fact that Article 33 of the Constitution of India confers unbridled powers on Parliament to bring into place a situation which severely abridges the Fundamental Rights of a citizen, it becomes the bounden duty of the Courts to ensure that the equality doctrine is not needlessly nullified. It also becomes essential that the Courts should interpret the law in a manner which will reduce to the minimum the inroads into the infringible rights contained in Chapter III of the Constitution......A SCM must be an exception and not the rule. It can only be convened where the exigencies demand an immediate and swift decision without which the situation will indubitably be exacerbated with widespread ramifications....The decision to convene an SCM must be preceded by a reasoned order which itself will be amenable to judicial review." [86]

Such an arbitrary system of justice is not followed in any other democratic country. The SCM never existed under the British military justice system. The military justice systems followed in the USA, Israel, China, Russia, Canada and South Africa do not have such provisions either.

Unlike the GCM, DCM and FGCM, the finding and sentence of which are subject to confirmation, the sentence awarded by the SCM need not be confirmed. Section 133 (2) of the Pakistan Army Act provides: "Any person subject to this Act who considers himself aggrieved by the finding or sentence of a SCM may submit a petition to the Central Government, or the Commander-in-Chief, or any officer empowered to act." This right is available in other countries also, where an aggrieved person can present a grievance application against the decision of the SCM. However, these petitions become meaningless, as by the time they are put up to the authorities concerned or the government, the accused might have undergone the punishment.

Notes

1. Section 80, Pakistan Army Act.
2. Section 80, Bangladesh Army Act.
3. Section 67, Nepal Army Act, 2006.
4. Summary General Court Martial (SGCM) is known as Field General Court martial (FGCM) in Bangladesh, Pakistan and Sri Lanka.
5. Section 45, Sri Lankan Army Act.
6. Section 80, Nepal Army Act,
7. Section 128, Indian Army Act.
8. Section 127 Indian Air Force Act.
9. Section 102, Bangladesh Army Act.
10. Section 102, Pakistan Army Act.
11. Sections 46 (4), 48 (3) and 50 (2), Sri Lankan Army Act.
12 Section 97 (12), Indian Navy Act.
13. Section 119 (1) and (3), Nepal Army Act.
14. Section 62, Nepal Army Act.
15. Section 119 (4), Nepal Army Act.
16. Section 108, Bangladesh Army Act.
17. Section 108, Pakistan Army Act.
18. Section 45, Sri Lankan Air Force.
19. Section 33, Sri Lankan Navy Act.
20. Section 95, Indian Navy Act. A disciplinary court may consist of not less than three nor more than five officers.
21. Clode, Charles M. 1874. *Military and Martial Law.* London: John Murray, p.58.
22. Under the British system, till 2006, the court martial were of two kinds—the general and the district. The third kind, a field general court martial existed within the Royal Air Force, but never assembled in the last two decades. An amendment by the Armed Forces Act 2001, enabled warrant officers to be members of a court martial, providing the accused soldier was lower in rank. The presence of judge advocate in both the kinds of court martial was must. The European Court of Human Rights in *Morris v. United Kingdom*, judgement of 26 February 2002, (2002) 34 EHHR 1253 that the military members of court martial lacked the appearance of independence and there were insufficient safeguards to prevent this. The Court noted that those officers had no legal training, that they remained subject to army discipline and reports, and there was no statutory or other bar to their being subject to external army influence when sitting in the case. The procedure has been amended in the new tri-service Armed Forces Act, 2006.

23. Section 102, Pakistan and Bangladesh Army Acts and sections 46, 48, and 50, Sri Lankan Army Act.
24. Section 128, Indian Army Act.
25. Section 80, Nepal Army Act.
26. The Sri Lankan law is little different in this regards. Section 73 of the Army and the Air Force Acts, and section 50 of the Navy Act provides: At all the proceedings before a court martial the prosecution as well as the defence shall be entitled to be represented by a counsel.
27. The Nepalese Army Act (section 81) is an exception and provides that an accused may request for a judge advocate from JA Department to defend him during the trial by a court martial.
28. In Nepal, the department is headed by the Chief Judge Advocate.
29. Section 54, Sri Lankan Army Act.
30. Section 129, Indian Army Act.
31. Paragraph 33, Regulations for the Indian Army.
32. In India, the Command Judge Advocate is the head of the Legal Section at Command Headquarters and is responsible to render legal advice on all matters pertaining to Air Force Law. The duties of Command Judge Advocate are as follows:
    (a) To give advice to the AOC-in-C through SOA on matters relating to Air Force Law such as (i) Convening of GCM and DCM; (ii) Summary disposal of charges against officers and Warrant Officers; and (iii) Confirmation of proceedings of Courts Martial. (b) To advise all the Principal Staff Officers and commanding officers of formations under the command headquarters. (c) To examine summaries of evidence received in the section and render reports on 'Applications for Trial' in serious and complicated cases. (d) To examine Court martial Proceedings and render Reports on Trial. (e) To examine and advise on petitions received in connection with Court martial. (f) To detail judge advocates at trials by Court martial. (g) To impart training to officers in the units on matters relating to air force law. (h) To supervise all civil suits filed in Supreme Court, high courts and lower courts and administrative tribunals. (j) To render advice on statutory applications. (k) To examine courts of inquiry and advise on legal issues involved therein. (l) To examine the delay reports in respect of persons in custody beyond 8 days. (m) To advise on disciplinary matters relating to civilian employees. http://indianairforce.nic.in/RTI/RTI_WAC.pdfhttp://indianairforce.nic.in/RTI/RTI_WAC.pdf
33. Paragraph 470 and 471, Regulations for the Indian Army.
34. Whenever in the course of a trial by a court martial, it appears to the court that the examination of a witness is necessary for the ends of justice, and that the attendance of such witness cannot be procured without delay, expense or inconvenience, the court may address the judge advocate general in order that a commission to take evidence of such witness may be issued. The judge advocate general may then issue a commission to the district magistrate or magistrate of first class, within the local limits of whose jurisdiction such witness resides, to take evidence of such witness. The magistrate to whom the commission is issued shall proceed to the place where the witness is and shall take down his evidence. The prosecutor and the accused may forward any interrogatories in writing which are relevant and the magistrate shall examine the witness upon such interrogatories. After a commission has been executed, it shall be

returned, together with the disposition of the witness to the judge advocate general. It will be read in the court and shall form the part of the proceedings of the court martial. Section 137, Indian Army Act.

35. **The duties of JAG under the British military justice system include the following**: (i) To act as the Presiding Judge in the military criminal jurisdiction and leader of its judges, thereby supervising the jurisdiction, (ii) To provide guidance to all stakeholders in the military criminal justice system on practices and procedures, developments and reforms, (iii) To monitor the workings of the military criminal justice system and to advise on its efficiency and effectiveness, (iv) To appoint and allocate judges to conduct specific court martial trials in UK or abroad for the Royal Navy, the Army and the Royal Air Force, (v) To provide judges to conduct Summary Appeal Courts and Standing Civilian Courts, and to rule upon applications for detention in custody and for search warrants, (vi) To act as the trial judge personally conducting some of the most serious, sensitive or controversial Court martial trials (such as for murder), (vii) To provide advice to reviewing authorities on reviews and petitions following every conviction and sentence, (viii) To refer to the Court martial Appeal Court cases involving a point of law of exceptional importance, (ix) To keep the record of proceedings for not less than six years after trial in all cases, (x) If a serviceman or woman is to be detained in custody, or if private premises need to be searched in the course of investigations, the authority of a Judge Advocate acting as a judicial officer is required. JAG or one of the judges must be satisfied that the continued detention, or the search, is legally justified. Such cases are often heard by video link and a judge is on duty every day of the year to rule upon urgent applications if required.
36. Pitzul Brigadier General Jerry S.T., 'Operational Law and the Legal Professional: A Canadian Perspective', *The Air Force Law Review*, 2001, p. 311-321.
37. The Judge Advocate in the South Asian countries is the equivalent of the 'Military Judge' under the USA's Uniform Code of Military Justice.
38. There were reports that the Judge Advocate General (JAG) of the Indian Army was victimised for his uncompromising stance on a case of alleged irregularities in the army. The army chief had rejected the recommendations of the JAG for taking disciplinary action against the alleged corrupt officer and instead awarded a mild 'reprimand', who was then promoted to the rank of Lieutenant General. Since the JAG comes under the military chain of command, the officers of the judicial branch seem to have become infected by the social malaise that taints our public institution. In the Dock, *Business India* May 4, 2008, p. 119.
39. Rule 77, Army Rules, 1954.
40. Regulations for the Indian Army, paragraph 458.
41. Rule 96, Army Rules, 1954
42. Section 73 (1), Sri Lanka Army Act.
43. If, owing to military exigencies or for any other reason, no such officer is available for the purpose, the convening officer must give a written notice to the presiding officer of the court martial. The notice is attached to the proceedings of the court martial. Rule 95 (1) and (2), Indian Army Rules, 1954.
44. Section 81, Nepal Army Act.
45. The Human Rights Committee in the case of *Estrella v Uruguay* (74/180) 29 March 1983, has held that a military court had violated the defendant's right to choose counsel

by limiting him to a choice between two appointed attorneys.

46. Regulations for the Army, 1987, Para 479.
47. Article 27, UCMJ.
48. Court martial (Army) and (Air Force) Rules 1997, rule 15 and QR 6.085. A person charged with an offence under the British military system is entitled to a copy of *The Rights of a Soldier Charged with an Offence*, an official pamphlet his commanding officer is required to provide him. The pamphlet sets out, inter alia, the accused person's rights and duties when under arrest, the procedure for summary disposal and penalties that may be imposed, the procedure for electing trial by court martial, procedure and before a court martial, and the sentences that may be imposed by a court martial. The pamphlet alludes briefly to post-conviction procedures and states that if the accused is convicted, he will be supplied with another official pamphlet, *Appeals and Petition after Conviction by Court Martial*, setting out his rights if he is dissatisfied with his conviction and sentence.
49. Regulations for the Indian Army, 1987, Para 449 provides: A superior officer to whom a case is referred may deal with it as follows: 1. Refer the case to a superior officer. 2. Direct the disposal of the case summarily or by SCM. 3. Convene a DCM, if he has power to do so. 4. Convene a GCM or DCM, if he has power to do so. 5. Dispose of the charge summarily under the provision of Section 83 or 84 of the Act, if he is competent to do so.
50. If the accused objects to any of the officers, his objection and any evidence in support are recorded. The remaining officers of the court, in the absence of the challenged one, then vote on the disposal of the objection. The objection is allowed if one half or more of the officers entitled to vote support it. The member objected to retires immediately and the vacancy thus created is filled in by the senior-most of the waiting officers, subject to the right of the accused to object to him as well. Rule 45, Indian Army Rules, 1954.
51. The plea may be on the grounds that he has been tried previously for the same offence by a competent court; or he has been dealt with summarily; or a charge in respect of the offence in question had been dismissed by the commanding officer during the investigation by him; or the offence has been pardoned or condoned by competent military authority; or the trial is barred by limitation under the Army Act. Rule 53, Indian Army Rules.
52. However, before doing so, the presiding officer or the judge advocate, on behalf of the court, ensures that the accused understands the nature of the charge to which he has pleaded guilty. The accused is also informed of the general effect of that plea and of the difference in procedure, if he had not pleaded guilty. The accused is also advised to withdraw the plea if it appears from the summary of evidence that he ought not to plead guilty. Rule 52 (2), Indian Army Rules.
53. Rule 52 (4), Indian Army Rules.
54. Rule 56 (3), Indian Army Rules.
55. Rule 142, Indian Army Rules, 1954.
56. In 1993, an amendment was made to Rule 58 of the Indian Army Rules, 1954. The accused, if he wishes, may give evidence as a witness, on oath or affirmation, in disposal of charges against him. If he gives evidence on oath or affirmation, he shall be examined as first witness for defence and shall be liable to be cross-examined by the

prosecutor and to be questioned by the court. *Bhagat Chand v. Union of India,* 1983 Criminal LJ 1059 (Del): An accused has a right to examine himself as a witness in a court martial.

57. Indian Army Rules, Rule 57 (3): The court is to consider the plea in closed court and shall not allow the plea unless satisfied that (a) the prosecution has not established a prima facie case on the charge(s) as laid; and (b) it is not open to the court to make a special findings, on the evidence adduced i.e., conviction on offences not charged.
58. Rule 57 (7), Indian Army Rules, 1954. The court shall record brief reasons while arriving at the finding on the plea of "no case".
59. Rule 60, Indian Army Rules, 1954.
60. In the Indian Army, the judge advocate's presence is necessary, while the court deliberates on its findings (Rule 61, India Army Rules). Whereas in the Air Force (Rule 70) and the Navy (Section 116, Navy Act), the judge advocate is not required to be present in the court, while it deliberates on the findings.
61. Section 132, Indian Army Act, 1950.
62. Before voting, normally a discussion takes place in closed court in the presence of the judge-advocate. After the discussion, the presiding officer asks the members for their opinion, in order of seniority starting from the junior most. Thus the presiding officer is the last to give his opinion. This is done to ensure that juniors are free to express their opinion. The members express their opinion orally on each charge.
63. Rule 62 (1), Indian Army Rules, 1954.
64. Rule 62 (10), Indian Army Rules, 1954.
65. Rule 64, Indian Army Rules, 1954.
66. Indian Navy Act, section 120 provides that the trial judge advocate shall sit with the court while they are considering the sentence and assist the court in the determination of the sentence, but shall not vote thereon. However, under the Indian Army Rules (Rule 65) and the Air Force Rules (Rule 74), the judge advocate is not required to sit in the court, while it is considering the sentence.
67. Rule 65, Indian Army Rules, 1954.
68. Rule 66, Indian Army Rules, 1954.
69. Rule 67, Indian Army Rules, 1954.
70. *Ranjit Thakur v. Union of India* (1987) 4 SCC 611, and *Ex-Naik Sardar Singh v. Union of India* (1991) 3 SCC 213.
71. Pakistan Air Force Act, section 117.
72. Pakistan Army and Air Force Acts, section 112(a).
73. Section 84, Bangladesh Army Act.
74. Section 118, Army Act, 1950.
75. Section 112, Indian Army Act, 1950. The summary general court martial can be convened by an officer commanding, under clause 112 (c) without a warrant or authorisation: Note 2 to Section 112. *Kartar Singh Sardar Jit Singh v Emperor* AIR (1946), Lahore 103.
76. Indian Army Rules, 1954, Rules 151 to 165.
77. Rule 152, Indian Army Rules, 1954 states: "Charge--The statement of an offence may be made briefly in any language sufficient to describe or disclose an offence under the Act.
78. Indian Army Rules, 1954, Rule 96. The accused does not have a right to be represented

by a counsel in the SGCM. Army Rule 159 provides that an accused may be allowed to have any person to assist him during the trial.

79. Section 48, Sri Lankan Army Act.
80. Manual of Pakistan Military Law, Paragraph 106.
81. Section 120, Indian Army Act, 1950.
82. Indian Army Rules, 1954, Rules 106 -133.
83. Section 120 (2) of the Indian Army Act dealing with the powers of SCM provides: "When there is no grave reason for immediate action and reference can without detriment to discipline be made to the officer empowered to convene a district court martial or on active service a summary general court martial for the trial of the alleged offender, an officer holding a summary court martial shall not try without such reference any offence punishable under any of the sections 34 (offences in relation to enemy and punishable with death), 37 (mutiny) and 69 (civil offences), or any offence against the officer holding the court."
84. In *Ex-Havildar Mahipal Singh v. Union of India*, 1994 DLT 176, the Delhi High Court had held that NCO or Sepoy cannot be attached to another unit for purpose of summary court martial.
85. Rajasthan High Court in *Roop Singh v Union of India*, 2007 (6) SLR dismissed seven petitions relating to trial by summary court martial on the grounds that proceedings do not suffer from any error in procedure. The Rajasthan High Court perhaps failed to appreciate that the summary court martial is an exception and not rule, a stand taken subsequently by the Delhi High Court in *Lance Naik V.P. Singh v. Union of India* (2008).
86. *Lance Naik V.P. Singh v. Union of India,* WP (C) 2511/1992 decided on 25 January 2008.

6

Confirmation, Revision and Appeal

The findings and sentence of a court martial are required to be confirmed by the Central Government or any officer empowered in this behalf by warrant of the Central Government.[1] A confirming officer cannot substitute a special finding on any charge for the court's findings, he can only confirm, reserve confirmation for superior authority, refuse to confirm or send back the proceedings to the same court for revision. If a finding of 'guilty' or 'not guilty' is not confirmed, it becomes invalid; consequently there is no conviction or acquittal, as a result of which the accused is neither convicted nor acquitted by the court martial

The authority empowered to convene/confirm the court martial proceedings in the South Asian military law systems enjoys a mighty position. He is generally an officer above the rank of brigadier and holds an authoritative and influential position. He is responsible for making the decision to prosecute or not to prosecute and deciding the charges against the accused. He also appoints the military prosecutor or counsel for prosecution; the court-members of his choice and the defending officer. He is empowered to deny a counsel on the grounds of expediency. The convening authority details a judge advocate for trial and the judge advocate, the prosecutor and the court members come under his authority in the chain of command. As a reviewing authority, he reviews the sentence awarded by the court martial and may refer the proceedings back to the court for reconsideration (enhancing the punishment), even if an accused is acquitted by the court.[2] He considers the pre-confirmation petition of the accused and is empowered to confirm or not to confirm the sentence awarded by the court martial. Finally, he also considers the post-confirmation petition of the convicted person.

The convening authority's role in the South Asian military legal system is distinctive because of his dominant position and control over every aspect of disciplinary proceedings. Under the military regimes in Bangladesh and Pakistan, military rulers have issued specific orders excluding civil courts from reviewing military court decisions in which civilians were tried. Democracies, such as the UK, Australia, Canada, Israel and South Africa, have restricted the role of commanders in their military justice systems in order to limit actual bias, as well as accusations and perceptions of unlawful command influence in judicial proceedings.

An effective judicial review system balances the power of the convening authority in the USA. With the recent reforms in the British military justice system, the duties of the commander have been distributed among three separate bodies. An independent prosecuting authority decides whether to take a case to court martial, an administration officer selects the court martial panel members, and a reviewing officer justifies the decision. The health of the law relating to judicial review is a good indicator of the status of the rule of law in any State, or even in any international organisation. Open, transparent and genuine access to judicial review, and the ability and willingness of judicial institutions to examine the acts of the administration lie at the heart of good democratic structures of government and, indeed, are an essential aspect of good governance.[3]

Confirmation and Revision

The finding or sentence of a GCM, DCM or SGCM is not valid unless confirmed. The findings recorded by a GCM are in the nature of recommendations which may or may not be accepted by the authority empowered to confirm the findings and sentence. The findings and sentence of a GCM may be confirmed by the Central Government or by any officer empowered in this behalf by warrant of the Central Government.[4] The findings and sentence of a DCM may be confirmed by any officer with the power to convene a GCM or by any officer empowered in this behalf by warrant of such officer.[5] The findings and sentence of a SGCM may be confirmed by the convening officer or, if he so directs, by an authority superior to him.[6] However, in the case of award of the death sentence, it will be confirmed by the Central Government. [7]

In the event that a court martial finds the accused "not guilty" the power to confirm or non-confirm the proceedings rests with the COAS in cases: (a) when the offence charged against any officer is punishable with death, and (b) if the accused officer holds or held the rank of Brigadier or above at the time of commission of the offence. In all other cases of 'not guilty' the powers to confirm or non-confirm the proceedings rests with the GOC-in-C. [8]

If the confirming authority is dissatisfied with the findings of a GCM, DCM or SGCM, and a confirmation is required, the findings and sentence may be once revised by order of the confirming authority. Section 126 (1) of the Pakistan Army Act provides:[9]

> **Revision of finding and sentence**--Any finding or sentence of a Court martial which requires confirmation may be once revised by order of the confirming officer, and, on such revision, the Court, if so directed by him, may take additional evidence.

On such revision, the court, if so directed by the confirming authority, may take additional evidence. The court shall consist of the same officers as were present when the original decision was passed.[10] When the finding is sent back for revision, the court re-assembles in open court, the revision order is read and if the court is directed to take fresh evidence, the same is taken in open court. The court then deliberates on its finding in closed court. If it does not adhere to its earlier finding, it revokes the finding and sentence and records the new finding, and if necessary, passes a fresh sentence. When the sentence alone is sent for revision, the court cannot revise the finding. After revision, the proceedings are transmitted for confirmation.[11] The proceedings of the court martial are processed through the judge advocate for confirmation. The reports of the officers of the JAG department are confidential and are not communicated directly or indirectly to any lower authority to whom they are addressed. When the proceedings are forwarded to lower formations or to units, such reports are removed.[12]

The power of revision can only be exercised once. However, if the second verdict by the court martial is the same, the confirming officer has no option but to confirm the proceeding. The service Acts do not contemplate successive trials by a court martial till a verdict acceptable to the confirming authority is received. A second trial by a court martial for the same offence, whether any person subject to the Act has been convicted or acquitted, is prohibited.[13]

The confirming authority can itself mitigate or remit or commute the punishment awarded by the court martial.[14] Therefore, when a sentence is directed to be revised by the confirming authority, it necessarily means that the confirming authority considers that the punishment awarded by the court martial is not commensurate with the offence and it should, therefore, be revised upward. It is generally believed that the confirming officers exercise "command influence" over the court members while seeking the desired findings and sentences by taking recourse to revision. In India, a number of "revision orders" have been the subject matter of controversies that have come up before civil courts.[15] The law does not require the confirming authority to give a hearing to the petitioner either before ordering revision under the Army Act, or before confirming the revised sentence.

The confirming officer, on receipt of the proceedings of a court martial, may confirm or refuse confirmation or reserve confirmation for the superior authority. His decision in this regard is entered in and forms a part of the proceedings.[16]

Non-confirmation of the finding of guilty does not amount to acquittal of the accused. When confirming the sentence of a court martial, the confirming officer may mitigate or remit the punishment awarded or commute that punishment for any punishment(s) lower in the scale laid down in Section 71 of the Army Act.[17] The Central Government or the Commander-in-Chief or any prescribed officer may annul the proceedings of any court martial on the ground that they are illegal or unjust.[18] The finding or sentence of a court martial, once confirmed by the confirming officer, becomes final. There are no corresponding provisions of revision in the Navy Act.

In Sri Lanka, the President, the minister of defence, or any prescribed officer may revise any sentence passed by a court martial. While revising the sentence, the authority may (a) mitigate the punishment to a lesser amount of the same punishment; (b) remit the whole or a part of the punishment; or (c) commute the punishment to a different form lower in the scale of punishments authorised by the Army Act.[19]

The charge(s), findings, sentence, recommendations for mercy, if any, and confirmation or non-confirmation of the proceedings of a court martial are promulgated in all cases to the accused. Until promulgation, the findings and sentence are not held to have been confirmed.[20]

The findings and sentences of a summary court martial do not require confirmation, but may be carried out forthwith. However, it has been provided that that if the officer holding the trial is of less than five years' service, he shall not, except on active service, carry into effect any sentence until it has received the approval of an officer of the rank of brigadier.[21]

Appeal

In the South Asian countries, till recently, there has been no right of appeal as such against the finding or sentence of a court martial. In India, there has been a constitutional ban on appeals against the findings and sentences of courts-martial. Article 136(2) of the Constitution makes the provision that the Supreme Court [22] [Article 227 (4) in the case of a high court] cannot give special leave to appeal against any judgement, determination or sentence of a military court or tribunal. The military tribunals in India are not, however, exempt from the Supreme Court's writ jurisdiction under Article 32 and the high court's writ jurisdiction under Article 226 of the Constitution.

In India, the high courts and Supreme Court have entertained petitions from service personnel under their writ jurisdiction. In *Lt Col PSS Bedi's* case (1982), the Supreme Court held that the absence of even one appeal with power to review evidence, legal formulation, conclusion and the adequacy or otherwise of punishment in the laws relating to the armed forces was a distressing and glaring lacuna, and urged the Government to take steps to provide for at least one judicial review in service matters. This decision led to the passing of the Armed Forces Tribunal Act in 2007. More than 12,000 cases relating to courts-martial and service matters of the members of the Armed Forces pending in the higher courts will be transferred to the Armed Forces Tribunal.

The Armed Forces Tribunal and its Benches under the Act of 2007 have started functioning since August 2009.[23] The Tribunal has original jurisdiction over service matters and will hear appeals from the verdicts of courts-martial (appellate jurisdiction). A bench of the Tribunal will have two members--a judicial officer and a retired senior service officer. The term 'service matters' as defined in the Act, includes (i) remuneration and pension; (ii) tenure, including commission, appointment, enrolment, seniority, promotion, reversion, termination of service and penal deductions; and (iii) summary disposal and trials where the punishment of dismissal is awarded. The Tribunal will not have any jurisdiction in issues relating to (i) removal from service under President's pleasure; (ii) transfers and postings; (iii) leave; and (iv) summary court martial except where the punishment is of dismissal or imprisonment for more than three months. The lack of jurisdiction in matters relating to leave, transfers and postings, and summary trials is a serious lacuna in Tribunal's original jurisdiction.[24]

In Nepal, the Army Act, 2006, has created a Special Court to hear appeals from courts-martial. The Special Court in Nepal consists of a judge of an appellate court, who functions as chairman, the Secretary Ministry of Defence and the Chief Judge Advocate.[25] In India and Nepal, appeals against the decision of Armed Forces Tribunal or Special Court could be taken up in the Supreme Court.

The military Acts of Bangladesh and Pakistan provide a remedy against finding and sentence of court martial. Section 131(1) of the Army Acts provides: "Any person subject to this Act who considers himself aggrieved by the finding or sentence; of a general, field general or district court martial may submit a petition, before confirmation of such finding or sentence, to the officer empowered to confirm it and, after confirmation to the Central Government, or the Commander-in-Chief or to any prescribed officer, provided that such prescribed officer is higher in rank than the one who confirmed such finding or sentence." The similar provision existed in the Indian Army Act, 1950.[26] The Law Commission of India examined the provisions contained in Section 164 of the Army Act and was of the view that **"In sum there is no right of appeal against the order of the court martial."**[27] However, with the establishment of the Armed Forces Tribunal and its benches, the provision has become redundant in India.

In Bangladesh and Pakistan, the army Acts ban any appeal against the decision of a court martial. Section 133 of the Acts states:

> **Bar of appeals** - No remedy shall lie against any decision of a court martial save as provided in this Act, and for the removal of doubt it is hereby declared that no appeal or application shall lie in respect of any proceeding or decision of a court martial to any court exercising any jurisdiction whatever.

The prohibition, however, is not absolute and the high courts in Pakistan have entertained collateral attacks on court martial proceedings on limited jurisdictional grounds. On 12 January 2009, the Lahore High Court set aside a 1999 sentence of the FGCM against a lieutenant colonel it found guilty of filing fake income tax returns, apart from other instances of fraud. Lt Col Munir Ahmed Gil, had invoked the jurisdiction of the court in the year 2000 against his 1999 conviction by the FGCM on charges of concealing his property which enabled him to claim financial benefits from the army. He had cited ministry of defence and the chief of the army staff (COAS) as respondents in his petition. Lt. Col. Munir Ahmed Gil was arrested in June 1997 by the special investigation branch on charges of receiving commission in the purchase of about 6,000 tons of sugar for military's use. In 1999 he was convicted by the FGCM in Rawalpindi for receiving commission, concealing his property and filing fake income tax returns. He was sentenced to one-year rigorous imprisonment and dismissal from service. Other charges against him were dropped. In August, 1999, COAS pardoned his prison sentence but upheld the others. The petitioner's plea to the Lahore High Court was that FGCM had overstepped its jurisdiction while convicting him for filing fake income tax returns as this can only be tried by the civilian court of law. The decision is being considered important by the analysts because it could open a flood of pleas to the civilian courts against the decisions of military courts.[28]

The Dhaka High Court has recently restored the rank of four-star general to a former chief of the Bangladesh Army, declaring that the government's decision to strip him of his rank was illegal. Upholding Muhammad Mustafizur Rahman's entitlement to the general's rank, the court said the government's decision to take away the rank four years after awarding it was politically motivated and done without following any rules and regulations. The Bangladesh Army was headed by a three-star general till 2007, when the army-backed caretaker government upgraded the rank of all the three services chiefs and awarded promotions to several top military officers. A two-judge Bench of the High Court held that the allegation that Rahman obtained the rank by influencing the government had not been proved.[29]

The Sri Lankan Constitution empowers the Supreme Court to issue writs of mandamus, certiorari and prohibition in respect of any court martial or of any military authority exercising judicial functions. In addition, the writs of habeas corpus shall be deemed to apply in respect of any person illegally detained in custody by order of a court martial or other military authority. [30]

Since Sri Lanka is a signatory to the Protocol to the UN International Covenant on Civil and Political Rights, 1966 (ICCPR), its citizens are empowered to approach the Human Rights Committee in case of breach of their fundamental rights. However, this is on condition that the individual must have exhausted local remedies. Further, his petition should not be under another procedure of international investigation or settlement. In a communication to the Human Rights Committee Lt Raththinde of the Sri Lankan Army alleged that on the night of 21 October 2000, he was tortured by two military officers and sustained severe injuries, which caused permanent disability. He further alleged that the military court as well as the Supreme Court had failed to give him justice. He had filed a civil complaint before the district court of Anuradhapura, for damages from the perpetrators, but the proceedings had been repeatedly adjourned, without the court giving any decision.

The Human Rights Committee decided that the State party was under a duty to thoroughly investigate the alleged violations of human rights, and to prosecute and punish those held responsible for such violations. The Committee reiterated that under paragraph 3, Article 2 of the ICCPR, the State party had an obligation to ensure that the remedies were effective. Expedition and effectiveness are particularly important in the adjudication of cases involving torture and other forms of mistreatment. The Committee was of the view that the State party had violated paragraph 3, Article 2, read together with Article 7 of the ICCPR. The State party was under an obligation to take effective measures to ensure that the magistrate's court proceedings were expeditiously completed and that the officer was granted full reparation. The State party was also under an obligation to (i) take measures to prevent similar violations in the future, and (ii) provide the officer with an effective remedy, including adequate compensation. The Committee wanted the State party's response regarding the measures taken to give effect to the Committee's views within 180 days.[31]

Although Sri Lanka has signed the Protocols to ICCPR in 1980, it has subsequently removed itself from the judgments of the United Nations Committee of Human Rights with respect to appeals from persons convicted in Sri Lanka courts. In 1993, Nallaratnam Singarasa, an illiterate Ceylone Tamil arrested for putative LTTE involvement in Batticaloa. The individual was abused and forced to sign a confession set down in Sinhala (falsely implicating him in the murder of Buddhist monks among other innocents) and, upon conviction in 1995 solely on the basis of confession was sentenced to 10 years imprisonment. The case was heard by a trial court, a Court of Appeal, and the Supreme Court. Singarasa appealed to the UN Committee on Human Rights (CHR) in Geneva in 2001, which heard the case, ruled that "the State party is under an obligation to provide the petitioner with an effective and appropriate remedy, including release or retrial and compensation." It further held that Sri Lanka is under an obligation to avoid similar violations in future, should ensure that sections of the Prevention of Terrorism Act are made compatible with provisions of the ICCPR, and the CHR wished to receive from the State, within 90 days, "information about the measures taken to give effects to its views." The case again went to Sri Lanka's Supreme Court which, on 15 September 2006, up held Singarasa's conviction arguing that "the Petitioner cannot seek to vindicate and enforce his rights through the CHR at Geneva, which is not reposed with judicial power under our Constitution."

In the UK, a service man convicted by a court martial may appeal to the Court Martial Appeal Court (CMAC), established in 1951. The importance of the CMAC lies not only in the fact that it provides a means by which an accused can argue that his conviction was wrong, but it also enables a civilian court to oversee the military legal system. The judges of the court are those who would hear appeals from the Crown Court and they are not, therefore, within the military command structure. The appellant is entitled to free legal aid during the appellate process.

The US military justice system offers the accused extraordinary access to the appeal process. Following trial, the convening authority may approve the findings and sentence, dismiss them, or change them in any way that benefits the convicted soldier. If the sentence includes death, a discharge from the military, or confinement for one year or more, a panel of at least three appellate military judges of the Court of Criminal Appeals of the individual's branch of service will automatically review the case. The Judge Advocate General of the relevant service reviews all other general courts-martial, whereas a judge advocate must review all special courts-martial not resulting in a discharge.

An important distinction between the military Courts of Criminal Appeals and their civilian counterparts is that while most civilian appellate courts must accept the facts as found by the trial-level court, the Courts of Criminal Appeals are permitted to reconsider such matters as disputed issues of fact, the credibility of witnesses and the appropriate weight to be accorded to evidence. The courts may correct legal errors made by the lower court and reduce sentences they deem excessive.

Further appeal is possible to the US Court of Appeals for the Armed Forces (USCAAF). The USCAAF exercises worldwide appellate jurisdiction over members of the armed forces on active duty and other persons subject to the Uniform Code of Military Justice (UCMJ). The Court is composed of five civilian judges appointed for 15-year terms by the President with the advice and consent of the Senate. The USCAAF is an independent tribunal established under Article I of the Constitution. It regularly interprets federal statutes, executive orders, and departmental regulations. The Court also determines the applicability of constitutional provisions to members of the armed forces. Through its decisions, the Court has a significant impact on the state of discipline in the armed forces, military readiness, and the rights of service-members. The Court plays an indispensable role in the military justice system.[32]

The USCCAF's primary jurisdictional statute is Article 67(a) of the UCMJ, which provides:

- The Court of Appeals for the Armed Forces shall review the record in:
- all cases in which the sentence, as affirmed by a Court of Criminal Appeals, extends to death;
- all cases reviewed by a Court of Criminal Appeals which the Judge Advocate General orders sent to the Court of Appeals for the Armed Forces for review; and
- all cases reviewed by a Court of Criminal Appeals in which, upon petition of the accused and on good cause shown, the Court of Appeals for the Armed Forces has granted a review.[33]

The USCAAF also has the jurisdiction to consider petitions for extraordinary relief under the All Writs Act. The Supreme Court of the United States has discretion to review cases under the UCMJ on direct appeal where the USCAAF has conducted a mandatory review (death penalty and certified cases), granted discretionary review of a petition, or otherwise granted relief. If the USCAAF has denied a petition for review or a writ appeal, consideration by the Supreme Court may be obtained only through collateral review (e.g., a writ of habeas corpus). The military appellant is entitled to counsel free of charge throughout the appellate process.

The Supreme Court of India has decided few interesting case relating to the award of disproportionate punishments by military courts and jurisdiction of military courts over the criminal offence, not relating to the service, allegedly committed by military personnel.

Case I. *Ranjit Thakur v Union of India* (1987) 4 SCC 611

Appellant Ranjit Thakur joined the Indian Army on September 7, 1972 and at the time of alleged offence, was serving as Signalman in 4 Corps Operating Signal Regiment. On March 29, 1985 he was undergoing a sentence of 28 days of rigorous imprisonment imposed on him for violating the norms for presenting representation to higher officers of the Army. He has sent representations to higher officers complaining ill-treatment at the hands of his commanding officer. For this act he was tried summarily by his commanding officer and awarded punishment under Section 80 of the Army Act. He was held in the quarter-guard cell to serve the sentence of 28 days of rigorous imprisonment.

While serving the above sentence, appellant is stated to have committed another offence (refused to eat when ordered by the orderly officer) on March 29, 1985. He was charged under section 41(2) of the Army Act. The charge sheet stated,

> Accused 1429055-M Signalman Ranjit Thakur of 4 Corps Operating Signal Regiment is charged with 'Disobeying a Lawful Command' given by his superior officer (under section 41(2) of the Army Act), in that he at 15.30 hours on Mar 29, 1985 when ordered by JC 106251-P Subedar Ram Singh, the Orderly Officer of the same Regiment to eat his food, did not do so.

To try this offence a summary court martial was assembled the very next day i.e., March 30, 1985. Commanding Officer of the appellant and two other officers serving under him were on the court martial. Appellant is stated to have pleaded guilty. The accused has no right of being defended by any defending officer in the summary court martial. A sentence of rigorous imprisonment for one year and dismissal from service was imposed by the summary court martial. In pursuance to the punishment of one year of rigorous imprisonment, the appellant was removed immediately to the civil prison to serve out the sentence. Appellant served the sentence in the civil jail. His representation to the confirming authority under Section 164 of the Army Act was rejected by the general officer commanding on May 24, 1985.

Thereafter, he challenged the proceedings of the summary court martial before the High Court, which also dismissed his writ petition in limini. Feeling aggrieved by the order of the high court, the appellant approached the Supreme Court by way of a Special Leave Petition. The issues raised by the appellant were summed up by the court as follows:

(a) (i) the proceedings of the court martial are vitiated by non-compliance with the mandate of Section 130(1) of the Army Act in that the summary court martial did not afford to the appellant an opportunity to challenge its constitution as required by the section;

(ii) the proceedings of the court martial were vitiated by bias on the part of commanding officer who participated and dominated the proceedings;

(b) inasmuch as the appellant was then serving a sentence of rigorous imprisonment, he was not in "active service" and that no question of disobeying any lawful command could at all arise;

(c) Appellant's refusal, while serving a sentence to accept food did not amount to disobedience, under section 41 of the Army Act, relating to any lawful command of a superior officer in such manner as to show a willful defiance of authority.

(d) At all events, the punishment handed down is so disproportionate to the offence as to amount, in itself to conclusive evidence of bias and vindictiveness.

While the Supreme Court did not find much substance in the submissions contained in paras (b) and (c) above, the court upheld the submissions vide paras (a) and (d). While the decision of the court at para (a) (i) was subsequently reversed by the court in a review petition because the provisions of the Army Act section 130 are not applicable to summary court martial. Nevertheless, on the grounds of bias the court quoted with approval the observation of Lord Denning M. R. in *Metropolitan Properties Co. (F.G.C.) Ltd. V. Lannon*, (1969) 1 QB 577 at p.599: "In considering whether there was a real likelihood of bias, the court does not look at the mind of the justice himself or at the mind of the chairman of the tribunal, or whoever it may be, who sits in a judicial capacity. It does not look to see if there was a real likelihood that he would, or did, in fact favour one side at the expense of the other. The court looks at the impression which would be given to other people. Even if he was as impartial as could be nevertheless if right minded persons would think that in the circumstances there was a real likelihood of the bias on his part, then he should not sit." Accordingly, the court having regard to the case, came to the conclusion that participation of the commanding officer rendered the proceedings *coram non-judice*.

With regard to the point at sub para (d) above, the court found the punishment awarded to be strikingly disproportionate to the offence committed. In the result, the appeal was allowed and the proceedings of the court martial and the subsequent orders were quashed. The pertinent observation of the supreme court with regard to the severity of sentence were, "Judicial review generally speaking, is not directed against a decision, but is directed against the, 'decision making process'. The question of the choice and quantum of punishment is within the jurisdiction and discrction of the court martial. But the sentence has to suit the offence and the offender. It should not be vindictive or unduly harsh. It should not be so disproportionate to the offence as to shock the conscience and amount in itself to conclusive evidence of bias. The doctrine of proportionality, as part of the concept of judicial review, would ensure that even on an aspect which is, otherwise, within the exclusive, province of the court martial, if the decision of the court even to the sentence is an outrageous defiance of logic, then the sentence would not be immune from correction. Irrationality and perversity are recognised grounds of judicial review." The court ordered reinstatement of the appellant with all monetary and service benefits but did not grant any compensation for punishment of one year RI already undergone by him.

The Supreme Court remarked, "The judicial review generally speaking, is not directed against a decision, but is directed against the "decision making process". The question of choice and quantum of punishment is within the jurisdiction and discretion of the court martial. But the sentence has to suit the offence and the offender. It should not be vindictive or unduly harsh. It should not be so disproportionate to the offence as to shock the conscience and amount in itself to conclusive evidence of bias. The doctrine of proportionality, as part of the concept of judicial review, would ensure that even on an aspect which is, otherwise, within the exclusive province of the court martial, if the decision of the court even as to sentence is an outrageous defiance of logic, the sentence would not be immune from correction. Irrationality and perversity are recognised grounds of judicial review."

Lord Diplock in *Council of Civil Services Unions v. Minister for the Civil Services* held:[34] "Judicial review has I think developed to a stage today when, without reiterating any analysis of the steps by which the development has come about, one can conveniently classify under three heads the grounds on which an administrative action is subject to control by judicial review. The first ground I would call 'illegality', the second 'irrationality' and the third 'procedural impropriety'. That is not to say that further development on a case by case basis may not in course of time add further grounds. I have in mind particularly the possible adoption in the future of the principle of 'proportionality' which is recognised in administrative law of several of our fellow members of the European Economic Community..."

The Supreme Court while referring its decision in *Bhagat Ram v. State of Himachal Pradesh* [35] that a punishment disproportionate to the gravity of the misconduct is violative of Article 14 of the Constitution, held that, "In the present case the punishment is so strikingly disproportionate as to call for and justify interference. It cannot be allowed to remain uncorrected in judicial review".

Case II: *Union of India v LD Balam Singh* (2002) 9 SCC 73.

LD Balam Singh joined the Indian Army on 28 October 1976. While serving the army, he was posted at a unit in Punjab and was residing with family in the government allotted house. On 28 December 1991 a search of his residence was conducted by army officers and other officials and allegedly opium (a contraband), weighing 4.900 kg was recovered from his house. Balam Singh was thereafter placed under arrest and was put in the quarter guard of his unit. A first information report (FIR) was also lodged at nearby civil police station on the same date. A sample of the opium recovered from his house was forwarded to the chemical examiner for analysis and the remaining quantity was kept with the civil police.

The summary of evidence was ordered by the commanding officer of 64 Cavalry, the unit where Balam Singh was serving. On the basis of the convening order issues by the Brigade Commander, Balam Singh was tried by the general court martial (GCM) under Section 69 of the Army Act for an offence punishable under Section 18 of the Narcotic Drugs and Psychotropic Substances Act, 1985 (NDPS Act). The charge-sheet read as follows.

> The accused No 1059403N LD (Subs) Balam Singh of 18 Cavalry, attached to 64 Cavalry is charged under section 69 of the Army Act with 'Committing a civil offence, that is to say, possessing opium in contravention of Section 18 of the Narcotic Drugs and Psychotropic Substances Act, 1985', in that he, at Patiala on 28 Dec 91 was found in illegal possession of 4 kgs and 900 grams of opium." The charge sheet was signed by his commanding officer and countersigned by general officer commanding with an endorsement, 'To be tried by General Court Martial.

Balam Singh was convicted and sentenced by the GCM. Incidentally, his two civilian co-accused were acquitted by the civil court. Aggrieved by the findings and sentence of GCM, Balam Singh challenged his conviction through a writ petition under Article 226 and 227 of the Constitution, before the High Court. The High Court quashed the charge-sheet, and finding and sentence awarded by the GCM.

The matter came before the Supreme Court by way of an appeal filed by the Central Government. The Supreme Court considered the charge-sheet and Section 69 and 109 of the Army Act, under which Balam Singh was tried by the court martial.

Section 69 of the Army Act, 1950, under which Balam Singh was tried relates to civil offences. It states:

> **Civil offences:** Subject to the provisions of Section 70, any person subject to this Act who at any place in or beyond India, commits any civil offence, shall be deemed to be guilty of an offence against this Act and, if charged therewith under this section, shall be liable to be tried by a court- martial and, on conviction, be punishable as follows, that is to say, -

- if the offence is one which would be punishable under any law in force in India with death or with transportation, he shall be liable to suffer any punishment, other than whipping, assigned for the offence, by the aforesaid law and such less punishment as is in this Act mentioned; and

- in any other case, he shall be liable to suffer any punishment, other than whipping, assigned for the offence by the law in force in India, or imprisonment for a term which may extend to seven years, or such less punishment as is in this Act mentioned."

The Supreme Court considered various provisions of the NDPS Act. The Act admittedly contains certain safeguards which are mandatory in nature. Section 18 of NDPS Act, provides punishment for cultivation, possession, sale and transport of certain contrabands; whereas Section 42 deals with the power of entry, search, seizure and arrest without warrant or authorisation. Section 50 of the Act lays down the conditions under which search to be conducted. The Court also considered Section 109 of the Army Act, which deals with the power to convene a general court martial and states: "A general court martial may be convened by the Central Government or the Chief of the Army Staff or by any officer empowered in this behalf by warrant of the Chief of the Army Staff."

The issue before the Supreme Court was: whether by reason of the respondent being a member of the armed forces would stand denuded of such a safeguard in the event the general court martial takes note of an offence under a specific statute. Article 33 of the Constitution though conferred a power but has not been taken recourse to put a bar or restraint as regards the non-availability of the statutory safeguards in terms therewith. It reads:

> **33. Power of Parliament to modify the rights conferred by this Part in their application to Forces, etc**. - Parliament may, by law, determine to what extent any of the rights conferred by this Part shall, in their application to, (a) the members of the Armed Forces; or (b) the members of the Forces charged with the maintenance of public order; or (c) persons employed in any bureau or other organisation established by the State for purposes of intelligence or counter intelligence; or (d) persons employed in, or in connection with, the telecommunication system set up for the purposes of any Force, bureau or organisation referred to in clauses (a) to (c), be restricted or abrogated so as to ensure the proper discharge of their duties and the maintenance of discipline among them.

As regards the mandatory effect of the provisions as contained in Section 50 of the NDPS Act, the Supreme Court referred the decision of the Constitutional Bench in *State of Punjab v Baldev Singh*: [36]

> 24. There is, thus, unanimity of judicial pronouncements to the effect that it is an obligation of the empowered officer and his duty before conducting the search of the person of a suspect, on the basis of prior information, to

inform the suspect that he has the right to require his search being conducted in the presence of a Gazetted officer or a Magistrate and that the failure to so inform the suspect of his right, would render the search illegal because the suspect would not be able to avail of the protection which is inbuilt in Section 50. Similarly, if the person concerned requires, on being so informed by the empowered officer or otherwise, that his search be conducted in the presence of a Gazetted officer or a Magistrate, the empowered officer is obliged to do so and failure on his part to do so would also render the search illegal and the conviction and sentence of the accused bad.

25. To be searched before a Gazetted officer or a Magistrate, if the suspect so requires, is an extremely valuable right which the legislature has given to the person concerned having regard to the grave consequences that may entail the possession of illicit articles under the NDPS Act. It appears to have been incorporated in the Act keeping in view the severity of the punishment. The rationale behind the provision is even otherwise manifest. The search before a Gazetted officer or a Magistrate would impart much more authenticity and creditworthiness to the search and seizure proceedings. It would also verily strengthen the prosecution case. There is, thus, no justification for the empowered officer, who goes to search the person, on prior information, to effect the search, of not informing the person concerned of the existence of his right to have his search conducted before a Gazetted officer or a Magistrate, so as to enable him to avail of that right. It is, however, not necessary to give the information to the person to be searched about his right in writing. It is sufficient if such information is communicated to the person concerned orally and as far as possible in the presence of some independent and respectable persons witnessing the arrest and search. The prosecution must, however, at the trial, establish that the empowered officer had conveyed the information to the person concerned of his right of being searched in the presence of a Magistrate or a Gazetted officer, at the time of the intended search. Courts have to be satisfied at the trial of the case about due compliance with the requirements provided in Section 50. No presumption under Section 54 of the Act can be raised against an accused, unless the prosecution establishes it to the satisfaction of the court that the requirements of Section 50 were duly complied with."

The Supreme Court also considered its recent decision in *Roy VD v State of Kerala* [37] dealing with Sections 41 and 42 of the NDPS Act.

> 15. It is thus seen that for exercising powers enumerated under sub-section (1) of Section 42 at any time whether by day or by night a warrant of arrest or search issued by a Metropolitan Magistrate or a Magistrate of the First Class or any Magistrate of the Second Class who has been specifically empowered by the State Government in that behalf or an authorisation under sub-section (2) of Section 41 by an empowered officer is necessary. Without such a warrant or an authorisation, an empowered officer can exercise those powers only between sunrise and sunset. However, the proviso permits such an empowered or authorised officer to exercise the said powers at any time between sunset and sunrise if he has reason to believe that such a search warrant or authorisation cannot be obtained without affording opportunity for the concealment of evidence of facility for the escape of an offender and he records the grounds of his belief.
>
> 16. Now, it is plain that no officer other than an empowered officer can resort to Section 41(2) or exercise powers under Section 42(1) of the NDPS Act or make a complaint under clause (d) of sub-section (1) of Section 36-A of the NDPS Act. It follows that any collection of materials, detention or arrest of a person or search of a building or conveyance or seizure effected by an officer not being an empowered officer or an authorised officer under Section 41(2) of the NDPS Act, lacks sanction of law and is inherently illegal and as such the same cannot form the basis of a proceeding in respect of offences under Chapter IV of the NDPS Act and use of such a material by the prosecution vitiates the trial.

The Supreme Court was of the view that if an arrest or search contemplated under Sections 41 and 42 is made under a warrant issued by any other Magistrate or is made by any officer not empowered or authorised, it would per se be illegal and would affect the prosecution case and consequently vitiate the trial. In this regard, the Court also rejected two contentions of the Central Government. First, since LD Balam Singh was a 'person' belonging to the Armed Forces, question of usual formalities as regards the procedural aspect under NDPS Act would not arise, as such infraction of Section 42 of the NDPS Act cannot be said to be of any consequence. Second, since Section 50 specifically records "about to search any person" and since the contraband item has been in fact recovered from the private residence of the respondent, Section 50 cannot be said to be of any application.

The Supreme Court opined: "While it is true that Army personnel ought to be subjected to strictest form of discipline and Article 33 of the Constitution has conferred powers on to the Parliament to bridge the rights conferred under Part III of the Constitution in respect of the members of the Armed Forces, but does that mean and imply that the Army Personnel would be denuded of the Constitutional privileges as guaranteed under the Constitution? Can it be said that the Army Personnel form a class of citizens not entitled to the Constitution's benefits and are outside the purview of the Constitution? To answer above in the affirmative would be a violent departure to the basic tenets of the Constitution. An Army Personnel is as much a citizen as any other individual citizen of this country. Incidentally, the provision as contained in Article 33 does not by itself abrogate any rights and its applicability is dependent on Parliamentary legislation. The language used by the framers is unambiguous and categorical and it is in this perspective Article 33 may be noticed at this juncture.

A plain reading thus would reveal that the extent of restrictions necessary to be imposed on any of the fundamental rights in their application to the armed forces and the forces charged with the maintenance of public order for the purpose of ensuring proper discharge of their duties and maintenance of discipline among them would necessarily depend upon the prevailing situation at a given point of time and it would be inadvisable to encase it in a rigid statutory formula. The Constitutions makers were obviously anxious that no more restrictions should be placed than are absolutely necessary for ensuring proper discharge of duties and the maintenance of discipline amongst the Armed Force Personnel and therefore Article 33 empowered the Parliament to restrict or abridge within permissible extent, the rights conferred under Part III of the Constitution in so far as the Armed Force Personnel are concerned.

The Court also referred to its earlier decision in the case of *Prithi Pal Singh v The Union of India*:[38]

> It is one of the cardinal features of our Constitution that a person by enlisting in or entering armed forces does not cease to be a citizen so as to wholly deprive him of his rights under the Constitution. More so when this Court held in *Sunil Batra v Delhi Administration* (1979) 1 SCR 392 that even prisoners deprived of personal liberty are not wholly denuded of their fundamental rights. In the larger interest of national security and military discipline Parliament in its wisdom may restrict or abridge such rights in their application to the Armed Forces but this process should not be carried so far as to create a class of citizen not entitled to the benefits of liberal spirit of the Constitution. Persons subject to Army Act are citizens of this ancient land having feeling of belonging to the civilized community governed by the liberty oriented Constitution.

The Supreme Court, while dismissing the appeal of the Central Government, concluded:

> In the event, a particular statute is taken recourse to, question of trial under another statute without taking recourse to the statutory safeguards would be void and the entire trial would stand vitiated unless, of course, there are existing specific provisions therefor in the particular statute. Needless to record that there were two other civilian accused who were tried by the civil court at Patiala but were acquitted of the offence for non-compliance of the mandatory requirements of the NDPS Act. Once the petitioner was put on trial for an offence under the NDPS Act, the general court martial and the army authorities cannot reasonably be heard to state that though the petitioner would be tried for an offence under Section 18 of the NDPS Act, yet the procedural safeguards as contained in the statutory provision would not be applicable to him being a member of the armed forces. The Act applies in its entirety irrespective of the jurisdiction of the general court martial or other courts. Since the army authorities did not take into consideration the procedural safeguards as is embodied under the Statute, the question of offering any credence to the submissions of Union of India in support of the appeal does not and cannot arise. There is no material on record to show that the authorities who conducted the search and seizure at the house of the respondent complied with Section 42 of the statute which admittedly stand fatal for the prosecution as noticed above as a matter of fact, two of the civilians were acquitted. While answer to the first question posed above is in the affirmative, the contextual facts bear out and pose a further issue as regards availability of substantive and procedural safeguards under a specific legislation the High Court answered it in the affirmative since such procedural safeguards are said to be mandatory in nature.

The power of review by the military commander in the South Asian countries is coercive and unique. This power of review was criticised almost two-centuries ago by the Earl of Bath who held the office of Secretary of War during the rebellion of 1715:

> Nothing can be more terrible than that called a revision of the sentence of a court martial, which is in so many respects different from that of a judge sending's sending a jury out again. When a judge sends a jury out again, it is done immediately whilst the looks and behaviour of the witnesses examined upon the trial are fresh in every one of their memories, and before anyone can have an opportunity to converse with or influence any of them. Whereas a commander-in-chief by his order of revision, may order them to revise the sentence three

> months later after its having been passed, when the behaviour of the witnesses must be entirely forgotten by most of them, and when they have been properly spoken to, and persuaded to alter their sentences. Besides these there is another material difference, which is, that a judge who sends a jury out again, and thereby shows himself displeased with their verdict, has no power or compulsive influence over any one man of the jury; but a commander, who orders a court martial to revise their sentence, and thereby shows himself displeases with it has an almost irresistible influence over every member of the court martial, so that the order for a revision is, and often proves to be an order for altering the sentence and making it more severe; for this must in general always be the design of a revision, because when the first sentence is too severe, there is no necessity for a revision as the commander may remit the whole or any part of the punishment he pleases. When we consider this, we may easily see the danger every gentleman of the army must be exposed to it he ventures to disobey or refuses to execute the orders of the commander of the army, let those orders be ever so illegal.[39]

In India, an army officer was tried by a summary general court martial and sentenced to be cashiered. The general officer commanding was dissatisfied with the sentence. While sending the court martial proceedings back to the same court for revision of the sentence, he made the following order:

> It would be appreciated that the charge of which the accused was convicted is of a very serious nature. The punishment of 'cashiering', therefore, awarded for the offence appears to be very lenient. Even though the proper amount of punishment to be inflicted is the least amount by which discipline can be effectively maintained, it is nevertheless equally essential that the punishment awarded should be appropriate and commensurate with the nature and gravity of the offence and adequate for the maintenance of the high standard of discipline in the armed forces....A person of the rank of an officer, who indulges in such a serious offence, should, therefore, be awarded suitable punishment.[40]

The same court martial, in revision, enhanced the punishment to two years of rigorous imprisonment. Such powers of review held by military commanders in the UK, Canada and Australia have been abolished. Since the appellate military courts do not exist in Bangladesh, Nepal, Pakistan and Sri Lanka, the military law system does not appear a 'justice system', either in design or in practice. It is disciplinary system and has a number of shortcomings relating to the 'rights to a fair trial' as enshrined in international documents.

Notes

1. Finding and sentence not valid unless confirmed: Section 153, Indian Army Act; Section 119, Pakistan Army Act and Bangladesh Army Act; Section 108, Nepal army Act and Section 64, Sri Lankan Army Act.
2. Except in the court martial held under the Indian Navy Act.
3. Laurence W Gormley, 'Judicial Review: Advice for the Deaf?' 29 (4) *Fordham International Law Journal,* 2006, p. 655.
4. Section 154, Indian Army Act, 1950.
5. Section 154, Indian Army Act, 1950.
6. Section 157, Indian Army Act, 1950.
7. Regulations for the Indian Army, 1987, Para 472 (a).
8. Regulations for the Indian Army, 1987, Para 472 (d).
9. Similar provisions are contained in the Indian Army Act, section 160; Bangladesh Army Act, section 126; Nepal Army Act, section 114; and Sri Lankan Army Act, section 65.
10. Section 160, Indian Army Act, 1950.
11. Rule 68, Indian Army Rules, 1954.
12. Para 471, Regulations for the Indian Army, 1987.
13. Section 121, Indian Army Act, 1950.
14. Section 158, Indian Army Act, 1950.
15. *Union of India v. Bajpai AP Capt*, SC Civil Appeal No. 9190 of 1995; *Capt Harish Uppal v. Union of India* AIR 1973 SC 258, and *Union of India v. Sub Avtar Singh,* Supreme Court of India SLP No. 868 of 1990.
16. Rule 70, Indian Army Rules, 1954.
17. Section 158, Indian Army Act, 1950; Section 143, Pakistan Army Act.
18. Section 132, Pakistan Army Act.
19. Section 67, Sri Lanka Army Act.
20. Rule 71, Indian Army Rules, 1954; and Para 473, Regulations for the Indian Army, 1987.
21. Similar provisions are contained in the Indian Army Act, section 161; Bangladesh Army Act, section 127; and Nepal Army Act, section 115.
22. Constitution of India, Article 227 (4), debars the High Courts in entertaining appeals from the decisions of military tribunals.
23. The Tribunal was inaugurated by the President of India on 8 August, 2009.
24. Jha U C. 2008. 'The Armed Forces Tribunal Act, 2007: A Critical Analysis', *Economic & Political Weekly*, March 15, 2008, p. 25-27.
25. Section 119, Nepal Army Act.
26. Section 164, Indian Army Act, 1950.
27. 169th Report of the Law Commission of India on "Amendments of Army, Navy and Air Force Acts", was forwarded to the Ministry of Law, Justice and Company Affairs on 3 May 1999.
28. http://letusbuildpakistan.blogspot.com/2009/01/lahore-high-court-makes-history-by.html
29. Dhaka, Feb 20, 2008. Rahman was promoted to the rank on the day he retired from service in December 2000, when the Awami League regime of Sheikh Hasina was in office. Almost four years later, on Oct 10, 2004, the Bangladesh Nationalist

Party-Jamaat alliance government cancelled his promotion on the recommendation of the parliamentary standing committee on defence. The cancellation order said the Bangladesh Army does not provide for the post of general and that the promotion was given in violation of army rules. Available at: http://www.thaindian.com/newsportal/uncategorized/court-restores-rank-to-former-bangladesh-army-chief_10019315.html

30. Constitution of Sri Lanka, Article 140 and 141. Section 79, Sri Lankan Army Act.
31. Communication No. 1426/2005, CCPR/C/91/D/1426/2005, 13 November 2007.
32. Senate Report No. 101-81, at 171 (1989).
33. Rule 4, United States Court of Appeals for the Armed Forces, Rules of Practice and Procedure, 1996.
34. *Council of Civil Services Unions v. Minister for the Civil Services* (1984) 3 WLR 1174 (HL): (1984) 3 All ER 935, 950.
35. AIR 1983 SC 454: (1983) 2 SCC p. 442.
36. *State of Punjab v Baldev Singh* (1999) 6 SCC 172.
37. *Roy VD v State of Kerala* (2001) SCC (Cri) 42.
38. *Prithi Pal Singh v Union of India* AIR 1982 SC 1413.
39. Clode Charles M. 1869. Military Forces of Crown, Vol. I, London: John Murray, p. 165-66.
40. *Captain Harish Uppal v Union of India* AIR (1973) SC 258.

7

The Right to A Fair Trial

International concern for human rights, human welfare and human dignity has evolved along with the evolution of the state system and out of the process of organising the international system of states. In 1948 when the UN General Assembly adopted the Universal Declaration of Human Rights (UDHR), it proclaimed that it is a common standard of achievement for all people of all nations. The importance of UDHR can hardly be exaggerated; it has influenced the subsequent constitutional developments in most countries of the world, including the South Asian countries. It has triggered the evolution of a host of international instruments of human rights, both global as well as regional.

International Law and the Right to a Fair Trial

The right to a fair trial is a norm of international human rights law, designed to protect individuals from the unlawful and arbitrary curtailment or deprivation of their basic rights and freedoms, the most prominent of which are the rights to life and liberty. Article 10 of the UDHR declares: "Everyone is entitled in full liberty to a fair and public hearing by an independent and impartial tribunal, in determination of his rights and obligations and of any criminal charges against him." Article 11 (1) of the Declaration further states: "Everyone charged with a penal offence has the right to be presumed innocent until proved guilty according to law in a public trial at which he has had all the guarantees necessary for his defence." These two rights are further elaborated under Article 14 of the International Covenant on Civil and Political Rights,[1] which provides that "everyone shall be entitled to a fair and public hearing by a competent, independent and impartial tribunal established by law." The fundamental importance of the right to a fair trial is illustrated not only by the extensive body of interpretation it has generated but, most recently, by a proposal to include it in the non-derogable rights provided for in Article 4(2) of the ICCPR.[2]

The UN General Assembly has adopted the Basic Principles on the Independence of the Judiciary, in 1985, which provides that "everyone shall have the right to be tried by ordinary courts or tribunals using established legal procedures."[3] In addition the Commission on Human Rights resolution 2002/37, entitled "Integrity of the judicial system", also reiterates that "everyone has the right to be tried by ordinary courts or tribunals using duly established legal procedures and that tribunals that do not use such procedures should not be created to displace the jurisdiction belonging to the ordinary courts or judicial tribunals." The provisions on the right to a fair trial and judicial guarantees are also contained in regional human rights instruments like the American Convention on Human Rights (Article 8),[4] the European Convention on Human Rights (Article 6)[5] and the African Charter on Human and Peoples' Rights (Article 7).

Article 6 of the European Convention on Human Rights (ECHR) guarantees the right to a fair and public hearing in the determination of an individual's civil rights and obligations or of any criminal charge against him. The text of Article 6 reads:

- In the determination of his civil rights and obligations or of any criminal charge against him, everyone is entitled to a fair and public hearing within a reasonable time by an independent and impartial tribunal established by law. Judgement shall be pronounced publicly but the press and public may be excluded from all or part of the trial in the interests of morals, public order or national security in a democratic society, where the interests of juveniles or the protection of the private life of the parties so require, or to the extent strictly necessary in the opinion of the court in special circumstances where publicity would prejudice the interests of justice.
- Everyone charged with a criminal offence shall be presumed innocent until proved guilty according to law.
- Everyone charged with a criminal offence has the following minimum rights:
    - to be informed promptly, in a language which he understands and in detail, of the nature and cause of the accusation against him;
    - to have adequate time and facilities for the preparation of his defence;
    - to defend himself in person or through legal assistance of his own choosing or, if he has not sufficient means to pay for legal assistance, to be given it free when the interests of justice so require;
    - to examine or have examined witnesses against him and to obtain the attendance and examination of witnesses on his behalf under the same conditions as witnesses against him;
    - to have the free assistance of an interpreter if he cannot understand or speak the language used in court. [6]

The right to a fair trial is applicable both to the determination of an individual's rights and duties in a suit at law and with respect to the determination of any criminal charge against him or her. The term "suit at law" refers to various types of court proceedings, including administrative proceedings. The standards against which a trial is to be assessed in terms of fairness are numerous, complex and constantly evolving.[7] They may constitute binding obligations that are included in human rights treaties to which the State is a party. They may also be found in documents which, though not formally binding, can be taken to express the direction in which the law is evolving.[8]

The Human Rights Committee did not consider initially that the trial of civilians by military courts was, per se, incompatible with the ICCPR, provided that the jurisdiction of such courts was in keeping with the provisions of article 14 of the Covenant. However, the Committee gradually came to criticise such tribunals during its consideration of periodic reports.[9] The Committee subsequently made it increasingly clear that it was in favour of limiting the jurisdiction of military tribunals for the trial of civilians by military tribunals was incompatible with the administration of fair, impartial and independent justice.[10]

The Basic Principles on the Independence of the Judiciary, adopted in September 1985, provide that "everyone shall have the right to be tried by ordinary courts or tribunals using established legal procedures". The Commission on Human Rights in its resolution of 22 April 2002,[11] entitled "Integrity of the judicial system", had declared that the Commission:

> Reiterates that every person is entitled, in full equality, to a fair and public hearing by a competent, independent and impartial tribunal, in the determination of his/her rights and obligations and of any criminal charge against him/her;
>
> Also reiterates that everyone has the right to be tried by ordinary courts or tribunals using duly established legal procedures and that tribunals that do not use such procedures should not be created to displace the jurisdiction belonging to the ordinary courts or judicial tribunals;
>
> Underlines that any court trying a person charged with a criminal offence must be based on the principles of independence and impartiality;
>
> Calls upon States that have military courts for trying criminal offenders to ensure that such courts are an integral part of the general judicial system and use the duly established legal proceedings.

The World Conference on the Independence of Justice, held in Canada, in June 1983, adopted the Universal Declaration on the Independence of Justice.[12] It provides: "The jurisdiction of military tribunals shall be confined to military offences committed by military personnel. There shall always be a right of appeal from such tribunals to a legally qualified appellate court."

The issue of the administration of justice through military tribunals is, also explicitly addressed by certain standards of a non-treaty nature. Article 5 of the draft declaration on the independence and impartiality of the judiciary, jurors and assessors and the independence of lawyers, referred to as the "Singhvi declaration",[13] provides that the jurisdiction of military tribunals should be confined exclusively to "military offences". Article 5 reads as follows:

- No ad hoc tribunals shall be established to displace jurisdiction properly vested in the courts;
- In such times of emergency, the State shall endeavour to provide that civilians charged with criminal offences of any kind shall be tried by ordinary civilian courts...;
- The jurisdiction of military tribunals shall be confined to military offences. There shall always be a right of appeal from such tribunals to a legally qualified appellate court or tribunal or a remedy by way of an application for annulment;

Although the Singhvi declaration has not been adopted by the Commission on Human Rights, the Commission, in its resolution[14] had invited Governments to take into account the principles set forth in the draft declaration.

In the context to the South Asian military law systems, the right to a fair trial needs to be examined in the three different scenarios. First, the trial of military combatants; second, the trial of civilians who have ties to the military (camp followers and other civilians working in the military), and third, the trial of civilians who have no functional ties with to the military, but become subject to military tribunals due to special legislations. The military courts while trying military offender in the South Asian countries, have jurisdiction to both, exclusive military offences as well as civil offences committed by military personnel.

Pre-Trail Rights

The prohibition of arbitrary arrest and detention.

Article 9(1) of the ICCPR provides that "everyone has the right to liberty and security of person". The liberty of a person has been interpreted narrowly, to mean freedom of bodily movement, which is interfered with when an individual is confined to a specific space, such as a prison or a detention facility. Under Article 9(1), "No one shall be subjected to arbitrary arrest or detention" and "No one shall be deprived of his liberty except on such grounds and in accordance with such procedure as are established by law." The principle of legality embodied in the latter sentence, both substantively ("on such grounds") and procedurally ("in accordance with such procedure"), mandates that the term "law" should be understood as referring to an abstract norm, applicable and accessible to all, whether laid down in a statute or forming part of the unwritten, common law. The prohibition of arbitrariness mentioned in the previous sentence serves to ensure that the law itself is not arbitrary, i.e., that the deprivation of liberty permitted by law is not "manifestly unproportional, unjust or unpredictable, and [that] the specific manner in which an arrest is made must not be discriminatory and must be able to be deemed appropriate and proportional in view of the circumstances of the case".

Article 6 of the ECHR guarantees a fair trial in the determination of a criminal charge against a person, and its guarantees apply from the moment a person is charged. In the case of *Deweer v. Belgium*[15] the Court stated that the word "charge" should be given a substantive rather than a formal meaning. The example what constitutes a "charge", could be when a person is first questioned as a suspect;[16] or his arrest for a criminal offence is ordered;[17] or he is officially informed of the prosecution against him.[18]

The right to know the reasons for arrest.

Article 9(2) of the ICCPR provides that "anyone who is arrested shall be informed, at the time of arrest, of the reasons for his arrest and shall be promptly informed of any charges against him". These provisions have been interpreted to mean that anyone who is arrested must be informed of the general reasons for the arrest "at the time of arrest", while subsequent information, to be furnished "promptly", must contain accusations in the legal sense.

The right to legal counsel.

The right to be provided and communicate with counsel is the most scrutinised specific guarantee of a fair trial, because it has been demonstrated to be the one that is violated the most often. Principle 1 of the Basic Principles on Lawyers states that "all persons are entitled to call upon the assistance of a lawyer of their choice to protect and establish their rights and to defend them in all stages of criminal proceedings". This right is particularly relevant in the case of pre-trial detention. Principle 5 of the Basic Principles on Lawyers specifically provides that when a person is arrested, charged or detained, he or she must be promptly informed of the right to legal assistance of his or her choice. Article 7 of the Basic Principles on Lawyers requires governments to ensure that all persons arrested or detained should have access to a lawyer within 48 hours of arrest or detention. [19]

The right to a prompt appearance before a judge to challenge the awfulness of arrest and detention.

Article 9(3) of the ICCPR refers specifically to the rights of a person arrested or detained on a criminal charge to "be brought promptly before a judge or other officer authorised by law to exercise judicial power and Rome Statute of the International Criminal Court (ICC) shall be entitled to trial within a reasonable time or to release". Article 9(4) of the ICCPR provides for the right to habeas corpus, that is, the right of anyone deprived of liberty by arrest or detention to "take proceedings before a court, in order that that court may decide without delay on the lawfulness of his detention and order his release if the detention is not lawful". In this context, the term "court" signifies not only a regular court, but a special court, including an administrative, constitutional or military court.[20] Lastly, Article 9(5) of the ICCPR provides that "anyone who has been the victim of unlawful arrest or detention shall have an enforceable right to compensation". Such a claim arises when the arrest or detention has contravened the provisions of Article 9(1) to (4) and/or a provision of domestic law.

The prohibition of torture and the right to humane conditions during pre-trial detention.

Article 7 of the ICCPR prohibits torture—or cruel, inhuman or degrading treatment or punishment—and is a norm of customary international law that also belongs to the category of *jus cogens.* The definition of torture,[21] which is prohibited by the Rome Statute of the International Criminal Court (ICC) as a crime against humanity when committed on a widespread or systematic basis, is slightly broader in that Statute than in the Torture Convention.

The prohibition on incommunicado detention.

The Human Rights Committee has found that incommunicado detention may violate Article 7 of the ICCPR which prohibits torture, as well as inhuman, cruel and degrading treatment. Principle 19 of the Body of Principles states that a "detained or imprisoned person shall have the right to be visited by and to correspond with, in particular, members of his family and shall be given adequate opportunity to communicate with the outside world, subject to reasonable conditions and restrictions as specified by law or lawful regulations". At a minimum, the right to communicate with "the outside world" includes the right to communicate with one's family, a lawyer and a doctor.[22]

Rights during Hearing

Equal access to, and equality before, the courts.

The first sentence of Article 14(1) of the ICCPR provides that "all persons shall be equal before the courts and tribunals", and has been interpreted to signify that all persons must be granted, without discrimination, the right of equal access to a court.[23] This, on the one hand, means that establishing separate courts for different groups of people on the basis of their race, colour, sex, language, religion, political or other opinion, national or social origin, property, birth or other status would be a contravention of Article 14(1). On the other hand, the establishment of certain types of special courts with jurisdiction over all persons belonging to the same category, such as military personnel, remains a thorny issue. The second sentence of Article 14(1) relates to the right to a fair and public hearing by a competent, independent and impartial tribunal established by law. It includes the basic components of due process of law which is, in criminal cases, further supplemented by the other provisions of Articles 14 and 15.

The right to a fair and public hearing.

The right to a fair hearing as provided for in Article 14(1) of the ICCPR encompasses the procedural and other guarantees laid down in paragraphs 2 to 7 of Article 14 and Article 15. However, the right is wider in scope, as can be deduced from the wording of Article 14(3) which refers to the concrete rights enumerated as "minimum guarantees". The right to a public hearing in both civil and criminal cases is expressly guaranteed by article 6(1) of the ECHR, although the press and public "may be excluded from all or part of" a trial for certain specified reasons, namely, in the interest of morals, public order or national security in a democratic society, in the interest of the parties' private lives, or where the interest of justice otherwise so requires. The single most important criterion in evaluating the fairness of a trial is the observance of the principle of equality of arms between the defence and the prosecution.

Article 14(1) of the ICCPR also guarantees the right to a public hearing as one of the essential elements of the concept of a fair trial. However, it also permits several exceptions to this general rule under specified circumstances. The publicity of a trial includes both the public nature of the hearings in all the stages of the proceedings, as well as the publicity of the judgement eventually rendered in a case. It is a right belonging to the parties, but also to the general public in a democratic society. The right to a public hearing means that the hearing should as a rule be conducted orally and publicly, without a specific request by the parties to that effect. The court or tribunal is, *inter alia*, obliged to make information about the time and venue of the public hearing available and to provide adequate facilities for attendance by interested members of the public, within reasonable limits. The public, including the press, may be excluded from all or part of a trial for the reasons specified in Article 14(1), but such exclusion must be based on a decision of the court rendered in keeping with the respective rules of procedure. Article 14(1) is violated in cases where the hearing has taken place in camera when the State party has failed to justify this measure in accordance with the terms of the ICCPR.[24]

A public hearing is an essential feature of the right to a fair trial. As the European Court stated in *Axen v. the Federal Republic of Germany*, "The public character of proceedings before the judicial bodies referred to in Article 6 (1) protects litigants against the administration of justice in secret with no public scrutiny; it is also one of the means whereby confidence in the courts, superior and inferior, can be maintained. By rendering the administration of justice visible, publicity contributes to the achievement of the aim of Article 6 (1), namely a fair trial, the guarantee of which is one of the fundamental principles of any democratic society, within the meaning of the Convention."[25]

The Court has stated that prison disciplinary hearings can be held in private. In the case of *Campbell and Fell v. the United Kingdom* the Court declared that consideration must be given to the public order and security problems that would be involved if these proceedings were conducted in public. This would impose a disproportionate burden on the authorities of the State.[26]

The right to a competent, independent and impartial tribunal established by law.

The right to be tried by an independent and impartial tribunal must be applied at all times and is a right contained in article 14(1) of the ICCPR, which provides that "in the determination of any criminal charge against him, or of his rights and obligations in a suit at law, everyone shall be entitled to a fair and public hearing by a competent, independent and impartial tribunal established by law." Although article 7(1) of the African Charter on Human and Peoples' Rights speaks only of a "competent" (art. 7(1)(b)) or "impartial" (art. 7(1)(d)) court or tribunal, article 26 of the Charter imposes a legal duty on the States parties also "to guarantee the independence of the Courts". Article 8(1) of the American Convention refers to "a competent, independent, and impartial tribunal, previously established by law", and article 6(1) of the European Convention on Human Rights to "an independent and impartial tribunal established by law".

The basic prerequisite for individuals to enjoy the right to a fair trial is that proceedings in any criminal case should be conducted by a competent, independent and impartial tribunal established by law.[27] The rationale of this provision is to avoid the arbitrariness and/or bias that would potentially arise if criminal charges were to be decided on by a political body or an administrative agency. When saying that a tribunal should be established by law, the term "law" denotes legislation passed by the habitual law-making body empowered to enact statutes or an unwritten norm of common law, depending on the legal system. In either case, the important feature is that the law must be accessible to all who are subject to it. The general aim of this provision is to ensure that criminal charges are heard by a court set up in advance and independently of a particular case—and not prior to and specifically for the offence involved.

The right to a presumption of innocence.
According to Article 14(2) of the ICCPR, "everyone charged with a criminal offence shall have the right to be presumed innocent until proved guilty according to law". As a basic component of the right to a fair trial, the presumption of innocence, *inter alia*, means that the burden of proof in a criminal trial lies on the prosecution and that the accused has the benefit of doubt. The presumption of innocence must, in addition, be maintained not only during a criminal trial *vis a vis* the defendant, but also in relation to a suspect or accused throughout the pre-trial phase. It is the duty both of the officials involved in a case as well as all public authorities to maintain the presumption of innocence by "refraining from prejudging the outcome of a trial".

The right to prompt notice of the nature and cause of criminal charges.
Everyone against whom any criminal charge is brought shall be entitled, in full equality, "to be informed promptly and in detail in a language which he understands of the nature and cause of the charge against him". This duty to inform relates to an exact legal description of the offence ("nature") and of the facts underlying it ("cause"), and is thus broader than the corresponding rights granted under Article 9(2) of the ICCPR applicable to arrest. The rationale is that the information provided must be sufficient to allow the preparation of a defence.

The right to adequate time and facilities for the preparation of a defence.
Article 14(3)(b) of the ICCPR provides that everyone is entitled in the determination of any criminal charge against him or her "to have adequate time and facilities for the preparation of his defence and to communicate with counsel of his own choosing". The right to adequate time and facilities for the preparation of a defence applies not only to the defendant, but to his or her defence counsel as well and is to be observed in all stages of the proceedings. What constitutes "adequate" time

will depend on the nature of the proceedings and the factual circumstances of a case. The factors to be taken into account include the complexity of the case, the defendant's access to evidence, and the time limits provided for in domestic law for certain actions in the proceedings.

The right to a trial without undue delay.

Everyone shall be entitled in the determination of any criminal charge against him/her, "to be tried without undue delay".[28] This provision has been interpreted to signify the right to a trial that produces a final judgement and, if appropriate, a sentence without undue delay. The time limit "begins to run when the suspect (accused, defendant) is informed that the authorities are taking specific steps to prosecute him". The assessment of what may be considered undue delay will depend on the circumstances of a case, i.e., its complexity, the conduct of the parties, whether the accused is in detention, etc. The right is not contingent on a request by the accused to be tried without undue delay.

The right to defend oneself in person or through legal counsel.

Article 14(3)(d) of the ICCPR, article 7(1)(c) of the African Charter on Human and Peoples' Rights, article 8(2)(d) of the American Convention on Human Rights and article 6(3)(c) of the ECHR all guarantee the right of anyone charged with a criminal offence to defend himself in person or through legal assistance of his own choice. The right of access to legal assistance must be effectively available, and the accused or his lawyer must have the right to act diligently and fearlessly in pursuing all available defences and the right to challenge the conduct of the case if they believe it to be unfair. In cases where the court is empowered to award the death sentence, the legal assistance to the accused must be provided in ways that adequately and effectively ensure justice.

According to the Human Rights Committee's jurisprudence under article 14(3)(d): "The court should ensure that the conduct of a case by a lawyer is not incompatible with the interests of justice. .... in a capital case, when counsel for the accused concedes that there is no merit in the appeal, the Court should ascertain whether counsel has consulted with the accused and informed him accordingly. If not, the Court must ensure that the accused is so informed and given an opportunity to engage other counsel."[29]

The right to counsel in the pre-trial stages of a criminal trial is clearly linked to the right to a defence during trial, as set out in Article 14(3)(d) of the ICCPR. The provision states that everyone shall be entitled, in the determination of any criminal charge against him/her, "to be tried in his presence, and to defend himself in person or through legal assistance of his own choosing; to be informed, if he does not have legal assistance, of this right; and to have legal assistance assigned to him, in any case where the interests of justice so require, and without payment by him in any such case if he does not have sufficient means to pay for it". This provision includes the following specific rights: (i) the right to be tried in one's presence, which means that the trial would not be in absentia; (ii) the right to defend oneself in person; (iii) the right to choose one's own counsel; (iv) the right to be informed of the right to counsel; and (v) the right to receive free legal assistance.

Article 14(3)(d) of the ICCPR provides that in the determination of any criminal charge, everyone shall be entitled "to have legal assistance assigned to him, in any case where the interests of justice so require, and without payment by him in any such case if he does not have sufficient means to pay for it". Article 6(3)(c) of the European Convention on Human Rights also provides for the right of a person not having "sufficient means to pay for legal assistance, to be given it free when the interests of justice so require". Article 8(2)(e) of the American Convention refers back to the provisions of national law in this respect, while the African Charter on Human and Peoples' Rights is silent on the question of free legal aid.

For the granting of free legal aid, article 14(3)(d) of the ICCPR and article 6(3)(c) of the European Convention set two conditions: first, the unavailability of sufficient funds to pay for a lawyer and, second, that the interests of justice require such aid. As seen in the preceding subsection, the interests of justice would require the granting of legal aid in capital punishment cases where the accused wishes for such aid and cannot pay for it himself. Assignment of counsel by the court contravenes the principle of fair trial if a qualified lawyer of the accused's own choice is available and willing to represent him or her. Court-appointed counsel must be able effectively to defend the accused, that is, to freely exercise his/her professional judgement and to actually advocate in favour of the accused.

The European Court has observed with respect to article 6(3)(c) of the ECHR that "the right of an accused to be given, in certain circumstances, free legal assistance constitutes one aspect of the notion of a fair trial in criminal proceedings". In determining whether the interests of justice require the granting of free legal aid, the European Court has regard to various criteria, such as "the seriousness of the offence" committed, "the severity of the sentence" the accused person risks and "the complexity of the case".[30]

The right to examine witnesses.

Article 14(3)(e) of the International Covenant provides that, in the determination of any criminal charge against him, everyone shall be entitled to "examine, or have examined, the witnesses against him and to obtain the attendance and examination of witnesses on his behalf under the same conditions as witnesses against him".

Article 6(3)(d) of the ECHR contains an identically worded provision, while article 8(2)(f) of the American Convention on Human Rights contains the "right of the defence to examine witnesses present in the court and to obtain the appearance, as witnesses, of experts or other persons who may throw light on the facts".

This right is an essential element of the principle of equality of arms. The terms "to examine" and "have examined" should be read as recognition of the two main systems of criminal justice, the inquisitorial and accusatorial one. However, the defence does not have an unlimited right to obtain the compulsory attendance of witnesses on the defendant's behalf, but only "under the same conditions" as witnesses against him/her.

In addition, Article 14(3)(e) has been concretely interpreted to mean that the prosecution must inform the defence of the witnesses it intends to call at trial within a reasonable time prior to the trial, so that the defendant may have sufficient time to prepare his/her defence. The defendant also has the right to be present during the testimony of a witness and may be restricted in doing so only in exceptional circumstances, such as when the witness reasonably fears reprisal by the defendant.

The right to an interpreter.

According to article 14(3)(f) of the Covenant and article 6(3)(e) of the European Convention, everyone shall be entitled to "have the free assistance of an interpreter if he cannot understand or speak the language used in court". [31] Article 8(2)(a) of the American Convention guarantees "the right of the accused to be assisted without charge by a translator or interpreter, if he does not understand or does not speak the language of the tribunal or court".

The prohibition on self-incrimination.

In the determination of any criminal charge against him/her, everyone is entitled "not to be compelled to testify against himself or to confess guilt".[32] This provision aims to prohibit any form of coercion, whether direct or indirect, physical or mental, and whether before or during the trial, that could be used to force the accused to testify against him/herself or to confess guilt. The judge must have the authority to consider an allegation of coercion or torture at any stage of the proceedings. In addition, silence by the accused may not be used as evidence to prove guilt and no adverse consequences may be drawn from an accused's exercise of the right to remain silent.

The prohibition on retroactive application of criminal laws.

Article 15(1) of the ICCPR, which embodies the principle *nullum crimen sine lege* (a crime must be provided for by law), can, in fact, be taken as a point of departure in any consideration of the fairness of a trial. In the broad sense, it expresses the principle of legality, according to which "no one shall be held guilty of any criminal offence on account of any act or omission which did not constitute a criminal offence, under national or international law, at the time when it was committed".[33] In the narrow sense, it is aimed at prohibiting the retroactive application of substantive criminal law and thus chronologically precedes a determination of the procedural fairness of a trial pursuant to Article 14.[34] It is one of the few non-derogable rights provided for in Article 4(2) of the ICCPR.

The prohibition on double jeopardy.

The ICCPR contains the prohibition of double jeopardy or the principle of *ne bis in idem*, according to which "no one shall be liable to be tried or punished again for an offence for which he has already been finally convicted or acquitted in accordance with the law and penal procedure of each country".[35] Article 8(4) of the American Convention guarantees this principle in the following words: "An accused person acquitted by a non-appealable judgement shall not be subjected to a new trial for the same cause". Protocol No. 7 to the European Convention provides in its article 4(1) that "no one shall be liable to be tried or punished again in criminal proceedings under the jurisdiction of the same State for an offence for which he has already been finally acquitted or convicted in accordance with the law and penal procedure of that State". However, according to article 4(2) of the Protocol, these provisions "shall not prevent the re-opening of the case ... if there is evidence of new or newly discovered facts, or if there has been a fundamental defect in the previous proceedings, which would affect the outcome of the case". The principle of *ne bis in idem* is non-derogable under the ECHR (art. 4(3) of Protocol No. 7).

The right to a reasoned judgement.

Although not expressly mentioned in the four main human rights treaties, the right to a reasoned judgement is inherent in the provisions regarding a "fair trial", including the right to a public judgement. The Human Rights Committee has examined numerous complaints concerning the failure of courts to issue a reasoned judgement. These complaints have been examined under article 14(3)(c) and (5) of the Covenant, which "are to be read together, so that the right to review of conviction and sentence must be made available without delay". According to the Human Rights Committee's case-law under article 14(5), "a convicted person is entitled to have, within reasonable time, access to written judgements, duly reasoned, for all instances of appeal in order to enjoy the effective exercise of the right to have conviction and sentence reviewed by a higher tribunal according to law".[36] According to the European Court of Human Rights, judgements of courts and tribunals should adequately state the reasons on which they are based.

Post-Trial Rights

The right to appeal

The ICCPR provides that "everyone convicted of a crime shall have the right to his conviction and sentence being reviewed by a higher tribunal according to law".[37] The existence of a right to appeal is a right guaranteed by the Covenant itself and its existence is thus not in theory dependent on domestic law; the reference to "according to law" refers here exclusively to "the modalities by which the review by a higher tribunal is to be carried out". Article 7(1)(a) of the African Charter on Human and Peoples' Rights provides that "every individual shall have the right to have his cause heard", a right which includes "the right to an appeal to competent national organs against acts violating his fundamental rights as recognised and guaranteed by conventions, laws, regulations and customs in force". Article 8(2)(h) of the American Convention on Human Rights stipulates that in criminal proceedings "every person is entitled, with full equality [to] the right to appeal the judgement to a higher court".

Article 6 of the European Convention does not, per se, guarantee a right of appeal, but this right is contained in article 2 of Protocol No. 7 to the Convention, although it "may be subject to exceptions in regard to offences of a minor character, as prescribed by law, or in cases in which the person concerned was tried in first instance by the highest tribunal or was convicted following an appeal against acquittal" (art. 2(2) of the Protocol).

The Human Rights Committee has made it clear that, regardless of the name of the remedy or appeal in question, "it must meet the requirements for which the Covenant provides",[38] which implies that the review must concern both the legal and material aspects of the person's conviction and sentence. In other words, in addition to pure questions of law, the review must provide "for a full evaluation of the evidence and the conduct of the trial".[39] The Committee has consistently held that legal aid be available to a convicted prisoner under sentence of death, and that this applies to all stages of the legal proceedings.

The right to appeal as guaranteed by Article 8 (2)(h) of the American Convention on Human Rights was violated in the case of *Castillo Petruzzi* where the victims had only been able to file an appeal with the Supreme Court of Military Justice against the judgement of the lower military court. As noted by the Inter-American Court of Human Rights, the right to appeal the judgement as guaranteed by the Convention "is not satisfied merely because there is a higher court than the one that tried and convicted the accused and to which the latter has or may have recourse"; on the contrary, for "a true review of the judgement, in the sense required by the Convention, the higher court must have the jurisdictional authority to take up the particular case in question".[40] In this case, where the victims had been tried by a military court with an appeal possible to the Supreme Court of Military Justice, "the superior court was part of the military structure and as such did not have the independence necessary to act as or be a tribunal previously established by law with jurisdiction to try civilians"; consequently, "there were no real guarantees that the case would be reconsidered by a higher court that combined the qualities of competence, impartiality and independence that the Convention requires". Although the right to appeal is not guaranteed as such by article 6 of the ECHR, the European Court has consistently held that the contracting State which sets up an appeal system is required to ensure that persons within its jurisdiction enjoy fundamental guarantees before appellate courts as contained in the article.

The right to compensation for miscarriage of justice.

"When a person has by a final decision been convicted of a criminal offence and when subsequently his conviction has been reversed or he has been pardoned on the ground that a new or newly discovered fact shows conclusively that there has been a miscarriage of justice, the person who has suffered punishment as a result of such conviction shall be compensated according to law, unless it is proved that the non-disclosure of the unknown fact in time is wholly or partly attributable to him."[41] The compensation for miscarriage of justice may be granted only after a conviction has become final, and the claim may be brought regardless of the severity of the offence involved. There are three additional conditions that must be cumulatively met: (i) a miscarriage of justice must have been subsequently officially acknowledged by a reversal of the conviction or by pardon; (ii) the delayed disclosure of the pertinent fact(s) must not be attributable to the convicted person; and (iii) the convicted person must have suffered punishment as a result of the miscarriage of justice. The phrase "according to law" does not mean that States can ignore the right to compensation by simply not providing for it, but rather that they are obliged to grant compensation pursuant to a mechanism provided for by law.

The Right to a Fair Trial and Military Tribunals

The Commission on Human Rights in its Sixty-second session has considered the report submitted by the Special Rapporteur on the issue of the administration of justice through military tribunals.[42] The report contains an updated version of "draft principles governing the administration of justice through military tribunals".

These principles emphasise that the military justice must be "an integral part of the general judicial system", it should have minimum level of universally applicable rules, leaving scope for stricter standards to be defined under domestic law. These principles are as follows.

Principle No. 1: Establishment of military tribunals by the constitution or the law. Military tribunals, when they exist, may be established only by the constitution or the law, respecting the principle of the separation of powers. They must be an integral part of the general judicial system.

Principle No. 2: Respect for the standards of international law. Military tribunals must in all circumstances apply standards and procedures internationally recognised as guarantees of a fair trial, including the rules of international humanitarian law.

Principle No. 3: Application of martial law. In times of crisis, recourse to martial law or special regimes should not compromise the guarantees of a fair trial. Any derogation "strictly required by the exigencies of the situation" should be consistent with the principles of the proper administration of justice. In particular, military tribunals should not be substituted for ordinary courts, in derogation from ordinary law.

Principle No. 4: Application of humanitarian law. In time of armed conflict, the principles of humanitarian law, and in particular the provisions of the Geneva Convention relative to the Treatment of Prisoners of War, are fully applicable to military courts.[43]

Principle No. 5: Jurisdiction of military courts to try civilians. Military courts should, in principle, have no jurisdiction to try civilians. In all circumstances, the State shall ensure that civilians accused of a criminal offence of any nature are tried by civilian courts.[44]

Principle No. 6: Conscientious objection to military service. Conscientious objector status should be determined under the supervision of an independent and impartial civil court, providing all the guarantees of a fair trial, irrespective of the stage of military life at which it is invoked.[45]

Principle No. 7: Jurisdiction of military tribunals to try minors under the age of 18. Strict respect for the guarantees provided in the Convention on the Rights of the Child and the United Nations Standard Minimum Rules for the Administration of Juvenile Justice (Beijing Rules) should govern the prosecution and punishment of minors, who fall within the category of vulnerable persons. In no case, therefore, should minors be placed under the jurisdiction of military courts.[46]

Principle No. 8: Functional authority of military courts. The jurisdiction of military courts should be limited to offences of a strictly military nature committed by military personnel. Military courts may try persons treated as military personnel for infractions strictly related to their military status.

Principle No. 9: Trial of persons accused of serious human rights violations.

In all circumstances, the jurisdiction of military courts should be set aside in favour of the jurisdiction of the ordinary courts to conduct inquiries into serious human rights violations such as extrajudicial executions, enforced disappearances and torture, and to prosecute and try persons accused of such crimes.[47]

Principle No. 10: Limitations on military secrecy. The rules that make it possible to invoke the secrecy of military information should not be diverted from their original purpose in order to obstruct the course of justice or to violate human rights. Military secrecy may be invoked, under the supervision of independent monitoring bodies, when it is strictly necessary to protect information concerning national defence. Military secrecy may not be invoked:

- Where measures involving deprivation of liberty are concerned, which should not, under any circumstances, be kept secret, whether this involves the identity or the whereabouts of persons deprived of their liberty;
- In order to obstruct the initiation or conduct of inquiries, proceedings or trials, whether they are of a criminal or a disciplinary nature, or to ignore them;
- To deny judges and authorities delegated by law to exercise judicial activities access to documents and areas classified or restricted for reasons of national security;
- To obstruct the publication of court sentences;
- To obstruct the effective exercise of habeas corpus and other similar judicial remedies.

Principle No. 11: Military prison regime. Military prisons must comply with international standards, including the Standard Minimum Rules for the Treatment of Prisoners, the Basic Principles for the Treatment of Prisoners, and the Body of Principles for the Protection of All Persons under Any Form of Detention or Imprisonment, and must be accessible to domestic and international inspection bodies.[48]

Principle No. 12: Guarantee of habeas corpus. In all circumstances, anyone who is deprived of his or her liberty shall be entitled to take proceedings, such as habeas corpus proceedings, before a court, in order that that court may decide without delay on the lawfulness of his or her detention and order his or her release if the detention is not lawful. The right to petition for a writ of habeas corpus or other remedy should be considered as a personal right, the guarantee of which should, in all circumstances, fall within the exclusive jurisdiction of the ordinary courts. In all circumstances, the judge must be able to have access to any place where the detainee may be held.[49]

Principle No. 13: Right to a competent, independent and impartial tribunal.

The organisation and operation of military courts should fully ensure the right of everyone to a competent, independent and impartial tribunal at every stage of legal proceedings from initial investigation to trial. The persons selected to perform the functions of judges in military courts must display integrity and competence and show proof of the necessary legal training and qualifications. Military judges should have a status guaranteeing their independence and impartiality, in particular vis-à-vis the military hierarchy. In no circumstances should military courts be allowed to resort to procedures involving anonymous or "faceless" judges and prosecutors.[50]

Principle No. 14: Public nature of hearings. As in matters of ordinary law, public hearings must be the rule, and the holding of sessions in camera should be altogether exceptional and be authorised by a specific, well-grounded decision the legality of which is subject to review.

Principle No. 15: Guarantee of the rights of the defence and the right to a just and fair trial. The exercise of the rights of the defence must be fully guaranteed in military courts under all circumstances. All judicial proceedings in military courts must offer the following guarantees:

- Everyone charged with a criminal offence shall be presumed innocent until proved guilty according to law;
- Every accused person must be informed promptly of the details of the offence with which he or she is charged and, before and during the trial, must be guaranteed all the rights and facilities necessary for his or her defence;
- No one shall be punished for an offence except on the basis of individual criminal responsibility;
- Everyone charged with a criminal offence shall have the right to be tried without undue delay and in his or her presence;
- Everyone charged with a criminal offence shall have the right to defend himself or herself in person or through legal assistance of his or her own choosing; to be informed, if he or she does not have legal assistance, of this right; and to have legal assistance assigned to him or her, in any case where the interests of justice so require, and without payment by him or her in any such case if he or she does not have sufficient means to pay for it;
- No one may be compelled to testify against himself or herself or to confess guilt;
- Everyone charged with a criminal offence shall have the right to examine, or have examined, the witnesses against him or her and to obtain the attendance

and examination of witnesses on his or her behalf under the same conditions as witnesses against him or her;

- No statement or item of evidence which is established to have been obtained through torture, cruel, inhuman or degrading treatment or other serious violations of human rights or by illicit means may be invoked as evidence in the proceedings;
- No one may be convicted of a crime on the strength of anonymous testimony or secret evidence;
- Everyone convicted of a crime shall have the right to have his or her conviction and sentence reviewed by a higher tribunal according to law;
- Every person found guilty shall be informed, at the time of conviction, of his or her rights to judicial and other remedies and of the time limits for the exercise of those rights.

Principle No. 16: Access of victims to proceedings. Without prejudice to the principles relating to the jurisdiction of military courts, such courts should not exclude the victims of crimes or their successors from judicial proceedings, including inquiries. The judicial proceedings of military courts should ensure that the rights of the victims of crimes - or their successors - are effectively respected, by guaranteeing that they:

- Have the right to report criminal acts and bring an action in the military courts so that judicial proceedings can be initiated;
- Have a broad right to intervene in judicial proceedings and are able to participate in such proceedings as a party to the case, e.g. a claimant for criminal indemnification, an *amicus curiae* or a party bringing a private action;
- Have access to judicial remedies to challenge decisions and rulings by military courts against their rights and interests;
- Are protected against any ill-treatment and any act of intimidation or reprisal that might arise from the complaint or from their participation in the judicial proceedings.

Principle No. 17: Recourse procedures in the ordinary courts. In all cases where military tribunals exist, their authority should be limited to ruling in first instance. Consequently, recourse procedures, particularly appeals, should be brought before the civil courts. In all situations, disputes concerning legality should be settled by the highest civil court. Conflicts of authority and jurisdiction between military tribunals and ordinary courts must be resolved by a higher judicial body, such as a supreme court or constitutional court, that forms part of the system of ordinary courts and is composed of independent, impartial and competent judges.

Principle No. 18: Due obedience and responsibility of the superior. Without prejudice to the principles relating to the jurisdiction of military tribunals:

- Due obedience may not be invoked to relieve a member of the military of the individual criminal responsibility that he or she incurs as a result of the commission of serious violations of human rights, such as extrajudicial executions, enforced disappearances and torture, war crimes or crimes against humanity;
- The fact that a serious violation of human rights, such as an extrajudicial execution, an enforced disappearance, torture, a war crime or a crime against humanity has been committed by a subordinate does not relieve his or her superiors of criminal responsibility if they failed to exercise the powers vested in them to prevent or halt their commission, if they were in possession of information that enabled them to know that the crime was being or was about to be committed.

Principle No. 19: Non-imposition of the death penalty. Codes of military justice should reflect the international trend towards the gradual abolition of the death penalty, in both peacetime and wartime. In no circumstances shall the death penalty be imposed or carried out:

- For offences committed by persons aged under 18;
- On pregnant women or mothers with young children;
- On persons suffering from any mental or intellectual disabilities.

Principle No. 20: Review of codes of military justice. Codes of military justice should be subject to periodic systematic review, conducted in an independent and transparent manner, so as to ensure that the authority of military tribunals corresponds to strict functional necessity, without encroaching on the jurisdiction that can and should belong to ordinary civil courts.[51]

In General Comment No. 13, the Human Rights Committee stated with regard to the creation of military and other special tribunals:

> The provisions of Article 14 of the ICCPR apply to all courts and tribunals within the scope of that article whether ordinary or specialised. The Committee notes the existence, in many countries, of military or special courts which try civilians. In the case of South Asian countries, particularly Bangladesh and Pakistan, the reason for the establishment of such courts is to enable exceptional procedures to be applied which do not comply with normal standards of justice. This poses a serious problem as far as the equitable, impartial and independent administration of justice is concerned. While the Covenant does not prohibit such categories of courts, nevertheless the conditions which it lays

> down clearly indicate that the trying of civilians by such courts should be very exceptional and take place under conditions which genuinely afford the full guarantees stipulated in article 14 of the ICCPR.[52]

The Inter-American Court of Human Rights concluded that the military courts permitted to try civilians for treason in Peru violated article 8(1) of the American Convention on Human Rights because they were not independent and impartial and because, since the judges were "faceless", the defendants had no possibility of knowing their identity and of assessing their competence.[53]

Although there is no reason in principle why Article 6 guarantees cannot be observed in courts martial, the European Court of Human Rights has found a number of violations in respect of military tribunals. Where civilians are on trial for offences against national security the presence of military judges on State Security Courts has been held to violate Article 6 because, *inter alia*, the judges remained subject to military discipline.[54] Several cases have been decided concerning courts martial which try military personnel for offences which the Convention classifies as criminal. In *Grieves v. the United Kingdom* the Grand Chamber found that British Navy's court martial system violated Article 6 because of the *ad hoc* appointments of presidents for each court martial and the fact that judge advocates were serving naval officers.[55] In *Cooper v. the United Kingdom*, however, the Grand Chamber found that in army courts martial the presence of a civilian judge advocate and a permanent president did provide sufficient guarantees to comply with Article 6, particularly since the judicial decision-making of the military members of the tribunal was not subject to supervision and career assessment by senior officers.[56] The tribunal must have the power to give a binding decision which cannot be altered by a non-judicial authority. Courts martial and other military disciplinary bodies have been found to violate Article 6 in this context. The executive may issue guidelines to members about the general performance of their functions, as long as any such guidelines are not in reality instructions as to how specific cases are to be decided.

The adjective "independent" has been interpreted as meaning independent of the executive and of the legislature. Relevant factors for determining whether this requirement is met include the manner of appointment of the adjudicators, the duration of their term of office, the guarantees against outside pressures and the appearance of independence. Being independent of the parties is rather to be analysed as a question of impartiality. An instructive case is *Findlay v. United Kingdom* where it was held that a court martial convened pursuant to the Army Act, 1955 did not meet requirements of independence and impartiality set by Article 6 (1) in view, in particular, of the central role played in the prosecution by the "convening officer": he was responsible for convening the court martial and for appointing its members and the prosecuting officer, but was closely linked to the prosecuting authorities (he had the final decision on the nature and detail of the charges to be brought) and was superior in rank to the members of the court martial.

The Human Rights Committee in the case of *Estrella v Uruguay* (74/180) 29 March 1983, has held that a military court had violated the defendant's right to choose counsel by limiting him to a choice between two appointed attorneys. More and more countries are adopting legislation that excludes the jurisdiction of military tribunals over serious human rights violations committed by members of the armed forces or the police. In some countries, the constitution and the fundamental law provide that only civil courts are competent to try military personnel responsible for human rights violations.[57]

International human rights instruments specify how justice is to be administered and under what conditions. The notions of an independent and impartial tribunal, due process of law and the existence of judicial guarantees are essential components. The United Nations General Assembly is of the opinion that an independent and impartial judiciary and an independent legal profession are essential pre-requisites for the protection of human rights and to ensure that there is no discrimination in the administration of justice. [58] In all circumstances, the competence of military tribunals should be abolished in favour of those of the ordinary courts, for trying persons responsible for serious human rights violations, such as extrajudicial executions, enforced disappearances, torture and so on.

Notes

1. International Covenant on Civil and Political Rights, UN General Assembly resolution 2200A (XXI), December 16, 1966, entered into force March 23, 1976 [hereinafter ICCPR].
2. *See* Draft Third Optional Protocol to the ICCPR, Aiming at Guaranteeing Under All Circumstances the Right to a Fair Trial and a Remedy, Annex I, in: "The Administration of Justice and the Human Rights of Detainees, The Right to a Fair Trial: Current Recognition and Measures Necessary for Its Strengthening," Final Report, Commission on Human Rights, Sub-Commission on Prevention of Discrimination and Protection of Minorities, 46th Session, E/CN.4/Sub.2/1994/24, June 3, 1994, at 59-62. http://www.unhchr.ch/Huridocda/Huridoca.nsf/TestFrame/d8925328e178f8748025673d00599b81?Opendocument).
3. Basic Principles on the Independence of the Judiciary, UN General Assembly resolution 40/32, November 29, 1985 and resolution 40/146, December 13, 1985.
4. The Inter-American Court of Human Rights, in a case relating to civilians tried for acts of terrorism by a military tribunal, considered that the trial of civilians by a military tribunal was contrary to the right to a fair and just trial and the principle of the "natural judge" [Judgement of 30 May 1999, *Castrillo Petruzzi et al. v. Peru*]. For its part,

the Inter-American Commission on Human Rights has always considered that military tribunals do not meet the conditions of independence and impartiality required by the American Convention on Human Rights and the American Declaration of the Rights and Duties of Man [see E/CN.4/Sub.2/1992/Add.2, para. 103]. For example, it considered that a special military court was not an independent and impartial tribunal because it was subordinate to the Ministry of Defence and, therefore, to the executive [The annual report of the Inter-American Commission on Human Rights for 1994 (OAS/Ser.L/V/II.88, doc. 9 rev., 1995)]. It also considered that the trial of civilians, particularly for political offences, by military tribunals violated the right to an independent and impartial tribunal [The reports of the Inter-American Commission on Human Rights on the situation of human rights in Nicaragua (OAS/Ser.L/V/II.53, doc. 25, 1981].

5. The European Court of Human Rights (ECtHR), and previously the European Commission, has interpreted this provision broadly, on the grounds that it is of fundamental importance to the operation of democracy. The European Commission of Human Rights was a first tier filter for complaints which was abolished when Protocol No. 11 to the Convention came into force in 1998. All decisions are now taken by the European Court of Human Rights.
6. The first paragraph of Article 6 applies to both civil and criminal proceedings, whereas the second and third paragraphs apply only to criminal proceedings.
7. Dominic McGoldrick. 1994. *The Human Rights Committee, Its Role in the Development of the International Covenant on Civil and Political Rights, Oxford:* Clarendon Press, p. 415.
8. Non-binding documents of relevance to the conduct of criminal proceedings and to ascertaining fair trial standards include: the Basic Principles for the Treatment of Prisoners, UN General Assembly resolution 45/111, December 14, 1990; Standard Minimum Rules for the Treatment of Prisoners, UN Economic and Social Council resolution 663 C (XXIV), July 31, 1957 and resolution 2076 (LXII), May 13, 1977; Body of Principles for the Protection of All Persons under Any Form of Detention or Imprisonment, UN General Assembly resolution 43/173, December 9, 1988; Basic Principles on the Role of Lawyers, adopted by the Eighth United Nations Congress on the Prevention of Crime and the Treatment of Offenders, Havana, Cuba, August 27-September 7, 1990; UN Standard Minimum Rules for the Administration of Juvenile Justice, UN General Assembly resolution 40/33, November 29, 1985; Code of Conduct for Law Enforcement Officials, UN General Assembly resolution 34/169, December 17, 1979; Guidelines on the Role of Prosecutors, adopted by the Eighth United Nations Congress on the Prevention of Crime and the Treatment of Offenders, Havana, Cuba, August 27-September 7, 1990; Principles on the Effective Prevention and Investigation of Extralegal, Arbitrary and Summary Executions, UN Economic and Social Council recommended resolution 1989/65, May 24, 1989; Basic Principles on the Use of Force and Firearms by Law Enforcement Officials, adopted by the Eighth United Nations Congress on the Prevention of Crime and the Treatment of Offenders, Havana, Cuba, August 27-September 7, 1990.
9. Periodic Reports concerning Algeria, Colombia, Morocco, the Republic of Korea and Venezuela. See UN ECOSOC E/CN.4/Sub.2/2002/4 dated 9 July 2002.
10. In the cases of Cameroon, Chile, Egypt, Kuwait, Lebanon, Poland, the Russian Federation, Slovakia, the Syrian Arab Republic and Uzbekistan. See UN ECOSOC E/

CN.4/Sub.2/2002/4 dated 9 July 2002.

11. Resolution 2002/37 adopted 22 April 2002, paragraphs 1, 2, 5 and 8.
12. E/CN.4/Sub.2/1985/18/Add.6, annex IV), paragraph 2.06 (e).
13. E/CN.4/Sub.2/1988/20/Add.1 and Add.1/Corr.1.
14. 1989/32 of 6 March 1989.
15. *Deweer v. Belgium*, 27 February 1980, paras. 42, 44 and 46.
16. *Hozee v. the Netherlands*, 22 May 1998.
17. *Wemhoff v. the Federal Republic of Germany*, 27 June 1968.
18. *Neumeister v. Austria*, 27 June 1986.
19. The Human Rights Committee has stated that "all persons who are arrested must immediately have access to counsel." (Concluding Observations of the Human Rights Committee, Georgia, UN Doc. CCPR/C/79 Add.75, April 1, 1997 para 27).
20. The review by a superior military officer, government official or advisory panel would be insufficient. Regarding superior military officers, *Vuolanne v Finland* (Communication 265/1987, 7 April 1989, 1989 Report of the Human Rights Committee, UN Doc.A/44/40, at 265-257) stating that review of detention of a soldier by a superior military officer does not satisfy Article 9(4) of the ICCPR. As to government officials, the Human Rights Committee in *Torres v Finland* (Communication 291/1988, 2 April 1990, 1990 Report of the Human Rights Committee, Vol II, UN Doc.A/45/40, at 99-100), which states that the opportunity of an asylum-seeker to appeal to the Ministry of the Interior does not satisfy Article 9(4) of the ICCPR. Regarding advisory panels, see the European Court in *Chahal v United Kingdom* 70/1995/576/662, 15 November 1996, paras 130-133) which decided that an advisory panel which did not disclose its reasons for decision, had no binding decision-making power and which did not permit legal representation did not satisfy Article 5(4) of the European Convention.
21. The definition of and protection against torture was elaborated in the 1984 Convention against Torture: Art 1(1): ... the term "torture" means any act by which severe pain or suffering, whether physical or mental, is intentionally inflicted on a person for such purposes as obtaining from him or a third person information or a confession, punishing him for an act he or a third person has committed or is suspected of having committed, or intimidating or coercing him or a third person, or for any reason based on discrimination of any kind, when such pain or suffering is inflicted by or at the instigation of or with the consent or acquiescence of a public official or other person acting in an official capacity. It does not include pain or suffering arising only from, inherent in or incidental to lawful sanctions.
22. Principle 19, Body of Principles for the Protection of All Persons under Any Form of Detention or Imprisonment, UN General Assembly Resolution, 14/174, A/RES/43/173, dated 9 December 1988.
23. The right to equality before the law and equal treatment by the law, or, in other words, the principle of non-discrimination, conditions the interpretation and application not only of human rights law in strict sense, but also of international humanitarian law. For example articles 1, 2 and 7 of the Universal Declaration of Human Rights; articles 2(1), (3), 4(1) and 26 of the International Covenant on Civil and Political Rights; article 2(2) of the International Covenant on Economic, Social and Cultural Rights; articles 2, 3, 18(3) and 28 of the African Charter on Human and Peoples' Rights; articles 1, 24 and 27(1) of the American Convention on Human Rights; article 14 of

the European Convention on Human Rights; articles 2 and 15 of the 1979 Convention on the Elimination of All Forms of Discrimination against Women; article 2 of the 1989 Convention on the Rights of the Child; and the 1966 International Convention on the Elimination of All Forms of Racial Discrimination. Of the four 1949 Geneva Conventions, see e.g. articles 3 and 27 of the Geneva Convention relative to the Protection of Civilian Persons in Time of War; articles 9(1) and 75(1) of the 1977 Protocol Additional to the Geneva Conventions of 12 August 1949, and relating to the Protection of Victims of International Armed Conflicts (Protocol I); and articles 2(1) and 4(1) of the 1977 Protocol Additional to the Geneva Conventions of 12 August 1949, and relating to the Protection of Victims of Non-International Armed Conflicts (Protocol II).

24. Human Rights Committee, Communication No. 74/1980, *M. A. Estrella v. Uruguay* (Views adopted on 29 March 1983), in UN doc. *GAOR*, A/38/40, p. 159, para. 10.
25. *Axen v. the Federal Republic of Germany*, 8 December 1983, para. 25.
26. *Campbell and Fell v. the United Kingdom*, 28 June 1984, para. 87.
27. Article 14 (1), ICCPR.
28. Article 14(3)(c) of the ICCPR.
29. Communication No. 663/1995, *M. Morrison v. Jamaica* (Views adopted on 3 November 1998), in UN doc. *GAOR*, A/54/40.
30. ECtHR, Case of *Quaranta v. Switzerland*, judgment of 24 May 1991, Series A, No. 205, p. 16, paragraph 27.
31. Article 14(3)(f) of the ICCPR.
32. Article 14(3)(g) of the ICCPR.
33. Article 15 (1) of the ICCPR.
34. The one exception to the prohibition of retroactive domestic criminal legislation is contained in Article 15(2) of the ICCPR: "Nothing in this Article shall prejudice the trial and punishment of any person for any act or omission which, at the time when it was committed, was criminal according to the general principles of law recognised by the community of nations." This provision has been interpreted to mean that certain violations of customary international law, such as war crimes, torture, slavery, etc. may be punished by states applying retroactive domestic criminal laws. However, in effect, this provision simply restates the position that persons may held accountable for violations of international customary law: it merely facilitates the ability of States to legislate to this effect.
35. Article 14(7) of the ICCPR.
36. Communication No. 320/1988, *V. Francis v. Jamaica* (Views adopted on 24 March 1993), in UN doc. *GAOR*, A/48/40 (vol. II), p. 66, para. 12.2.
37. Article 14(5) of the ICCPR.
38. Communication No. 701/1996, *Gómez v. Spain* (Views adopted on 20 July 2000), in UN doc. GAOR, A/55/40 (vol. II), p. 109, para. 11.1.
39. Communications Nos. 623, 624, 626, 627/1995, *V. P. Domukovsky et al. v. Georgia* (Views adopted on 6 April 1998), in UN doc. GAOR, A/53/40 (vol. II), p. 111, para. 18.11.
40. I-A Court HR, *Castillo Petruzzi v. Peru,* judgment of May 30, 1999, Series C, No. 52, p. 208, para. 161
41. Article 14(6) of the ICCPR.

42. Report submitted by the Special Rapporteur of the Sub-Commission on the Promotion and Protection of Human Rights, Emmanuel Decaux, E/CN.4/2006/58 13 January 2006.
43. International humanitarian law also establishes minimum guarantees in judicial matters. Article 75, paragraph 4, of Protocol I to the Geneva Conventions of 12 August 1949 provides the fundamental guarantees in judicial matters that must be respected even during international conflicts, referring to an "impartial and regularly constituted court." Article 6, paragraph 2, of Protocol II refers to a "court offering the essential guarantees of independence and impartiality". According to the International Committee of the Red Cross (ICRC), "this sentence reaffirms the principle that anyone accused of having committed an offence related to the conflict is entitled to a fair trial. This right can only be effective if the judgement is given by 'a court offering the essential guarantees of independence and impartiality'".
44. While the ICCPR does not prohibit such categories of courts, nevertheless the conditions which it lays down clearly indicate that the trying of civilians by such courts should be very exceptional and take place under conditions which genuinely afford the full guarantees stipulated in article 14 of the Covenant.
45. When the right to conscientious objection is not recognised by the law, the conscientious objector is treated as a deserter and the military criminal code is applied to him or her. The United Nations has recognised the existence of conscientious objection to military service as a legitimate exercise of the right to freedom of thought, conscience and religion, as laid down in the Universal Declaration of Human Rights and the International Covenant on Civil and Political Rights. The Human Rights Committee has very clearly linked conscientious objection to the principle of freedom of conscience enshrined in article 18 of the ICCPR (General Observation No. 22 of 1993). It has expressed its concern on several occasions recently at the fact that military courts have punished conscientious objectors for failing to perform military service. It considers that a person may invoke the right to conscientious objection not only before entering military service or joining the armed forces but also once he or she is in the service or even afterwards.
46. United Nations Standard Minimum Rules for the Administration of Juvenile Justice ("The Beijing Rules"), Adopted by General Assembly resolution 40/33 of 29 November 1985
47. Contrary to the functional concept of the jurisdiction of military tribunals, there is today a growing tendency to consider that persons accused of serious human rights violations cannot be tried by military tribunals insofar as such acts would, by their very nature, not fall within the scope of the duties performed by such persons. Moreover, the military authorities might be tempted to cover up such cases by questioning the appropriateness of prosecutions, tending to file cases with no action taken or manipulating "guilty pleas" to victims' detriment. Civilian courts must therefore be able, from the outset, to conduct inquiries and prosecute and try those charged with such violations.
48. Military prisons must comply with international standards in ordinary law, subject to effective supervision by domestic and international inspection bodies. In the same way that military justice must conform to the principles of the proper administration of justice, military prisons must not depart from international standards for the protection of individuals subject to detention or imprisonment.

49. The right of access to justice - the "right to the law" - is one of the foundations of the rule of law. In the words of article 9, paragraph 4, of the ICCPR "Anyone who is deprived of his liberty by arrest or detention shall be entitled to take proceedings before a court, in order that that court may decide without delay on the lawfulness of his detention and order his release if the detention is not lawful." In wartime, the guarantees under humanitarian law, including the Geneva Convention relative to the Protection of Civilian Persons in Time of War, of 12 August 1949, apply in full.
50. The statutory independence of judges vis-à-vis the military hierarchy must be strictly protected, avoiding any direct or indirect subordination, whether in the organisation and operation of the system of justice itself or in terms of career development for military judges. Regarding the concept of an independent and impartial tribunal, a large body of case law has spelled out the subjective as well as the objective content of independence and impartiality. Particular emphasis has been placed on the English adage that "justice should not only be done but should be seen to be done". Emphasis should also be placed on the requirement that judges called on to sit in military courts should be competent, having undergone the same legal training as that required of professional judges. The legal competence and ethical standards of military judges, as judges who are fully aware of their duties and responsibilities, form an intrinsic part of their independence and impartiality.
51. Each such review of codes of military justice should be carried out by an independent body, which should recommend legislative reforms designed to limit any unjustified residual authority and thus return, to the greatest extent possible, to the jurisdiction of the civil courts under ordinary law, while seeking to avoid double jeopardy. More generally, this periodic review should ensure that military justice is appropriate and effective in relation to its practical justification. It would also embody the fully democratic nature of an institution that must be accountable for its operations to the authorities and all citizens. In this way, the fundamental discussion concerning the existence of military justice as such can be conducted in a completely transparent way in a democratic society.
52. United Nations Compilation of General Comments, p. 123, para. 4.
53. I-A Court HR, *Castillo Petruzzi* judgment of May 30, 1999, Series C, No. 52, pp. 196-197, paras. 129-134.
54. *Incal v. Turkey*, 9 June 1998.
55. *Grieves v. the United Kingdom*, 16 December 2003.
56. *Cooper v. the United Kingdom*, 16 December 2003.
57. Bolivia (Art. 34), Haiti (Art. 42.3) and Venezuela (Art. 29). In other countries, this exclusion is made under ordinary or military penal law: Colombia (Military Penal Code and the Act on Genocide, Enforced Disappearance, Torture and Illicit Displacement of Populations), Guatemala (Decree No. 41 of 1996) and Nicaragua. UN ECOSOC E/CN.4/Sub.2/2002/4 dated 9 July 2002.
58. UN General Assembly Resolution 46/120 of 17 December 1991.

8
Special and Emergency Laws

The militaries in the South Asian countries have been deployed in internal conflicts on a number of occasions when the existing police forces have proved inadequate to deal with perpetrators of large-scale violence. The armed forces have had to deal with violent conflicts arising out of what has variously been described as terrorism, insurgency, militancy, proxy war, armed rebellion and naxalism (the common term 'terrorism' will be used henceforth).[1] While being deployed in anti-terrorist operations, the armed forces function under special legalisations. There have been allegations that the members of the armed forces have taken advantage of the special legislations to unleash their own brand of terror. It has also been claimed by various national and international NGOs that the provisions of special legislations are against the international norms of human rights.

The Armed Forces (Special Powers) Act in India, the Armed Forces (Special Powers) Ordinance, 1942, in Bangladesh and the Public Security Ordinance (PSO) and Prevention of Terrorism Act (PTA) in Sri Lanka and the Terrorists and Disruptive Activities (Control and Punishment) Ordinance (TADO) in Nepal are a few of the legislations which accord special powers to the armed forces employed in anti-terrorist activities within the country. In Pakistan, the amendment of the Army Act of 1952 on various occasions gave powers to military courts to try civilians on charges of terrorism, anti-national activities, sedition, attacks on army personnel and attacks on the President.[2]

Human rights organisations have alleged that the security forces in Indian and Pakistan have been responsible for systematic and widespread human rights violations, including massive illegal arbitrary arrest, enforced disappearance, extrajudicial killings, illegal detention and torture.[3] Further, these violations are perpetrated with impunity.[4] This discussion deals with the special laws that have an impact on the functioning of the armed forces in the South Asian countries.

India

India has experienced violence related to separatist or insurgent movements in various parts of its territory. These include a Sikh separatist movement in Punjab in the early 1980s to the early 1990s, the ongoing cross-border insurgency in Jammu and Kashmir, which has been going on since 1989, and secessionist movements in the North-eastern states, such as Assam and Manipur. Moreover, recently there has been a significant rise in violence related to the left-wing extremist movement called "naxalism".[5]

Under normal circumstances, law and order is a provincial (state) subject in India. However, when a state becomes helpless in dealing with the law and order situation and discharging its primary duty of affording protection to citizens, the Union (Central) Government may declare the whole state or a part of it a disturbed area under the special law and send armed forces in aid of civil powers. The special laws in question are the Assam Disturbed Area (Special Power) Act, 1947; The Armed Forces (Special Powers), Act (AFSPA), 1958; and The Armed Forces (Jammu and Kashmir) Special Powers Act, 1990. These Acts contain similar provisions and are hereinafter referred to as AFSPA.

The excessive use of the armed forces to aid the civil authority has raised the question of violation of human rights. Various human rights organisations in the country and abroad, as well as the foreign and local media, have criticised the effectiveness of the Indian laws that deals with violations of human rights by armed forces personnel. They have also criticised the special laws that accord enhanced powers to the armed forces to deal effectively with disruptive activities in specific areas.[6] The armed forces have often been accused of extra-judicial execution of innocent civilians; illegal imposition of curfew; rape, molestation and sexual harassment of women; torture; forced labour; and large-scale looting of homes and granaries under the powers vested in them by the AFSPA.[7] The civil liberties organisations have dubbed the AFSPA a colonial instrument, modelled on the Armed Forces Special Power Ordinance, 1942, which was enacted to neutralise the Quit India Movement. They have accused the Indian government of violating the Constitution and the international standards of human rights, defined by International Bill of Human Rights.

The Armed Forces (Special Powers) Act (AFSPA)

The AFSPA is a small legislation with six sections. Section 1 contains the title of the Act and the territorial limits to which the provisions of the Act are applicable. Section 2 sets out the definition of terms like "armed forces". However, the term "disturbed area" has not been defined. It has been stated as "an area which is for the time being declared by notification under Section 3 to be a disturbed area". In the 1972 version of the AFSPA, the armed forces were defined as "the military and Air Force of the Union so operating". In the 1958 version of the Act, the definition was of the "military forces and the air forces operating as land forces". Section 2(c) states that all other words not defined in the AFSPA have the meanings assigned to them in the Army Act of 1950.

Section 3 of the Act states how an area can be declared disturbed. It grants the power to declare an area disturbed to the Central Government and the Governor of the state, but does not describe the circumstances under which the authority would be justified in making such a declaration. It only requires that such authority be "of the opinion that the whole or parts of the area are in a dangerous or disturbed condition such that the use of the Armed Forces in aid of civil powers is necessary." This definition was challenged in the case of *Indrajit Barua v. State of Assam* AIR 1983 Del 513. The Delhi High Court decided that the lack of precision in the definition of a disturbed area was not an issue since the government and the people of India understand its meaning. The Court held that the term "disturbed area" defies any definition. It held, "A disturbed area has to be adjudged according to the location, situation and circumstances of a particular case". Section 3 of the AFSPA lays down that a notification in respect of disturbed area may be issued in regard to an area which "is in such a disturbed or dangerous condition that the use of armed forces in aid of civil power is necessary".

However, there are acts which define the term more concretely. In the Disturbed Areas (Special Courts) Act, 1976, an area may be declared disturbed when "a state government is satisfied that (i) there was, or (ii) there is, in any area within a state extensive disturbance of public peace and tranquility, by reason of differences or disputes between members of different religions, racial, language, or regional groups or castes or communities."

The 1972 amendments to the AFSPA extended the power to declare an area disturbed to the Central Government. In the 1958 version of the AFSPA only the state governments had this power. The Central Government has the power to overrule the opinion of the Governor of a state and declare an area disturbed.

Section 4 sets out the powers granted to the military stationed in a disturbed area. These powers are granted to commissioned officers, warrant officers, or non-commissioned officers (NCO). This section allows armed forces personnel to use force for a variety of reasons. Section 4 of the Act [8] states:

Special Power of the Armed Forces – Any commissioned officer, warrant officer, non commissioned officer or any other person of equivalent rank in the armed forces may, in a disturbed area-

- if he is of opinion that it is necessary so to do for the maintenance of public order, after giving such due warning as he may consider necessary, fire upon or otherwise use force, even to the causing of death, against any person who is acting in contravention of any law or order for the time being in force in the disturbed area prohibiting the assembly of five or more persons or the carrying of weapons or of things capable of being used as weapons or of fire-arms, ammunition or explosive substances;

- if he is of opinion that it is necessary so to do, destroy any arms dump, prepared or fortified position or shelter from which armed attacks are made or are likely to be made or are attempted to be made, or any structure used as a training camp for armed volunteers or utilised as a hide-out by armed gangs or absconders wanted for any offence;
- arrest, without warrant, any person who has committed a cognizable offence or against whom a reasonable suspicion exists that he has committed or is about to commit a cognizable offence and may use such force as may be necessary to effect the arrest;
- enter and search without warrant any premises to make any such arrest as aforesaid or to recover any person believed to be wrongfully restrained or confined or any property reasonably suspected to be stolen property or any arms, ammunition or explosive substances believed to be unlawfully kept in such premises and may for that purpose use such force as may be necessary.

The designated member of the armed forces can shoot to kill, for the commission or suspicion of the commission of the following offences: acting in contravention of any law or order for the time being in force in the disturbed area prohibiting the assembly of five or more persons, carrying weapons, or carrying anything which is capable of being used as a fire-arm or ammunition. To justify the invocation of this provision, the officer need to be "of the opinion that it is necessary to do so for the maintenance of public order" and give "such due warning as he may consider necessary".

The armed forces officer/warrant officer or NCO can destroy property, if it is an arms dump, a fortified position or shelter from where armed attacks are made or are suspected of being made, if the structure is used as a training camp, or as a hide-out by armed gangs or absconders. They can arrest anyone without a warrant who has committed, is suspected of having committed a cognizable offence and use any amount of force "necessary to effect the arrest". They can enter and search without a warrant to make an arrest or to recover any property, arms, ammunition or explosives, which are believed to be unlawfully kept on the premises. Section 4 of the AFSPA also allows the use of force necessary for the search.[9]

There is a contention that drastic powers have been conferred on low-ranking officials like non-commissioned officers.[10] In the armed forces, an NCO holds a responsible position. When troops are deployed, the sections/patrols which go for search and patrolling operations are commanded by the NCO. In isolated places/ remote areas, while encountering insurgents, the NCO is expected to take a decision as regards the suitable use of force in the particular situation, for which he is trained.

The Supreme Court in the case of *Naga People's Movement of Human Rights*, held that the powers conferred under clauses (a) to (d) of Sections 4 and 5 on the officers and NCOs are not arbitrary and unreasonable, and are not violative of the provisions of Article 14, 19 and 21 of the Constitution.[11] However, in 1991, the United Nations Human Rights Committee had found Section 4 of the AFSPA to be incompatible with Articles 6, 9 and 14 of the International Covenant on Civil and Political Rights (ICCPR), 1966.[12]

Section 5 states that after the military has arrested someone under the AFSPA, they must hand that person over to the nearest police station with the "least possible delay". There is no definition in the Act of what constitutes the least possible delay. This provision has been interpreted as depending on the specific circumstances of each case; there is no precise amount of time after which the section is violated. In *Bacha Bora v. State of Assam*, the Divisional Bench of the Guwahati HC held that the words 'least possible delay' mean 'within the shortest possible time', though no arbitrary time limit can be set down as it may not be possible in many cases to precisely quantify the period of time in the terms of hours, dates or months.[13]

A few human rights organisations have claimed that the AFSPA is one of the more draconian legislations that the Indian Parliament has passed. Under this Act, all security forces are given unrestricted and unaccounted power to carry out their operations, once an area is declared disturbed. Even an NCO is granted the right to shoot to kill on the basis of the mere suspicion that it is necessary to do so in order to "maintain the public order". The AFSPA gives the armed forces wide powers to shoot, arrest and search, all in the name of "aiding civil power".

In reality, the imposition of the AFSPA and subsequent safeguards avoids any possibility of arbitrariness in the exercise of power under the Act. The provisions of the AFSPA can be applied in only the following special cases: (1) The Central Government is satisfied that the normal law and order situation has deteriorated up to the extent that it has created a disturbed or dangerous situation; (2) the state police force is not in a position to stop infiltration or the activities of undesirable forces; (3) the power conferred by the statute can be exercised only in the specified area and in no other state; (4) even in a disturbed area, the law has to be followed, for example, an order under Section 144 of the CrPC must be in force before the powers under Section 4 of the Act can be exercised;[14] (5) the powers can be exercised only in respect of those who are violating law and order; (6) before exercising the power, a warning is required to be given to those who are violating the law in force; and (7) The military person exercising the power is answerable to the organisation for any breach in the policy directives issued by the organisation.

Another condition is that in the event of deployment of armed forces, the said forces will operate in the state concerned in cooperation with the civil administration so that the situation that has necessitated the deployment of the armed forces is effectively dealt with and normalcy is restored. Thus, there are ample safeguards to prevent the wanton abuse of the power conferred by the AFSPA

Section 6 of the AFSPA stipulates that no legal proceeding can be brought against any member of the armed forces acting under the AFSPA without the permission of the Central Government. This does not amount to the granting of immunity to members of the armed forces. It only requires that permission be taken from the Central Government before prosecution. Section 6 gives the Central Government the discretion to grant or refuse sanction for instituting prosecution against any person in respect of anything done in the exercise of the powers conferred by the Act. This discretion cannot be termed arbitrary as any order of the Central Government refusing or granting sanction under Section 6, is subject to judicial review. Section 6 of the AFSPA was reviewed in the case of *Indrajit Barua v. Union of India*. The High Court justified this provision on the grounds that it prevents the filing of "frivolous claims".[15]

The armed forces need special legal protection and powers in the areas where they operate. It is imperative to use special legislation "from the point of view of morale as well as operational efficiency to protect the rights of soldiers". The Supreme Court of India, in the case of *Naga People's Movement of Human Rights* upheld the AFSPA. Upholding the instructions issued by the Central Government, a five-judge bench gave a list of do's and don'ts to be observed while acting under the AFSPA that provide effective checks against any misuse or abuse of the powers conferred. These are as follows.

List of do's and don'ts while acting under the Armed Forces Special Powers Act, 1958

Do's

- Action before operations
    - The armed forces should act only in an area declared a "disturbed area" under Section 3 of the Act.
    - The power to open fire, use of force or arrest is to be exercised under this Act only by an officer/JCO/WO or NCO.
    - Before launching any raid/search, definite information about the activity should be obtained from the local civil authority.

  - As far as possible, representatives of the local civil administration should be co-opted during the raid.
- Action during operation
  - In case it is necessary to open fire or use force against a suspect or any person acting in contravention to law and order, it should first ascertain that it is essential for the maintenance of public order. Fire should be opened only after due warning.
  - Only those who have committed a cognizable offence or are about to commit one or against whom a reasonable ground exists to prove that they have committed or are about to commit one should be arrested.
  - It should be ensured that troops under command do not harass innocent people, destroy the property of the public or unnecessarily enter the houses/dwellings of people not connected with any unlawful activity.
  - Women should not be searched or arrested in the absence of female police. In fact, women should be searched by female police only.
- Action after operation
  - After arrest, a list of the persons arrested should be prepared.
  - The arrested persons should be handed over to the nearest police station with the least possible delay.
  - While handing over arrested persons to the police, a report should also be submitted detailing the circumstances occasioning the arrest.
  - Every delay in handing over a suspect to the police must be justifiable and reasonable in terms of the place, time of arrest and terrain in which the person has been arrested. The least possible delay may be 2-3 hours, extendable to 24 hours or so, depending on the circumstance of the case.
  - After a raid, a list must be made of all arms, ammunition or any other incriminating material/ document taken into possession.
  - All such arms, ammunition, stores, etc. should be handed over to the police station, along with a seizure memo.
  - A receipt must be obtained of the persons, arms/ammunition, stores, etc. handed over to the police.
  - A record of the area where the operation is launched should be made, including the date and time and the persons participating in the raid.
  - A list of the commander and other officers/JCOs/NCOs forming part of the force should be made.
  - Medical relief must be given to any person injured during the encounter. If any person dies in the encounter, his dead body should be handed over immediately to the police, along with details of the circumstances leading to the death.

- Dealing with Civil Court.
  - Directions of the high courts and Supreme Court should be promptly attended to.
  - Whenever summoned by the courts, decorum of the court must be maintained and proper respect paid.
  - Questions put by the court should be answered politely and with dignity.
  - A detailed, correct and explicit record of the entire operation must be maintained.

Don'ts

- Persons should not be kept under custody for a period longer than what is absolutely necessary before they are handed over to the nearest police station.
- Force should not be used after arresting a person, except if he is trying to escape.
- Third-degree methods should not be used to extract information, a confession or details of other involvement in unlawful activity.
- After a person has been arrested by a member of the armed force, he shall not be interrogated by the members of the armed force.
- A person should not be released by the members of the armed forces who have apprehended him. If any person is to be released, he must be released through the civil authorities.
- One must not temper with official records.
- The armed forces shall not take back a person after he has been handed over to the civil police.

The Supreme Court opined that these instructions should be treated as binding by members of the armed forces while exercising their powers under the Act. It further observed that a complaint against misuse or abuse of the powers conferred by the Act should be thoroughly enquired into and if it is found that there is substance in the allegation, the victim should be suitably compensated by the state and the requisite sanction under Section 6 of the Act should be granted for institution of prosecution against the person responsible for such violation.

Parliamentary Competency

Parliament is competent to enact the AFSPA in exercise of the legislative power conferred on it under Entry 2 of List I and Article 248 of the Constitution, read with Entry 97 of List I. After the insertion of Entry 2A in List I by the Forty-Second

Amendment to the Constitution, the legislative power of Parliament to enact the Central Act flows from Entry 2A of List I. The expression "in aid of civil power" in Entry 2A of List I and in Entry I of List II implies that the deployment of the armed forces shall be for the purpose of enabling the civil power in the state to deal with a situation which is affecting the maintenance of public order and which the civil power cannot deal with without the aid of the armed forces. The word "aid" postulates the continued existence of the authority to be aided. This means that even after deployment of the armed forces, the civil power continues to function. If the armed forces are deployed, they operate in the state in cooperation with the civil administration so that the situation which has necessitated their deployment is effectively dealt with and normalcy restored.

Constitutional Provisions

It has been claimed that under section 4(a) of the AFSPA, which grants armed forces personnel the power to shoot to kill, the constitutional right to life (Article 21) is violated, and that the AFSPA is not fair, just or reasonable because it allows the armed forces to use an excessive amount of force. The AFSPA came under the scrutiny of the Delhi High Court in the case of *Indrajit Barua* as violative of Articles 14, 19 and 21 of the Constitution. The Delhi High Court held: "If to save hundred lives one life is put in peril or if a law ensures and protects the greater social interest then such law will be a wholesome and beneficial law although it may infringe the liberty of some individuals: it will ensure the liberty of greater number at the cost of one and a few. In any organised society claiming to be civilized and governed by the rule of law, social imperatives for the greater good must take precedence over individual rights."

Article 22 of the Indian Constitution states: "(1) No person who is arrested shall be detained in custody without being informed, as soon as may be, of the grounds for such arrest nor shall he be denied the right to consult, and to be defended by, a legal practitioner of his choice; and (2) Every person who is arrested and detained in custody shall be produced before the nearest magistrate within a period of twenty-four hours of such arrest, excluding the time necessary for the journey from the place of arrest to the court of the magistrate, and no such person shall be detained in custody beyond the said period without the authority of a magistrate." The remaining sections of the Article deal with the limits on these first two sections in the case of preventive detention laws. The safeguards under Article 22 are guaranteed to people arrested under Section 5 of the AFSPA. There are hundreds of cases in which captured militants have been handed over to the state police for subsequent trial.

AFSPA and International Human Rights Law

The Universal Declaration of Human Rights, adopted by the General Assembly in 1948, provided the basis for the formulation of covenants and conventions. Three documents—The Universal Declaration of Human Rights (UDHR), the International Covenant on Civil and Political Rights (ICCPR), 1966 and the International Covenant on Economic, Social and Cultural Rights (ICESCR), 1966, along with two protocols---the Optional Protocol to the ICCPR and the Second Optional Protocol to the ICCPR, constitute the International Bill of Human Rights. The Convention against Torture and other Cruel and Inhuman or Degrading Treatment or Punishment was adopted by the General Assembly on 10 December 1984 and came into force on 26 June 1987. The Convention on the Elimination of All Forms of Discrimination against Women was adopted by the General Assembly on 18 December 1979 and came into force on 3 September 1981. In addition, the Convention on the Rights of the Child was adopted by the UN General Assembly on 20 November 1989 and came into force on 2 September 1990. The World Conference on Human Rights was held in Vienna in 1993 and was attended by about 7000 participants, representing 171 countries, including India.

It has been claimed by certain bodies that the AFSPA, by its form and application, violates the UDHR, ICCPR, Convention Against Torture, UN Code of Conduct for Law Enforcement Officials, UN Body of Principles for Protection of All Persons Under any Form of Detention, and UN Principles on Effective Prevention and Investigation of Extra-Legal and Summary Executions. Specifically, the AFSPA violates the following provisions of the UDHR: (a) freedom and equal dignity and rights; (b) non-discrimination; (c) right to life, liberty, security of person; (d) provision against torture; (e) equality before the law; (f) right to effective remedy; (g) provisions against arbitrary arrest; and (h) right to property.

The Second Periodic Report under the ICPPR was submitted by India to the UN Human Rights Committee in March 1991. The members of the Committee pointed out that the AFSPA violates certain rights contained in the ICCPR. In response to the UN Human Rights Committee, the Attorney General of India justified the AFSPA under Article 355 of the Indian Constitution, which makes it the duty of the Union to protect each state from external aggression. He said the AFSPA was necessary, given the context of the North-East, where there is "infiltration of aliens into the territories mingling with the local public, and encouraging them towards this [secession]", and "that the ICCPR does not encourage secession and governments are not encouraged to promote it".

AFSPA and International Humanitarian Law

The four Geneva Conventions of 1949, along with the two Additional Protocols of 1977 constitute the body of international humanitarian law (IHL). The significant provisions of the four Geneva Conventions can be summarised as (1) outlawing violation of right to life; (2) prohibiting cruel treatment and torture; (3) protecting personal dignity; (4) providing for treatment of the wounded and sick during hostilities; and (5) prohibiting discrimination on the basis of race, colour, religion, nationality, etc. Article 3, common to all four Geneva Conventions, also extends basic protection to all personnel not taking part in hostilities. Protocol II of June 1977 introduces more detailed rules in the case of armed conflicts of a non-international nature. They: (1) guarantee the fundamental rights of all persons not directly involved in hostilities; (2) make special provisions in respect of persons where liberty is restricted; (3) entitle the civilian population to general protection; (4) prohibit forced movement and starvation as a method of combat; (5) protect objects indispensable to the survival of the civilian population, cultural objects and places of worship; (6) prohibit taking of hostages and outraging of personal dignity; and (7) prohibit violence to life and persons, in particular murder, mutilation, cruel treatment and torture.

The principles of IHL find fair mention in the different provisions of the Constitution of India. Part III (Fundamental Rights), Part IV (Directive Principles) and Part IVA (Fundamental Duties) of the Constitution together ensure the basic human rights embodied in IHL. The rights mentioned in Part III are enforceable by the courts. The Directive Principles mentioned in Part IV are non-justiceable, but are fundamental in the governance of the country. Further, the Indian Parliament has been empowered by Article 253 of the Constitution to make laws to give effect to the treaties and conventions to which India is a signatory.

National Human Rights Commission (NHRC)

The NHRC was set up under the provisions of the Protection of Human Rights Act, 1993, and came into being on 12 October 1993. Since its establishment, the Commission and the armed forces have made a major and reciprocal effort to exchange views on human rights, including the training of personnel of all ranks. Sections 17 to 19 of the Protection of Human Rights Act, 1993 relate to the procedure to be followed by the Commission for inquiring into the complaints of violation of human rights. Section 17 prescribes the general procedure for inquiring into such complaints, Section 18 specifies the steps (after inquiry) that may be taken by the Commission, and Section 19 prescribes the special procedure while dealing with such complaints. Under Section 19 of the Act, the Commission may seek a report from the Central Government in cases of complaints of violation of human rights by members of the armed forces. It is the responsibility of the Central Government to investigate such complaints in a fair and objective manner. The conclusion reached in the report must be the logical outcome and duly supported by the reasons given in the report. The Commission is empowered to make its recommendations to the Ministry of Defence for compliance. There have been a few cases of human rights violations by members of the armed forces, where the commission has directed the payment of compensation/interim relief to the victims/next-of-kin of the deceased. The NHRC has also taken cognizance of the action taken by the armed forces against its members accused of human rights violations.

Indian Armed Forces: Peacekeeping Missions

The Indian Army's participation in the UN peacekeeping operations spans a period of 57 years and has been spread over four continents. Over 90,000 Indian soldiers have served in 43 UN Missions in various parts of the world. In support of UN peacekeeping endeavours, the Indian Army has contributed outstanding force commanders, elite military contingents, impartial observers and dedicated staff officers. Their devotion to duty and excellent performance has been widely acclaimed. India's most significant contribution has been its participation in missions aimed at bringing peace and stability in Africa and Asia. It has demonstrated its unique capacity to sustain large troop commitments over prolonged periods. [16] The contribution of the Indian armed forces was outstanding in 1971, in particular, when they provided protection to about 20,000 civilians, including women and children, and kept about 95,000 prisoners of war, affording them treatment as per the principles of IHL. During the Kargil conflict in 1999, the armed forces again showed their adherence to IHL in the way they treated captured Pakistani soldiers.

Action on Human Rights Allegations

The Indian armed forces take serious note of all allegations of human rights violations brought against their members. Some of the steps taken in this regard are:

- A Human Rights Directorate has been constituted in the Army HQ to investigate, monitor, analyse and record all allegations of human rights violations.
- The Human Rights directorate functions under the Discipline and Vigilance Directorate, headed by a Major General together with one of the Brigadiers (DDG - B), and acts as a nodal agency for receiving allegations from various agencies.
- In addition, in each of its command headquarters an officer of the rank of Colonel has been specifically designated to monitor and follow up cases of human rights violations reported against army personnel.

- The directorate receives allegations of human rights violations from the public, NHRC, the ministries of home affairs and external affairs, the media and human rights organisations.
- Every human rights allegation is scrutinised. The directorate investigates the veracity of such allegations and ensures that corrective action is taken to minimise the abuse of human rights.
- On investigation, if an allegation is found to be true, suitable punishment is meted out to the defaulter and redress is given to the aggrieved, to the extent possible.
- Independent bodies like the Press Council of India, are invited to investigate allegations.

The Human Rights Cell of the Western Command has recently come out with a detailed report of all allegations of human rights violations against the Army in J&K during the last two decades. Its analysis shows that of the total 1,508 allegations of human rights violations received between 1990 and 2008, only 35 were found to be true. The remaining 1,453 charges (97.70 per cent) were "baseless and without an element of truth". The report mentions that strict action was taken in all cases in which Army personnel were found to be guilty of human rights violations. Thirty-nine officers and 61 personnel below officer rank (PBOR) were punished. Importantly, the investigations were conducted and the officers punished at Army's own initiative and not under pressure from any statutory authority. The Army has also extended all forms of assistance towards the rehabilitation of the victims.[17]

Of late, secessionist groups in India have been provoking the armed forces into over-reaction and this has mobilised public opinion against their alleged excesses. The militants have used human shields, predominantly women, to escape when confronted by the armed forces. This ruse has enabled them to allege misconduct on the part of the armed forces, with the help of a favourable media. The fact is that the Indian armed forces, while engaging in counter-insurgency operations, have been maintaining the principles of 'minimum force' and avoidance of collateral damage. Cordon and search operations are being conducted in accordance with the policy guidelines issued by the headquarters on the basis of intelligence, and in association with village elders.

Pakistan

In Pakistan, the militarised response to 'internal disturbance' in the past has led to the adoption of parallel justice systems – for example, the creation of military or special courts to try those accused of terrorist offences. In most instances, this approach departed from accepted legal procedures and safeguards. Typically, such courts lacked independence and impartiality, as well as exhibiting other shortcomings, such as limits on access to lawyers and witnesses. The three different systems in which the military was directly involved in imparting justice to civilians are discussed.[18]

Military Courts under Martial Law Regime

Rule by the military establishment has prevailed in Pakistan for almost half of its history. Military chiefs, such as the Chief Martial Law Administrator (CMLA), have established military courts and tribunals for the trial of offences punishable under the martial law regulations or martial law order or any other law, including special law. The provisions made under these orders allowed the transfer of a case from a civilian court to any military court. Once a military court or tribunal was established, no other court, including a high court, could grant any injunction, make an order, or entertain any proceedings in respect of any matter in which the military courts had jurisdiction or such a court or tribunal had taken cognizance of any matter. The constitutional amendments gave extraordinary powers to the existing the military courts constituted under the Army Act.

A constitutional amendment order was issued in 1979 for the addition of a new article, Article 212-A in the Constitution.[19] Section 2 of this order provided:

Addition of new Article 212-A in the Constitution.

In the Constitution, in Part VII, after Article 212, the following new Article shall be added, namely:

212A Establishment of Military Courts or Tribunals

- Notwithstanding anything herein before contained, the Chief Martial Law Administrator may, by a Martial Law Order, provide for the establishment of one or more Military Courts or Tribunals for the trial of offences punishable under the Martial Law Regulations or Martial Law Orders or any other law, including a special law, for the time being in force specified in the said Martial Law Order and for the transfer of cases to such Courts or Tribunals.
- The jurisdiction and powers of a Military Court or Tribunal shall be such as may be specified in a Martial Law Order issued by the Chief Martial Law Administrator.
- Notwithstanding anything herein before contained, where any Military Court or Tribunal is established, no other Court, including a High Court, shall grant an injunction, make any order or entertain any proceedings in respect of any matter to which the jurisdiction of the Military Court or Tribunal extends and of which cognizance has been taken by, or which has been transferred to, the

Military Court or Tribunal and all proceedings in respect of any such matter which may be pending before such other Court, other than an appeal pending before the Supreme Court shall abate.

When the higher civil courts questioned military judgements and occasionally overturned the convictions, the military courts acted like real courts rather than puppet tribunals. The regime reacted by severely restricting the purview of the higher civil courts to only the most neutral cases.[20] In order to curb the power of judicial review of the Supreme Court and the High Courts over the orders made by the CMLA or military courts, another constitutional amending order was issued in 1980.[21] Section 2 of this order stated:

Amendment of Article 199 of the Constitution

In the Constitution, in Article 199, after clause (3), the following new clauses shall be inserted, namely:

"(3A) Notwithstanding any judgement of any Court, including any judgement in respect of the powers of Courts relating to judicial review, a High Court shall not, under this Article-

- make an order relating to the validity or effect of any Martial Law Regulation made by the Chief Martial Law Administrator or any Martial Law Order made by the Chief Martial Law Administrator or a Martial Law Administrator or of anything done, or action taken, or intended to be done or taken, thereunder;
- make an order relating to the validity or effect of any judgement or sentence passed by a Military Court or Tribunal;
- grant an injunction, make any order or entertain any proceedings in respect of any matter to which the jurisdiction of a Military Court or Tribunal extends and of which cognizance has been taken by a Military Court or Tribunal ; or
- issue any process against the Chief Martial Law Administrator or a Martial Law Administrator or any person acting under the authority of either.

(3B) Every such order, injunction or process as is referred to in clause (3-A) made, granted or issued at any time before or after the commencement of the Constitution (Amendment) Order, 1980, shall, notwithstanding any judgement of any Court, be null and void and of no effect whatsoever and any proceedings for the making, granting or issue of such order, injunction or process which may be pending before any Court, including in the Supreme Court and a High Court, shall abate.

(3C) The proclamation of the fifth day of July 1977, all President's Orders,

> Orders of the Chief Martial Law Administrator, Martial Law Regulations and Martial Law Orders made on or after the fifth day of July 1977, are hereby declared, notwithstanding any judgement of any Court, to have been validly made."

The military courts constituted under martial law ended once the proclamation of withdrawal of martial law was issued by the CMLA.

The Pakistan Armed Forces (Acting in Aid of Civil Power) Ordinance, 1998

In order to curb violence in Sindh,[22] the Government of Pakistan imposed emergency (governor's rule) in the province. This led to an invitation to the military, acting in its capacity of "aid to civil power," to take over law and order duties in the Sindh province. The Pakistan Armed Forces (Acting in Aid of Civil Power) Ordinance, 1998, was enacted.[23] The purpose of the ordinance was to empower the governor to take all necessary actions "to create a peaceful environment in which ordinary citizens can conduct their day-to-day affairs in accordance with their constitutional rights and entitlement within the province."[24]

Promulgated on 20 November 1998, the ordinance, which had application only to the Sindh province, extended broad judicial powers to the military. The ordinance granted military officers of the rank of brigadier and above the right to "convene as many courts as may be deemed necessary to try offenders". Such courts could try civilians. Appeals against conviction by such courts would lie only with such appellate tribunals as the military authorities deemed necessary to establish. Moreover, cases pending before other courts (regular courts and anti-terrorism courts) could be transferred to such newly established military courts. The courts would have jurisdiction to award sentences, including the death penalty, for specified crimes. The ordinance also created a "new crime" punishable with a penalty of up to seven years of rigorous imprisonment—the crime of "civil commotion".[25]

On 30 January 1999, the jurisdiction of the ordinance was extended to the whole of Pakistan. Also, the ordinance was amended so that accused "absconders" from justice could be tried in absentia by any military court established in Pakistan.[26] The definition of the crime of "civil commotion", particularly subject to implementation by military courts, was very troublesome—many of the activities defined as "crimes" could also be interpreted as "normal" political behaviour. Numerous constitutional petitions were filed before the superior courts challenging the validity of the ordinance. The Supreme Court consolidated such petitions and heard the petitioners.

The Supreme Court, in its landmark decision in *Liaquat Hussain v. Federation of Pakistan,*[27] delivered one of the most unequivocal decisions ever rendered by the Supreme Court of Pakistan. It declared the Pakistan Armed Forces (Aid to Civil) Act "unconstitutional, without legal authority, and with no legal effect." Furthermore, the court, as per the unanimous decision of the nine-member full bench, rejected the duration the Act's validity only to the Sindh province. The court also rejected the government's contention that the ordinance was expedient and defensible under the so-called "doctrine of necessity".

The Supreme Court also found the ordinance to be unconstitutional in that: (i) civilians cannot be tried by military courts; (ii) the special courts cannot perform parallel functions to those assigned to regular courts; and (iii) the military's powers with regard to "aid to civil authority" do not extend to the creation of courts or the exercise of judicial functions. Given the forcefulness of the Supreme Court's verdict, on 27 April 1999, the Armed Forces (Acting in Aid of Civil Power) Act was repealed. However, "civil commotion" was made a crime under the Anti-Terrorism Act.[28]

The Pakistan Army while in the 'aid of civil power' was also authorised to court martial civilians accused of stealing electricity. The Offences in Respect of Electricity (Emergency Provisions) Ordinance, 1998 (Ordinance XIX of 1998)[29] provided that the armed forces called upon to act in aid of civil power[30] to combat the menace of stealing of electricity would be authorised to constitute courts-martial under chapter IX of the Pakistan Army Act. The person or authority empowered to convene a court martial would convene as many trial courts as may be necessary to try offenders, and would also establish 'military appeal courts' to hear appeals against the decisions made and sentences passed by the court martial. The decision of the court of appeal would be final and not be called in question in any court.

Anti-Terrorism Law in Pakistan

A new era began in Pakistan's legislative history when "special" laws and courts dealing with "terrorism" or "terrorist acts" became the norm. In October 1974, the government established "special" courts for "suppression of acts of sabotage, subversion, and terrorism".[31] The stated objective of the 1974 ordinance was to provide "special provisions" for suppressing such acts and to establish "special" courts with exclusive jurisdiction for "speedy trials" of such crimes. The creation of "special courts" in order to address violence and ensure swift justice meant a departure from the regular judicial system. The 1974 ordinance was approved by Parliament and in 1975, became the Suppression of Terrorist Activities (Special Court) Act.

The Act of 1975 incorporated a number of measures to expedite the slow legal process. Adjournments in court proceedings were not granted unless "necessary in the interest of justice".[32] The Act also provided that once the accused had appeared before the court, the remaining trial could proceed even if the accused subsequently absconded.[33] It departed from the universal principle of presuming the accused innocent until proven guilty. The law presumed the accused guilty when found in possession of any article which could be used in the commission of the offence he was accused of committing, or when apprehended "in circumstances which tend to raise a reasonable suspicion that he has committed such [an] offence".

The 1975 law remained in force until it was repealed and replaced by the Anti-Terrorism Act (ATA) of 1997,[34] which is the principal "special" anti-terror law currently in force.[35] In between these two laws, the government introduced a range of laws aimed at dealing with "special" needs, and the laws were mainly directed at expeditious adjudication of cases concerning acts of terrorism. These laws included the Special Courts for Speedy Trial Ordinance (1987), the Terrorist-Affected Areas (Special Courts) Ordinance (1990), and the Terrorist-Affected Areas (Special Courts) Act (1992).[36]

The Act defined terrorism as:

> Whoever, to strike terror in the people, or an any section of people, or to alienate any section of the people or to adversely affect harmony among different sections of the people, does any act or thing by using bombs, dynamite or other explosive or inflammable substance, or firearms, or other lethal weapons or poisons or noxious gases or chemical or other substances of a hazardous nature in such a manner as to cause the death of, or injury to, any person or persons, or damage to, or destruction of, property or disruption of any supplies or services essential to the life of the community or display firearms, or threaten with the use of force public servants in order to prevent them from discharging their lawful duties commits a terrorist act.[37]

On August 27, 1999, the government made amendment to the ATA 1997 to allow for the creation of anti-terrorism courts in any province of Pakistan.[38] The December 2, 1999, twin amendments to the anti-terrorism ordinance expanded the definition of the act of terrorism and enhanced the ambit of the anti-terrorism courts to include several other provisions of Pakistan's criminal court. According to the first amendment, the anti-terrorism courts' extended jurisdiction would now include: (1) Section 109 – abetment of offence; (2) Section 120 – concealing of a design to commit an offence; (3) Section 120 B – criminal conspiracy to commit a crime punishable by death or with the imprisonment greater than two years; (4) Section 121 – waging or attempting to wage war against Pakistan; (5) Section 121 A – conspiracy to commit certain offences against the state; (6) Section 122 – collecting arms with the intent to wage war ; (7) Section 123 – concealment of a design aimed at facilitating waging of a war; (8) Section 365 – kidnapping ; (9) Section 402 – being one of five or more persons assembled for the purpose of committing dacoity; and (10) Section 402 B – conspiracy to commit hijacking.[39]

The December 2 amendments set up two new special courts, to be empowered to "transfer, claim, or readmit any case within that province". These courts also served as appellate tribunals for the anti-terrorist courts.[40] During September and October 2001, eleven new courts were established in the NWFP (North West Frontier Province) and four in Sindh. By the end of October 2001, Pakistan had forty-one anti-terror courts. In January 2002, the Anti-terrorism (Amendment) Ordinance was promulgated. This enhanced the single-member bench of the anti-terror courts to three-members bench and introduced "military personnel" as a third member. The courts were to sit in cantonments or jail premises to ensure the security of the accused, witnesses and the judiciary. This act of military involvement in the judicial set up was criticized by lawyers, judicial circles, and international human rights groups. Further amendments to the Anti-Terrorism Act of 1997 were added in November 2004. The maximum jail term for supporters of militants was increased from 14 years to life imprisonment.

An amendment made to Section 2 (1-d) of the Pakistan Army Act, 1952, in 2007, added some more offences of the Pakistan Penal Code (PPC) and allowed the military courts to try and convict civilians. The amendment was made through an ordinance[41] that came into force at once and was deemed to have taken effect from January 2003. Under the amendment, a sub-clause (iia) was inserted into the sub-clause (ii), which says:

> Any offence, if committed in relation to defence or security of Pakistan or any part thereof or Armed Forces of Pakistan, punishable under the Explosive Substance Act, 1908 (VI of 1908), prejudicial conduct under the Security of Pakistan Act, 1952 (XXXV of 1952), the Pakistan Arms Ordinance, 1965 (WP Ordinance XX of 1965), the Prevention of Anti-national Activities Act, 1974 (VII of 1974) or Anti-terrorism Act, 1997 (XXVII of 1997), Sections 109 (punishment of abetment if the act abetted is committed in consequence and where no express provision is made for its punishment), 117 (abetting commission of offence by the public, or by more than ten persons), 120B (punishment of criminal conspiracy), 121 (waging or attempting to wage war or abetting waging of war against Pakistan), 121A (conspiracy to commit

> offences punishable by Section 121), 122 (collecting arms, etc., with intention of waging war against Pakistan), 123 (concealing with intent to facilitate design to wage war), 123A (condemnation of the creation of the state and advocacy of abolition of its sovereignty), 124 (assaulting president, governor, etc., with intent to compel or restrain the exercise of any lawful power), 124A (sedition), 148 (rioting, armed with deadly weapon), 302 (punishment of Qatl-i-amd), 353 (assault or criminal force to deter public servant from discharge of his duty) and 505 (statement conducive to public mischief) of the Pakistan Penal Code or attempt to commit any of the said offences.

The Army Act had a provision to try civilians by court martial only when at least one of the accused belonged to the armed forces. Under the amended Act, the Army could try civilians on charges ranging from treason, sedition and attack on army personnel to "assaulting the President with intent to compel or restrain the exercise of any lawful power" and "giving statements conducive to public mischief". One of the reasons cited for the amendment was said to be the inability of the existing anti-terrorism courts to hold proper or speedy trials of people involved in acts of terrorism or fanning religious or other brands of armed militancy in the country. [42]

Anti-terrorism laws are essentially of a preventative nature and can work only in conjunction with political, military, and administrative steps taken in response to terrorism. Such laws can be implemented successfully only when there is a political will complemented by public support and institutional capacity. In Pakistan, the application of anti-terror laws remains an unfulfilled objective. For example, at times, charges have been framed against a particular organisation or person, but action has been delayed on account of "unexplained reasons."[43]

Sri Lanka

The Constitution of Sri Lanka contains provisions allowing for emergency powers and limitation of certain rights in a state of emergency. The foundation of Sri Lanka's emergency laws dates back to British rule – the Public Security Ordinance 1947 (PSO), to suppress and control political dissent.[44] For over 60 years, the PSO has empowered successive Presidents to declare states of emergency and enact emergency regulations under Section 5 as appear necessary or expedient "in the interests of public security and the preservation of public order and the suppression of mutiny, riot or civil commotion, or for the maintenance of supplies and services essential to the life of the community". The second key legislation is the Prevention of Terrorism (Temporary Provisions) Act of 1979 ("PTA").[45] As the name implies, it was adopted as a temporary measure to address a sudden upsurge in political violence. It has remained in force for almost 30 years.

More recently, the Government of Sri Lanka, using powers derived from the PSO, enacted two new and far-reaching emergency laws in 2005 and 2006.[46] The Emergency (Miscellaneous Provisions and Powers) Regulation No. 1 of 2005 (EMPPR 2005) deals with powers of arrest and detention, powers of search and seizure, trial procedures, admissibility of confessions, bail, and other amendments to normal criminal procedure. The Emergency (Prevention and Prohibition of Terrorism and Specified Terrorist Activities) Regulations No. 7 of 2006 (Emergency Regulations 2006) define and criminalise "terrorism" and "acts of terrorism",[47] and create new offences, including engaging in transactions with a terrorist or terrorist group regardless of knowledge and intent.[48] These regulations compound pre-existing problems with Sri Lanka's emergency law framework.

The EMPPR 2005 and Presidential orders made under the PSO delegate sweeping powers to military personnel to perform functions usually carried out by law enforcement officials, including powers of investigation, search, arrest and detention.[49] Under the EMPPR 2005, persons "acting in any manner prejudicial to the national security or the maintenance of public order, or to the maintenance of essential services" may be arrested and held in detention for up to one year, without access to judicial review by an independent body. Persons may be similarly detained up to 18 months under the PTA or indefinitely pending trial. There is also provision for automatic detention of up to two years for a person who has surrendered for the purposes of "rehabilitation". A detainee can be moved from place to place during interrogation, and denied prompt access to a lawyer or judicial authority. Provisions under the EMPPR 2005 also reverse the normal burden of proof, undermining the principle of the presumption of innocence.

In Sri Lanka, the President has made several emergency regulations empowering government officials to order curfews, to restrict travel outside Sri Lanka and to prohibit movement in particular areas,[50] on grounds of national security, public order and maintenance of essential services. The decision of the executive is not subject to judicial review. The the International Commission of Jurists (ICJ), a Geneva based NGO, is of the view that the Government of Sri Lanka is justified in enacting emergency regulations to address a complex and challenging security situation that includes serious incidents of terrorism. However, such laws must be narrowly tailored to address the crisis without criminalising lawful conduct and free expression.

According to the ICJ, during the last few decades of conflict between the security forces and the LTTE in Sri Lanka, both sides have committed gross violations of human rights and humanitarian law, including massacres, extrajudicial killings, and enforced disappearances. It has been reported that Sri Lanka's emergency laws have delegated sweeping powers to the military and accorded arbitrary grounds for arrest and detention. The definition of "terrorism" under Emergency Regulations 2006 is too broad and vague. This has resulted in immunity from legal responsibility for human rights violations.[51]

Bangladesh

The extraordinary laws in Bangladesh too empower their armed forces to deal with emergent situations. In Bangladesh, on March 24, 1982, the army chief of staff, Lieutenant General Hussain Muhammad Ershad, seized control of the Bangladesh government in a military coup. He proclaimed martial law, made himself chief martial law administrator, and dismantled the structures of democratic government that the administration of the late president Zia had carefully built during the previous five years. Ershad suspended the Constitution, disbanded Parliament, prohibited all political activities, and deprived the president, vice president, and cabinet ministers of their offices. Three days after the coup, Supreme Court justice Abdul Fazal Muhammad Ahsanuddin Chowdhury became interim president. Ershad became chief minister of a new cabinet, and by December 1983 he took over the presidency.

During his tenure as chief martial law administrator, Ershad divided the country into five martial law zones, each headed by a handpicked senior army officer. Twenty-four special and summary martial law courts directly involved the military in local administration. Although the civilian court system continued to function, violations of martial law ordinances were handled by these extra-constitutional martial law tribunals, where active-duty military officers met in secret sessions to try cases ranging from violations of press censorship to vaguely defined 'anti-social activities'. Those convicted of political crimes had no right of appeal, and defendants were tried in absentia. Martial law deprived the Supreme Court of its jurisdiction over the protection of fundamental rights, and criticism of martial law was punishable by up to seven years' imprisonment.[52]

Nepal

In Nepal, the Communist Part of Nepal-Maoist (CPN-M) launched a people's war in February 1996. It was a reaction to the failed attempt by the National Congress-dominated government to establish a democracy and meet the demands of the CPN-M. The aim of the armed struggle was to overthrow the existing regime, to establish a democratic republic and to transform its economy and society. In the following months, the Maoists attacked police stations, banks, village development committee offices, local landlords and politicians. During the first years of the armed conflict, the ill-equipped and poorly trained Nepal Police bore the brunt of responsibility for fighting the CPN-M.[53]

As a key target of the CPN-M, hundreds of police officers lost their lives. A total of 1,271 out of 1,971 police posts across the country stopped functioning after they were destroyed during attacks by the CPN-M, or after police personnel were withdrawn for security reasons. The police, being in charge of law and order retaliated. The government also reactivated the Public Security Act of 1991, which allowed for people to be detained for up to 12 months without trial. The civil war prolonged without much success. In 1999, CPN-M announced formation of their People's Liberation Army (PLA). In order to attract cadre, PLA had promised that once a Maoists government takes over, the PLA cadre would be integrated with Nepal Army.

After 9/11, the Nepalese government supported war against terrorism. India also declared that Nepalese Maoists were terrorists and pledged its support for the Nepal government. Since the peace talk with CPN-M failed, the Nepal government declared Emergency and deployed the Royal Nepalese army (RNA) to fight Maoists. The government promulgated the Terrorists and Disruptive Activities (Control and Punishment) Ordinance (TADO), and declared CPN-M a terrorist organisation under the TADO. The TADO granted the police and army wide powers and suspended the rights of freedom of thought and expression; assembly and movement; right to information, property and privacy; and the right to constitutional remedy. Clause 9 of the TADO states: "If a security official feels the need to prevent a person from carrying out any terrorist and disruptive activity, such a person can be kept under house arrest for a maximum period of one year, six months at his [Security Official's] discretion and another six months after obtaining permission from the home ministry, in any place after fulfilling common humanitarian conditions."

With this legislation, the government of Nepal surrendered its authority to the military, and given it a green signal to continue with gross human rights violations including arbitrary detentions, torture, disappearances, and extrajudicial and summary executions. Most of the victims of the abuses committed by the state security forces working under the Joint Command of the Royal Nepal Army[54] --as well as those committed by the Maoists were ordinary people innocent of any crimes. The security forces also targeted journalists, lawyers, human rights defenders, victims and witnesses of their atrocities.[55] There were around 2000 cases of disappearances reported and army officers are said to have had involvement in a large number of the recorded cases.

On February 1, 2005, King Gyanendra declared a state of emergency and with the army's backing assumed all executive authority, citing the inability of the civilian government to resolve the conflict. He ordered the detention of thousands of political activists, journalists, and human rights monitors, and imposed severe restrictions on civil liberties. In the low intensity conflict, which followed, about 38,400 people were killed, the majority being supporters of CPN-M. The Maoists, taken prisoners were also eliminated. In November 2006, the government and CPN-M signed a Comprehensive Peace Agreement (CPA) to implement a peace process, redraft the country's constitution and establish an interim government. The RNA was renamed as Nepal Army (NA).

In the view of David Bonner (1985): "Special legal provisions pose dangers to democratic systems. The use of emergency powers can become a habit; it may de-sensitise the population to the problems of human rights involved and increased authoritarian tendencies in law and society; extraordinary laws can become de facto permanent features; new procedures may become the norms for criminal procedure; the dividing line between emergency laws and ordinary laws may become difficult to draw; such special laws may be used to cope up with ordinary crimes; and the dangerously seductive illusion of emergency law may indeed represent a victory for terrorists and insurgents."[56] An indiscriminate use of military might be successful in quelling insurgency and militancy, but it would also destroy community, friendship, justice and common good. To believe that depriving citizens of their individual rights and suspending the democratic process is necessary to maintain 'order' is to put oneself on the same moral plane as the terrorists who believe that the 'end justifies the means'."[57]

The use of the armed forces in internal security duties is not improper. According to Edmonds (1976): "If legitimate, there is no reason why a society should not be policed by the military completely; indeed in some under-developed countries for purely practical, as opposed to political, reasons, this is the case. In others, tradition plays a major part as does the prevailing political philosophy."[58] Therefore the need for the use of the armed forces for internal security duties must be analysed by the political leadership on merit. While defining counter-terrorism measures, the government must spell out the circumstances under which military aid to civil power would be invoked, the rights and responsibilities of the military personnel operating in the internal security role, and the lines of command and control. It must also accord full and proper support to the security forces personnel involved in counter-terrorist operations. The anti-terrorist response must be limited, well-defined, controlled and within the law.

State security and military courts in many countries of the Middle East illustrate the problems special courts can create. The State Security Court in Turkey (abolished in May 2004), for example, was criticised for procedural shortcomings in various rulings of the European Court of Human Rights.[59] As the name suggests, such courts tend to see their role as enforcing 'State security' rather than adjudicating impartially. In many countries, pre-existing regimes of martial law, or states of siege, provided for the trial of civilians by military courts. In other countries, emergency laws transferred jurisdiction on certain terrorist or subversive offences from civilian to military courts. In yet other countries, to allow for looser evidentiary rules and the curtailing of defence rights, the laws established specialised civilian or *ad hoc* courts to try suspected 'subversives'.

According to Huntington (1968), military intervention in politics, or political disorder, is the direct result of the inability of a country's political institutions to cope with the rising demands motivated by political participation resulting from economic and social change. This view assumes that the military merely reflects underlying political difficulties. It is a neutral force, which mechanically moves into the political arena when a vacuum is created. The armed forces are trained to cause death or serious injuries on the designated enemy. When they are entrusted with duties which, under normal circumstances, are the responsibility of the police force, they have to work with their hands tied behind their backs. They are expected to apprehend a violator and hand him over to the nearest police post for a judicial trial. A system in which a violator of the law of the land can be seized and brought to justice can work as long as the state machinery has physical control over the situation and is backed by a well-developed judicial process. Unfortunately, by the time the armed forces are called in, the State machinery and the judicial process are already influenced by the violators of law and their sympathisers.

Though it is true that under no circumstances should the use of counter-terrorism by the State be justified by the need to quell terrorism, we should perhaps view instances of excesses by the State machinery in the context of preserving national integrity and stability. We must keep in mind the inhumanity of terrorist acts like the killing of innocents, abductions, and political assassinations and the threat such acts pose to the integrity of the nations in the South Asian region.

The legal and constitutional framework of the South Asian countries, based on the respect for human rights, is extremely conducive, to the implementation of international norms. The armed forces of the South Asian countries have by now established a proud and enviable record of compliance with international standards, to which their military manuals, by and large, conform. Various engagements under the aegis of the United Nations in which South Asian peacekeeping forces have participated have largely demonstrated this compliance. The armed forces need special legal protection and powers in areas where they operate. Special legislation is necessary from the point of view of morale and operational efficiency to protect the rights of soldiers. However, while engaging in counter-insurgency operations, the armed forces need to maintain the principles of 'minimum force' and avoidance of 'collateral damage'.[60] There is a growing trend towards abolition of military courts for the trial of civilians. In several countries, a ban on such practice has been incorporated into the constitution. The governments in the South Asian countries need to ensure that civilians are not subjected to the jurisdiction of ad hoc military tribunals as the system provides a veneer of legality to cover up the impunity of the military members.[61]

Notes

1. There is no precise definition of these terms; therefore, common phrase 'terrorism' has been used. The term 'terrorism' and 'terrorist' have their roots in the French Revolution. Since then the term 'terrorism' has been used to denote almost every imaginable form of violence. The dividing line between terrorism and criminality has become less and less distinct. Wardlaw Grant. 1989. *Political Terrorism: Theory, Tactics and Counter-measures*, Cambridge: Cambridge University Press, p.18-33. The UN Security Council has also struggled to define terrorism in various resolutions. In one of the more recent attempts, UN Security Council Resolution (UNSCR) 1566, the Security Council defines terrorism as: "Criminal acts, including against civilians, committed with the intent to cause death or serious bodily injury, or taking of hostages, with the purpose to provoke a state of terror in the general public or in a group of persons or particular persons, intimidate a population or compel a government or an international organisation to do or to abstain from doing any act...U.N. Doc. S/RES/1566 (Oct. 8, 2004). In the body of UNSCR 1566, the Security Council identifies terrorism as a threat to international peace and security under Chapter VII, but goes on to describe it as a criminal act. In the *chapeau*, however, the Security Council reaffirms the need to "combat terrorism in all its forms and manifestations by all means, in accordance with the Charter of the United Nations and international law."
2. "Amendment to Army Act only to fight terrorism", *The Hindu*, India, 12 November 2007.
3. There were allegations that the Pakistan army personnel were involved in torturing suspected Taliban militants and sympathisers in Swat where the army recently carried out anti-Taliban operations. The 10.17 minute video, showing uniformed soldiers beating, kicking and whipping civilians was put on BBC website. There were also reports of hundreds of mutilated bodies of suspected Taliban at various places in Swat other parts of Malakand region. The bodies have given rise to allegations of extra-judicial killings by military; but Pakistan army strongly denied the allegation. *THE HINDU*, New Delhi, Saturday, October 3, 2009, p. 15. In the recent past similar allegations have been leveled against the armed forces of Bangladesh, India, Nepal, and Sri Lanka.
4. (i) Pakistan: Army as the Judge, Jury and Executioner, Asian Centre for Human Rights Report dated 8 February 2008; (ii) Manoharan N (2006), Counterterrorism Legislation in Sri Lanka: Evaluating Efficacy, Policy Studies 28, East-West Center, Washington; (iii) The State of Emergency in Bangladesh, Asian Legal Resource Centre, Hong Kong, Document: ALRC-SHRC-04-02-2007; (iv) Human Rights Watch, UPR Submission

Bangladesh, September 2008; and (v) *India: The Armed Forces Special Powers Act (AFSPA) Review Committee takes one step forward and two backwards*, 23 November 2006, Amnesty International, ASA 20/031/2006, available at: http://www.unhcr.org/refworld/docid/45a234212.html, accessed 5 September 2009.

5. The Indian Air Force (IAF) is associated with anti-naxal operations in certain part of Chattisgarh and Jharkhand. The Chief of the Air Staff has recently approached the Ministry of Defence to allow it to fire back in self-defence. 'IAF seeks nod to fire back at Maoists', *The Times of India*, Friday, October 2, 2009, p. 15. Also see: Jha U.C., Yes to armed forces, but as last resort, *THE HINDU*, June 6, 2010, p. 14.
6. Noorani A G. 2009. 'Armed Forces (Special Powers) Act: Urgency of Review', *Economic & Political Weekly*, Vol. XLIV No. 34, August 22, 2009, p. 8-11; Hargopal G. 2009. 'Terrorism and Human Rights: Indian Experience with Repressive Laws', *Economic & Political Weekly*, Vol. XLIV No. 38, July 11, 2009, p. 76-85.
7. In July 2004, there was an allegation of rape and murder of 33-year-old lady by security forces in Manipur. Following the incident were widespread protests and demands for the withdrawal of the AFSPA. The movement, spearheaded by 32 social organisations, spiralled into civil disobedience and turned violent after a student leader immolated himself. MANIPUR ON FIRE, *Frontline,* Volume 21, Issue 18, August 28 - September 10, 2004.
8. The Armed Forces (Special Powers) Act, 1958 [Act 28 of 1958, 11th September, 1958].
9. According to Human Rights Watch Report: The right to life is violated by section 4(a) of the AFSPA, which grants the armed forces power to shoot to kill in law enforcement situations without regard to international human rights law restrictions on the use of lethal force. Lethal force is broadly permitted under the AFSPA if the target is part of an assembly of five or more persons, holding weapons, or "carrying things capable of being used as weapons." The terms "assembly" and "weapon" are not defined. The right to liberty and security of person is violated by section 4(c) of the AFSPA, which fails to protect against arbitrary arrest by allowing soldiers to arrest anyone merely on suspicion that a "cognizable offence" has already taken place or is likely to take place in the future. Further, the AFSPA provides no specific time limit for handing arrested persons to the nearest police station. Section 5 of the AFSPA vaguely advises that those arrested be transferred to police custody "with the least possible delay." Getting Away With Murder: 50 Years of the Armed Forces (Special Powers) Act, *Human Rights Watch Report*, August 2008. There has been an increasing demand for revocation of AFSPA in Jammu& Kashmir. Mufti demands revocation of AFSPA in J&K, THE HINDU, 30 May 2010, p. 7.
10. Dhawan Rajeev, The Manipur Crisis, *The Hindu*, New Delhi, 20 August 04.
11. *Naga People's Movement of Human Rights v. Union of India* AIR 1998 SC 431.
12. The ICCPR was ratified by the India on 10 April 1979.
13. *Bacha Bora v. State of Assam* (1991) 2 GLR, 119.
14. The Criminal Procedure Code (CrPC) of India confers wide powers on an Executive Magistrate to deal with emergent situations. Under Section 144 of the CrPC the Magistrates have powers to impose restrictions on the personal liberties of individuals, in a specific locality or town, where the situation has the potential to cause unrest or danger to peace and tranquility.

15. *Indrajit Barua v. Union of India* AIR 1983 Del 513.
16. http://indianarmy.nic.in/un.html accessed on 10 September 2009.
17. Report available at: http://indianarmy.nic.in/nc/hr.html accessed on 10 September 2009. The report makes an interesting reading. One of its shocking revelations is that in several cases, inquiries revealed that it had not launched any operation in the area and on dates mentioned by the complainants. In numerous cases, persons mentioned as killed by the Army surfaced and admitted they were never taken into custody by the Army. The report also mentions specific cases in which persons who had filed FIRs about a missing person confessed that they were coerced by terrorists to file false complaints. In certain cases charges of torture and illegal detentions were made with the sole purpose of receiving compensation from the government. However, overwhelming evidence shows that most of the false allegations were made by persons actively associated with separatist groups with the evil design of maligning the Army and the country.
18. In Pakistan, Proclamation of Emergency was made on account of the 1965 and 1971 wars with India. In 1988, Emergency was proclaimed in the midst of nuclear experimentation by Pakistan. In addition to these Proclamation of Emergencies, the people of Pakistan have been subjected to 'extra-constitutional emergency' regimes or Martial Law, when the Constitution was either abrogated, or partially or wholly suspended. Omar Imtiaz. 2002. *Emergency Powers and the Courts in India and Pakistan*, The Netherlands: Kluwer Law International, p.6-7.
19. Constitutional (Second Amendment) Order, 1979, [Gazette of Pakistan, Extraordinary, Part 1, 18th October, 1979] No. F.17(2)/79-Pub.
20. Paula R. Newberg. 1995. *Judging the State: Courts and Constitutional Politics in Pakistan*, UK: Cambridge University Press, p. 194.
21. Constitutional (Amendment) Order, 1980, Presidential Order 1 of 1980. [Gazette of Pakistan, Extraordinary, Part 1, 27th May, 1980], No. F. 17(2)/80 Pub.
22. On 17 October 1998, Hakim Muhammad Said, one of Karachi's most well-known citizens, a former governor of Sindh and founder of the Hamdard Foundation (*Hamdard Islamicus)* and Hamdard University, was murdered. Under increasing pressure from within his own political circle—and most likely from the military—to do something to curb such lawlessness and violence, Nawaz Sharif chose to impose Article 232 and declare a state of emergency (Governor's Rule) in Sindh Province.
23. Pakistan Armed Forces (Acting in Aid of Civil Power) Ordinance, 1998 (20 November 1998). *PLD* 1999 Central Statutes 156.
24. Constitution of Pakistan (1973) Article 232 (30 October 1998). *PLD* 1999 Central Statutes 202.
25. "Civil commotion" means creation of internal disturbances in violation of law or intended to violate law, commencement or continuation of illegal strikes, go-slows, lock-outs, vehicle snatching/lifting, damage to or destruction of State or private property, random firing to create panic, charging protection money/extortion, acts of criminal trespass, distributing, publishing or pasting of a handbill or making graffiti or wall-chalking intended to create unrest or fear or create a threat to the security of law and order. Section 6, The Pakistan Armed Forces (Acting in Aid of Civil Power) Ordinance, 1998.

26. Pakistan Armed Forces (Acting in Aid of Civil Power) (Amendment) Ordinance, 1999 (30 January 1999) *PLD* 1999 Central Statutes 241.
27. *Liaquat Hussain v. Federation of Pakistan* PLD 1999 SC 504.
28. Anti-Terrorism (Amendment) Ordinance, 1999 (27 April 1999). *PLD* 1999, Central Statutes 289.
29. Available at: http://www.pakistani.org/akistan/legislation/1998/ord_XIX,html.
30. Under Article 245 of the Constitution of Pakistan.
31. *Preamble, Suppression of Terrorist Activities (Special Courts) Ordinance (XVIII),* 1974.
32. *Sec.5 (2), Suppression of Terrorist Activities (Special Courts) Act 1975.*
33. *Sec. 5(4), Ibid.*
34. Sec. 39 (c), *Anti-Terrorism Act (ATA), 1997.*
35. On October 2, 2009, Pakistan President Asif Ali Zardari has amended the Anti-Terrorism Act of 1997, allowing authorities to act against members of outlawed groups that set up new outfits with different name. PTI. 'New law to tackle 'front' outfits', The Times of India, New Delhi, October 4, 2009, p. 20.
36. Mian Ghulam Hussain. 2006. *Manual of Anti-Terrorism Laws in Pakistan,* Lahore: Afsari Printers.
37. *Anti-Terrorism Act, 1997 (20 August 1997)*, PLD 1997 Central Statutes (unreported) 537.
38. *Anti Terrorism (Second Amendment) Ordinance 1999 (27 August 1999) PLD 2000 Central Statues 2.*
39. Anti- Terrorism (Second Amendment) Ordinance 1999 (2 December 1999) *PLD 2000 Central Statues 8.*
40. Anti- Terrorism (Third Amendment) Ordinance 1999 (2 December 1999) *PLD 2000 Central Statues 78.*
41. The Government notification said: "In exercise of the powers conferred by clause (1) of Article 89 of the Constitution read with proclamation of emergency of the of third day of November 2007 and the Provisional Constitution Order (PCO) No 1 of 2007, the president is pleased to make and promulgate the Ordinance."
42. It was feared that the power under the amended Army Act will be interpreted loosely, abused, and the threat of their use will serve as a powerful tool to stifle dissent. **Pakistan Army: The Judge, The Jury, The Executioner;** The Asian Centre for Human Rights reports on the impact of governance by the army in Pakistan.
43. Fayyaz, Shabana, *Responding to Terrorism: Pakistan's Anti-Terrorism Laws: Part II*, available at: http://www.terrorismanalysts.com/pt/index.php?option=com_rokzine&view=article&id=45&Itemid=54.
44. In Sri Lanka, emergency provisions have been widely used to combat militancy. They are popularly known as 'Emergency Regulations' declared under the Public Security Ordinance (PSO) enacted just before independence to deal with the general strike of 1947. The PSO was passed as an urgent bill in ninety minutes despite warning from the floor of the House that the matter required careful consideration. The situation at that time did not seem to call for the stringent provisions incorporated into the ordinance, such as detention without trial, search and seizure, immunity from prosecution for security forces, absence of judicial scrutiny, and so on. Manoharan, M. 2006. *Counterterrorism Legislations in Sri Lanka: Evaluating*

Efficacy, The East-West Center, Washington. www.eastwestcenter.org/fileadmin/stored/pdfs/PS028.pdf.

45. Whilst not an emergency law *per se* the Prevention of Terrorism (Temporary Provisions) Act (PTA) is relevant to the emergency laws in Sri Lanka. Adopted in 1979 as a temporary measure in response to growing political violence in the North, it contains broad security-related offences, and wide powers of search, arrest and detention. It has also been strongly criticised by UN bodies, such as the Human Rights Committee (Concluding observations of the Human Rights Committee, CCPR/CO/79/LKA, 1 December 2003, para 13)
46. These laws were enacted in response to the assassination of Foreign Minister Lakshman Kadirgamar in August 2005 and the attempted assassination of the Secretary to the Ministry of Defence in December 2006. Under Section 5 of the PSO, the President made the EMPPR 2005, the Emergency Regulations 2006 and other emergency regulations creating prohibited zones in certain areas in Sri Lanka. These emergency regulations are only valid for one month at a time and require monthly parliamentary approval to remain valid. The President also has special powers under Section 12 (power to call out the armed forces), Section 16 (power to order curfews) and Section 17 (power to declare essential services), whether or not a state of emergency has been declared.
47. Regulation 6 of the Emergency Regulations 2006 prohibits "terrorism" or "specified terrorist activity", or any act in furtherance thereof. Regulation 20 defines "terrorism" to mean "any unlawful conduct", which, *inter alia*, "involves the use of violence", "threatens or endangers national security", "intimidates a civilian population or group thereof", "disrupts or threatens public order", "causing destruction or damage to property" - if such conduct is aimed at, *inter alia*, "threatening or endangering the sovereignty or territorial integrity" of Sri Lanka or "any other political or governmental change". The definition of terrorism is extremely broad and vague, and it is difficult to know with precision exactly what acts will amount to the offence.
48. Section 19 of the Emergency Regulations 2006 provides specific immunity for actions taken under the Regulations. It states: *"No action or suit shall lie against any Public Servant or any other person specifically authorised by the Government of Sri Lanka to take action in terms of these Regulations, provided that such person has acted in good faith and in the discharge of his official duties."* Similar immunity provisions are contained in Regulation 73 of the EMPPR 2005, and the PSO (Sections 9 and 23) and the PTA (Section 26).
49. Regulations 19 and 20 of the EMPPR 2005 give the armed forces powers of search and seizure, arrest and detention without warrant; powers in dealing with prisoners; and the power to question a person in detention. The use of armed forces to carry out normal policing functions gravely increases the risk of human rights violations, as the armed forces are not trained to act as an investigating body or as law enforcers.
50. Regulation 18 (1) (a) and (b), EMPPR 2005 gives the Secretary to the Minister of Defence discretion to use a wide array of powers to restrict freedom of movement to prevent a person "acting in any manner prejudicial to the national security or to the maintenance of public order, or to the maintenance of essential services".
51. International Commission of Jurists, *Briefing Paper: Sri Lanka's Emergency Laws*, March 2009. Available at: http://www.icj.org/IMG/SriLanka-BriefingPaper-Mar09-FINAL.pdf

52. In March 1986, Ershad removed military commanders from key civil posts and abolished martial law offices and the military courts in an attempt to ease martial law restrictions. The martial law lasted until November 1986. <http://countrystudies.us/bangladesh/90.htm>
53. Oije P.J.C. Schimmelpenninck van der, International Humanitarian Law from a Field Perspective—Case Study Nepal, *Yearbook of International Humanitarian Law*, Vol. 9, 2006, p. 394-417.
54. In November 2003, the government put the police and the paramilitary Armed Police Force (APF) under the unified command of the army.
55. The Asian Human Rights Commission statement available at: <http://www.globalpolicy.org/component/content/article/154-general/26730.html>
56. David Bonner. 1985. *Emergency Powers in Peacetime*, London: Sweet & Maxwell.
57. Wardlaw Grant. 1989. Political Terrorism: Theory, Tactics and Countermeasures, Cambridge: Cambridge University Press, p. 69.
58. Edmonds M. 1976, 'The Role of armed forces in the maintenance of law and order in Britain: A Discussion' in C.H. Enloe and U. Semin-Panzer (eds.), *The Military, the Police and Domestic Order: British and Third World Experiences*, London: Richardson Institute for Conflict and Peace Research, p.26.
59. ECtHR, Grand Chamber Judgment of 12 May 2005, *Öcalan v. Turkey*, Application No. 46221/99.
60. Jha UC. 2009. 'Terrorism and Human Rights Laws: A Comment', *Economic & Political Weekly*, Vol XLIV, No. 37, p. 70-71.
61. In the case of *Rodrigo Rojas De Negri and Carmen Gloria Quintana Arancibia v. Chile*, in which two young people were detained by a military patrol and then beaten, doused in petrol and set on fire and which had been dealt with by the Chilean military courts, the Inter-American Commission on Human Rights Commission pointed to "the various irregularities pertaining to legal process inherent in the military justice system in Chile" and stated that "the actions of these military courts have served to provide a veneer of legality to cover up the impunity which the members of the Chilean Security Forces enjoy when they are found to be involved in flagrant violations of human rights".The Commission also stated that, "these irregularities pertaining to legal process inherent in Chilean military justice are reflected in the abusive recourse to secrecy in the conduct of the proceedings. The situation that has thereby arisen has made it virtually impossible to gain access to basic elements of the trial and allows the military authorities to control the evidence submitted. Annual Report of the Inter-American Commission on Human Rights, 1987-1988, OEA/Ser.L/V/II.74, Doc. 10 Rev. 1, 16 September 1988, Resolution No 01a/88, Case 9,755 (Chile), Considerings 7(c).

9

Impact of Human Rights Laws

Unlike any other institution in a state, the armed forces are charged with safeguarding nation's vital interests and their main purpose is effective participation in war.[1] Since war involves loss of life and destruction of property, some might argue that during a war there is little room to consider the human rights of those who are fighting.[2] Generally speaking, human rights are those rights which allow an individual freedom to live a dignified life of her/his choice. Human rights are applicable at all times, whether in peace or during armed conflicts, by virtue of the fact that people are human and should thus always possess these rights. Though human rights treaties allow parties to derogate them in times of war, the 'hard-core' rights remain non-derogable.[3] Human rights jurisprudence has stressed the importance of this and the continued applicability of certain judicial guarantees that are essential in order to give effective protection to the 'hard-core' rights.

Like human rights law, international humanitarian law (IHL) is based on the premise that the protection accorded to victims of war must be without any discrimination. This is also a fundamental rule of human rights and is specified in the UN Charter, as well as in all human rights and humanitarian law treaties.[4] In recent years, scholars have noted a substantial convergence between international human rights law and IHL. This convergence is due in large measure to the distressing proliferation of violent internal armed conflicts in South Asia and other parts of the world.[5]

Armed Forces and Human Rights

Since the last three decades, the armed forces of Bangladesh, India, Nepal, Pakistan and Sri Lanka have been engaged in internal conflicts. In the past, the concept of human rights was rarely used in relation to the armed forces because a soldier remained at the mercy of his military superiors, whose task was to enforce military discipline. Today, there are a large number of international human rights instruments which have a bearing on the human rights of soldiers. This chapter discusses the applicability of international human rights laws in the military systems of South Asian countries. As representatives of the State, the armed forces of the South Asian countries are bound to respect human rights in the exercise of their duties. It follows that they must be entitled to the same rights and protections as all other persons, subject to certain limitations imposed by military life.

Role of the Armed Forces

The armed forces are an integral part of a democratic state and society. Their role is not merely to defend the State and its citizens against internal and external threats, but also to protect and uphold the human rights and fundamental freedoms on which democratic societies are based. As the fundamental purpose of the armed forces is to fight during an armed conflict, the needs of the individual were (earlier) treated as subservient to this purpose. The armed forces also had a hierarchical structure based on rank, with an obligation to obey the orders of superiors. In the past, the officers had formal education, while the soldiers were generally uneducated. Military organisations usually considered it inappropriate to treat all ranks equally in relation to certain aspects of military life.

However, all this has changed in the last 50 years, due largely to the international human rights laws. The impact of international human rights laws will be examined in the context of the changing role of the armed forces and awareness of human rights. While employed in internal conflicts, the armed forces of the South Asian countries have been accused of human rights violations. However, this chapter takes a view that when the human rights and fundamental freedoms of the members of the armed forces are protected within their institution, they will be more likely to uphold these while carrying out their duties.

International Human Rights Laws

The human rights are conceptually indivisible and an entitlement of being human. The concept of human rights developed after World War II. The modern law of international human rights is based on the UN Charter,[6] supplemented by the Universal Declaration of Human Rights, the International Covenant on Civil and Political Rights, and the International Covenant on Economic, Social and Cultural Rights. In addition, there are UN treaties dealing with discrimination with respect to race and women; the Convention on the Rights of the Child; the Convention against Torture and Other Cruel, Inhuman or Degrading Treatment; and conventions concerned with refugees and citizenship.[7] Human rights law is also complemented during times of armed conflict by international humanitarian law (IHL). The main IHL treaties are the Geneva Conventions of 1949, with the 1977 Protocols to those Conventions. A number of other treaties also protect human rights by dealing with the criminal liability of individuals, rather than State liability. This includes treaties on genocide and slavery, and the Rome Statute on the International Criminal Court.

A number of these provisions can potentially apply to armed forces personnel. However, in the South Asian region, the enjoyment of human rights by the members of the armed forces has been restricted by the countries' constitutions[8]or by law. The core human rights treaty, the International Covenant on Economic, Social and Cultural Rights (ICESCR) has been signed and ratified by all the countries in South Asia. The International Covenant on Civil and Political Rights (ICCPR) has been signed and ratified by all the countries, except Pakistan which has only signed it in 2008.[9] Nepal is the lone signatory to the Optional Protocols to the ICCPR. The Convention on the Elimination of All Forms of Discrimination against Women (CEDAW) and the Convention on the Rights of the Child (CRC) have been signed and ratified by all the South Asian countries. The International Convention on the Elimination of All Forms of Racial Discrimination has been signed and ratified by all, whereas the Convention against Torture and Other Cruel, Inhuman or Degrading Treatment or Punishment has not been ratified by India[10] and Pakistan. As for the major IHL treaties, all the South Asian countries have signed and ratified the four Geneva Conventions of 1949, but only Bangladesh has signed and ratified the 1977 Additional Protocols I and II to the Geneva Conventions of 1949.

Today, there are a large number of rights contained in these international human instruments which have a bearing on the human rights of soldiers. Some of these rights relate to the right to life; the right to liberty—detention under military justice systems; the right to equality—differences in treatment of women and minorities; the right to a fair trial and hearing during summary trials and courts-martial; the right to freedom of thought, conscience, religion or belief, subject to military requirements; the right not to be subjected to cruel, inhuman or degrading treatment in military service; the right to freedom of opinion and expression—with limits on public statements by members of the armed forces; and the right to peaceful assembly or protest by service personnel. A very obvious feature of human rights instruments is that they recognise, at least implicitly, that some human rights are deserving of a higher degree of protection than others and that they may not be abrogated.

The Military Legal System

Armed forces the world over are governed by an independent and special code of conduct designed to ensure the highest standard of discipline among the members. In the South Asian countries armed forces do not have a common code, and services are governed by the respective military acts. In Indian military laws are contained in the Army Act, 1950, and the Air Force Act, 1950, and Indian Navy Act, 1957.

In essence, these laws were replicas of the British-Indian laws and only a few cosmetic changes have been made in them.[11] In Pakistan, the three services' laws are the Pakistan Army Act of 1952,[12] the Pakistan Navy Ordinance of 1961 and the Pakistan Air Force Act of 1953. Bangladesh has not carried out any significant change in the Pakistan military laws, adapted after Independence in 1972.[13] The Bangladesh Army is governed by the Act of 1952, the Air Force by the Act of 1953 and the Navy by the Ordinance of 1961. In Bangladesh, the military laws have been amended on a few occasions, though no substantial changes have been made in them. In essence, the military legal systems of India, Pakistan and Bangladesh are identical. The Sri Lankan armed forces are governed by the Army Act, 1949, the Air Force Act, 1949, and the Navy Act, 1950.[14] The democratic government in Nepal has passed the Nepalese Army Act, 2006.[15] These legal systems regulate the rights and discipline of the armed forces personnel in the following way.

Human Rights in Discipline System

Respect for human rights and fundamental freedoms for all, including armed forces personnel, is not just a moral obligation. It is part of international human rights law, and states are thus obliged to respect and protect the rights of personnel serving in their armed forces. The right to a fair trial is a norm of international human rights law designed to protect individuals from the unlawful and arbitrary curtailment or deprivation of their basic rights and freedoms, the most prominent of which are the rights to life and liberty. It is guaranteed under Article 14 of the ICCPR, which provides that "everyone shall be entitled to a fair and public hearing by a competent, independent and impartial tribunal established by law". Article 14 of the ICCPR, contains a catalogue of 'minimum procedural guarantees' for an individual undergoing a trial for criminal charges.[16]

Military commanders the world over have been given statutory powers to dispose of minor offences committed by members. This is an informal way of dealing with disciplinary matters that can be termed non-judicial summary trial. It has many advantages. The summary trial can be held quickly and avoids the formality of a court martial. The punishment awarded is not expected to have any adverse effect on the career of the accused. The human rights issues that might arise in these cases are whether (a) the punishments awarded could amount to torture, or degrading or inhuman treatment, (b) if the cumulative effect of the punishment is serious, whether the accused had the right to refuse summary trial and face a court martial instead, where detailed procedural rights are available, and (c) the accused has a right to appeal against the punishment awarded in a summary trial.

The observance of human rights may not be necessary in summary trials. However, the impact of a minor punishment on the future career of a soldier demands the observance of the rules of 'natural justice'. For instance, a single punishment entry in the conduct sheet may make a soldier ineligible for promotion or certain privileged missions. In cases where the punishment available to a commanding officer (CO) is such as to amount to deprivation of the soldier's liberty, the observance of the rules of fair trial becomes mandatory.

For maintaining operational efficiency and discipline, there is nothing wrong with empowering a CO to impose the punishment of deprivation of liberty or fine. To both the soldier and the superior, the informal disciplinary system has advantages. The soldier avoids any serious record of disciplinary offence and superior avoids the bureaucracy involved in bringing formal disciplinary process.[17] However, what is necessary is to afford a soldier the right to trial by a military court-martial, instead of dealing with him summarily. An affected person must be given the right to appeal against the decision of a summary trial to the judicial tribunal or court. Incidentally, the military legal systems of the South Asian countries do not provide for judicial review of the punishment awarded by a commanding officer. In contrast, the establishment of a Summary Appeals Court in the UK, in 2000, has had a beneficial effect on the summary process by laying down principles with which commanding officers would be unlikely to disagree.[18]

The governments in the South Asian countries must ensure that the punishment awarded in a summary trial is not degrading and humiliating. It must not be such as to arouse feelings of fear, anguish and inferiority in its victim. In 1992, the Indian Army Act, 1950 was amended to abolish the award of 'field punishment', which was considered degrading and inhuman. However, the award of 'field punishment' (or 'battlefield penalty' in Nepal) still continues in the Bangladesh, Nepal, Pakistan and Sri Lankan armed forces. The Rules provide that during the field punishment the military accused may be kept in irons (in fetters or handcuffs or both fetters and handcuffs), and may be secured so as to prevent his escape. Field punishment amounts to cruel, inhuman and degrading treatment and needs to be abolished.[19] In the South Asian context, an affected person does not have the right to represent himself against minor punishments, as well as the right to appeal in the higher tribunals.

As far as the formal disciplinary system is concerned, the military justice systems of the South Asian countries fall short of the international legal standards in that they do not provide free legal aid, they are not free from command pressure and there are chances of their being applied with discretion.[20] Since the military judicial system is archaic, both the persons tried by it as well as outsiders do not perceive of it as just and fair. To a military accused, the system does not provide the necessary safeguards required by a fair trial. The courts-martial can readily be subject to manipulation by the convening authority.[21] The officer who convenes a court-martial selects the panel from among the officers under his command. The officers constituting the court, though untrained in law, decide the guilt of the military accused and award punishment. Ultimately the military justice system is seen as being unjust and unfair. In countries like the US, the UK, Australia, Canada, China, Israel, Switzerland and the Republic of South Africa, the military justice system has been amended in the recent past to make it compatible with the international norms.

A Summary Court Martial (SCM) is another peculiarity of the armies of the South Asian countries, except that of Sri Lanka.[22] It may try any person subject to the Army Act and under the command of the officer holding the court, except an officer, junior commissioned officer or warrant officer. A SCM may pass any sentence, except the sentence of death or imprisonment for a term exceeding one year in case the officer holding the trial is of or higher than the rank of Lieutenant Colonel, and three months, if such officer is below that rank. A SCM is legally authorised to take cognizance of all military offences committed by a soldier and the accused has no right to challenge his trial by the commanding officer on the ground of bias or personal interest. It can award punishment of dismissal with one-year imprisonment after a summary trial. In India, the high courts and the Supreme Court have criticised the trials held under the SCM,[23] as it is felt that the SCM awards excessive and harsh punishments and denies the procedural rights guaranteed under Article 14 of the Constitution. Such an arbitrary system of justice is not followed in any other democratic country. The SCM never existed under the British military justice system.

The Right to Appeal

In the South Asian countries, till recently, there has been no right of appeal as such against the finding or sentence of a court-martial. In Bangladesh and Pakistan,[24] the Army Acts ban any appeal against the decision of a court-martial. The prohibition, however, is not absolute and the high courts in Pakistan have entertained collateral attacks on court-martial proceedings on limited jurisdictional grounds.[25] In India, there had been a constitutional ban on appeals against the findings and sentences of courts-martial. However, since August 2009, the Armed Forces Tribunal and its Benches created under the Act of 2007, have been entertaining appeals against the findings and sentences of a court martial.[26] Similarly, in Nepal, the Army Act, 2006, has created a Special Court to hear appeals from courts-martial, and appeals can be taken up further to the Supreme Court.

The Sri Lankan Constitution empowers the Supreme Court to issue writs of mandamus, certiorari and prohibition in respect of any court-martial or of any military authority exercising judicial functions. In addition, the writs of habeas corpus shall be deemed to apply in respect of any person illegally detained in custody by order of a court martial or other military authority.[27] Since Sri Lanka is a signatory to the Protocol to the UN International Covenant on Civil and Political Rights, 1966 (ICCPR), its citizens are empowered to approach the Human Rights Committee (HRC) in case of breach of their fundamental rights. However, the Supreme Court of Sri Lanka in Nallaratnam Singarasa's case ruled that a Sri Lankan citizen can not enforce their rights through the HRC at Geneva, since it is not reposed with judicial power under our Constitution.[28] The South Asian countries need to establish an independent judicial forum to hear appeals from the court martial.

Freedom of Association

In the South Asian countries, the right to the freedom of association is severely restricted for members of the armed forces.[29] The freedom of association could give rise to two distinct problems with regard to armed forces personnel. The first is the question of military discipline and possible interference with the *esprit de corps*. The second relates to issues of allegiance and outside influence. It is feared that soldiers (or sailors or airmen) will act together in defiance of the orders of superiors in the military chain of command. The weight of numbers could lead to senior officers losing control of an army unit. In most of the armed forces mutiny is considered to be a serious military offence. However, in some countries representative bodies are permitted and certain constraints have been placed to limit their membership to members of the armed forces or restrict their powers, for instance forbidding strikes or other forms of industrial action. The right of armed forces personnel to the freedom of association is granted in 22 out of 39 countries of the Council of Europe. Of these, only seven allow the right to collective bargaining and none afford the right to collective action. Democracies like Hungary, Sweden[30] and Germany[31] allow trade unions in the armed forces. In Russia, the All-Russian Professional Union of Servicemen was set up in 1992, a period during which the army was facing many challenges brought about by the disintegration of the Soviet Union. The organisation concentrated its initial efforts on the establishment of regional organisations and is now represented in 70 out of the 80 national regions. At the State level, it promotes the social, legal, economic and professional interests of armed forces personnel. Many of its members are active at various levels of parliament and government and public administration. One of the Union's major achievements has been the provision of protection and assistance to families of military personnel who died during missions.

In the South Asian context, the restriction on the right of assembly can be used to conceal poor physical treatment of soldiers, unpopular activities required of a soldier, poor leadership, discriminatory treatment of soldiers, irrational orders and poor management. While officers and soldiers are permitted by military law to make individual complaints about their treatment at the hands of superiors, the processing of the complaints remains outdated. In some cases, the relatives of members of the armed have taken the lead and attracted considerable publicity. Thus, there is a need for an independent body to consider the requirements of various segments within the armed forces. Recognition of the rights of armed forces personnel is a reflection of the maturity of a democracy.

Gender Discrimination and the Right to Equality

The issue of gender discrimination in the armed forces has been raised on a number of occasions. Though women have been working in the armed forces as medical and nursing officers in the South Asian countries, the armed forces have been skeptical of their ability to perform the role of a soldier. In India, though women officers started being inducted in the non-combat branches of the services in 1991, they were not given permanent commission[32] and also not assigned any combat-related task.[33] There have been reported cases in India where women officers have alleged sexual harassment. The cases of sexual harassment can be significantly reduced by: (a) developing a definitive policy that is clearly and regularly communicated to all the ranks; (b) providing a grievance procedure for reporting sexual harassment to one other than the alleged harasser; (c) prompt, thorough and documented investigations of all complaints; (d) swift remedial action to protect the victim from further harassment; and (e) enforcing policies against sexual harassment quickly, consistently and aggressively. The present procedure of addressing all grievance applications to the commanding officer needs change.

The greatest challenge before the South Asian countries in the context of removing gender-related inequality is to create an enabling environment and make institutional arrangements that would ensure the equal participation of women in every sphere. In pursuance of this goal, efforts must be made to ensure that all members of the armed forces receive the same benefits and are treated equally, as mandated by the countries' respective constitutions. Hopefully, the defence system will become more technologically advanced in the years to come and battles will increasingly depend more on technology than on muscle power. Also, perhaps the physical and psychological differences between men and women will be taken into consideration in the future while designing training programmes and creating functional environments to enable women to perform combat roles.

Redress of Grievances

In a civilized democratic society, the State guarantees that every citizen can approach prescribed forums for the redress of grievances against an individual or the State. In relation to the armed forces, this right has been expressly provided in the respective service Acts, whereby an individual may complain up to the Chief of the Staff (Central Government in the case of officers) for the redress of grievances. However, the processing of grievance petitions is faulty. The officials who may be the root cause of the grievance process the complaint. The complainant is not informed about the comments of his superiors on his petition and there is no independent judicial forum to review the executive decision.[34]

In the armed forces, morale and discipline are enhanced when the troops understand that they are being treated with dignity, fairness and equality under the law. Thus, there is a need for a system for redressing grievances that is administered fairly, effectively and promptly to improve transparency. The hostile environment in which the armed forces operate today demands better protection of their rights than what was available to them two decades ago.

Allegations of Human Rights Violations

In the last three decades, South Asian countries have witnessed an increase in instances of violent conflict which have been called by various names, like terrorism, insurgency, militancy, proxy war and armed rebellion. The existing police forces in the countries have often proved inadequate to deal with the perpetrators of large-scale violence and the armed forces have been called upon to aid the civil power. The involvement of the armed forces in such operations has become a controversial issue. There have been allegations that members of the armed forces have taken advantage and unleashed their own brand of terror.

Various human rights organisations in the region and the foreign and local media have criticised the effectiveness of military laws dealing with the violation of human rights by armed forces personnel. They have also criticised the special laws giving enhanced powers to the armed forces for dealing effectively with disruptive activities in specific areas. The armed forces have often been accused of extra-judicial execution of innocent civilians; illegal imposition of curfew; rape, molestation and sexual harassment of women; torture; forced labour; and largescale looting of homes and granaries under the powers vested in them by the special Acts.[35] Though the armed forces can effectively prosecute soldiers and officers for abuses committed under special powers, the civil liberties organisations doubt the effectiveness of the military judicial system. Human rights activists and national and international NGOs have urged the Government of India to repeal the Armed Forces (Special Powers) Act and hold trials of human rights abuses in civilian courts.

Conscientious Objection to Military Service

The Universal Declaration of Human Rights and the International Covenant for Civil and Political Rights (ICCPR) do not explicitly mention the right to conscientious objection to military service.[36] However, a large number of military personnel in the US, the UK and Israel have claimed the right to refuse to perform military service (conscientious objection) on the basis that such rights derived from their freedoms under Article 18 of the ICCPR. The laws of a growing number of States have exempted from compulsory military service citizens who genuinely hold religious or other beliefs that forbid the performance of military service and have replaced it with alternate national service.[37] The Israeli military justice system has tackled conscientious objection to military compulsory service, as well as the use of force in a particular operation. Military service and conscientious objection in Israel are regulated by the Defence Service law of 1986.[38]

The British Human Rights Act, 1998 implements the European Convention on Human Rights and Fundamental Freedoms. Article 9 of the Act guarantees the 'right to freedom of thought, conscience and religion'.[39] The South Asian armed forces may have to face similar situations in the near future as the ICCPR and national constitutions give the right to freedom of expression, which has been influenced by 'new developments in political and ethical thoughts'.

The armed forces in the South Asian countries consist of volunteer service personnel. Armed forces personnel are not a homogeneous group and there are various branches of the armed forces, like the army, the air force, the navy and the coast guards. Within each branch there may be different categories of personnel, like commissioned officers, junior commissioned officers, non-commissioned officers and enrolled combatant soldiers. In a few services, there may also be non-combatant personnel who accompany the armed forces. They become subject to the respective service Act when specified conditions of the respective Act become operative. The Indian Supreme Court has held that persons in active service, in camps, although non-combatant, are an integral part of the armed forces.[40]

As human rights are inherently a part of being human and that being a member of military service should not affect the enjoyment of human rights. As far as armed forces personnel are concerned, human rights may by clustered into four groups: (1) civil and political rights; (2) rights related to equal opportunities and non-discrimination in the armed forces; (3) rights related to military life; and (4) procedural rights related to implementing and ensuring human rights in the barracks.[41] While individuals do not lose their human rights when they enter the armed forces, the State can limit their enjoyment of human rights due to requirements related to the particular characteristics of military life. The particularities of military life that are used to justify restrictions on the exercise of human rights are often related to preserving order and discipline in the military; establishing the political neutrality of the armed forces; maintaining operational effectiveness; protecting classified information; obeying orders; and maintaining the hierarchical structure of the military organisation.

There is a need to consider the human rights of military personnel. The 'civilianisation' of the military justice system has taken place in a number of democratic countries. In some countries, military discipline procedure is used to deal with only relatively minor military offences, while more serious offences are dealt with by civilian courts. In Germany, military offences are also tried by the civil courts. In some States, where the European Convention on Human Rights has been in force from early 1950s, soldiers have themselves initiated the drive to make the disciplinary procedure compliant with human rights standards. They have appealed in the European Court of Human Rights against alleged breaches of human rights. This has resulted in a change in the military disciplinary procedures to ensure compliance with the Convention.

The human rights of the members of the armed forces have additional importance in the contemporary context for two reasons. The first is the changing nature of military operations. Armed forces are now more likely to be deployed in peacekeeping operations than in conventional warfare. Servicemen and women in peacekeeping operations are frequently called upon to assist political institutions within societies fractured by conflict to re-establish a culture of respect for human rights in their area of operations. They will be in a better position to do this if they themselves have knowledge of, and are accustomed to, such a culture within their own armed forces. Also, where armed forces are not engaged in conventional combat but in roles analogous to policing, the case for restrictions on their rights for reasons of military discipline is substantially weakened.

Second, the increasing use of multinational military task forces in these and other operations draws attention to differences in the working conditions and rights enjoyed by members of the armed forces in different States. Unless there are good reasons to justify such variations, the differences will inevitably impact the morale and effectiveness of those units enjoying fewer rights. Therefore, limitations on the rights of the members of the armed forces must be "in accordance with law" or "authorised by law" and "necessary in a democratic society" for one of a number of specified interests.

The governments in the South Asian nations should ensure that military personnel are able to enjoy and exercise their human rights and fundamental freedoms in conformity with the relevant constitutional and legal provisions and with the requirements of service. There is a need to treat members of the armed forces as citizens in uniform, i.e., military personnel retain their civil and political rights, although they could be modified in accordance with the military context. Indeed, respect for human rights and fundamental freedoms for all, including armed forces personnel, should be the aim of the governments in the South Asian countries.

In the South Asian countries, the enjoyment of human rights by members of the armed forces is disproportionately restricted by the law. The military law in Bangladesh, Nepal, Pakistan and Sri Lanka does not provide for any right to appeal against the decision of the military courts, a legacy inherited from the British. In none of the South Asian countries are armed forces personnel allowed to fully exercise their rights to freedom of speech and freedom of assembly. As a consequence, armed forces personnel are hindered from speaking for themselves or voicing concern about cases of human rights violations.

The questions come up: Do military personnel deserve fundamental human rights? If yes, then to what extent? Can all the fundamental rights mentioned in a Constitution be abridged or restricted for military personnel by legislation? Has there been any change in the perspective of the world in the last 60 years? Answers to these questions can be found in the Vienna World Conference on Human Rights, held in 1993, which emphasized the unity of the normative framework of human rights. All human rights are universal, indivisible and interdependent and interrelated. The international community must treat human rights globally in a fair and equal manner, on the same footing, and with the same emphasis. While the significance of national and regional particularities and various historical, cultural and religious backgrounds must be borne in mind, it is the duty of States, regardless of their political, economic and cultural systems, to promote and protect all human rights and fundamental freedoms.

Democracy, development and respect for human rights and fundamental freedoms are interdependent and mutually reinforcing. Democracy is based on the freely expressed will of the people to determine their own political, economic, social and cultural systems and their full participation in all aspects of their lives. In the context of the above, the promotion and the protection of human rights and fundamental freedoms at the national and international levels should be universal and conducted without conditions attached. The international community should support the strengthening and promotion of democracy, development and respect for human rights and fundamental freedoms in the entire world.

Human rights are conceptually indivisible and an entitlement of being human. Indeed, the exercise of some human rights cannot be limited at all. These are human rights from which there can be no derogation, including the right to life; prohibition of torture; prohibition of slavery; prohibition of imprisonment on the grounds of the inability to fulfil a contractual obligation; prohibition of being found guilty of any criminal offence, when the act committed did not constitute a criminal offence under national or international law at the time that it was perpetrated; and the right to be recognised as a person before the law. However, the exercise of other human rights may be adapted or limited under specific conditions and situations. Several factors may be taken into account when adapting human rights standards to the armed forces: the nature of military discipline, the hierarchical organisation of military ranks, the need to obey orders and the protection of morale. Unlike any other group of citizens, members of the armed forces can, in the course of their official duties, be called upon to kill other people and to sacrifice their own lives. Military life may involve serving under harsh or extreme conditions. Even in normal circumstances, there may be relatively little separation between private life and official duties, e.g., where personnel live in barracks.

These special factors, distinctive to life in the armed forces, confirm the need for placing limitations on the human rights of armed forces personnel. Some take the view that the military is a unique institution entirely different from civilian institutions. This uniqueness is imperative for militaries of all times and all countries, as it is the only way of preserving operational effectiveness. According to this view, a member of the armed forces is not an ordinary public servant but is someone who answers a calling, is dedicated to duty, country and honour. Contrary to this position, other commentators take the view that the distinctiveness of the military is only of relative importance because the military was subject to "civilianising" trends in the 20th century as a result of political, legal, cultural, technological and economic pressures from society.

Therefore, the military profession of today has taken a different shape due to broader transformations in society. The military profession is shifting away from an institutional format to one that is similar to the occupational format of other professions in society. It is increasingly becoming "just another job", with those joining it being driven by financial incentives, job security and attractive working conditions, instead of a unique institution based on considerations of country, duty and honour. According to the institution model, soldiers' human rights will be greatly restricted because the military profession cannot be compared with any other profession in society. According to the occupation model, however, soldiers will generally have the same rights as other citizens because of the commonalities between the military profession and other professions in society.

It is imperative, however, that such restrictions satisfy several criteria. They must be rationally related to military needs and not merely the result of arbitrary practice or tradition. They should be firmly based upon law, preferably legislation that has been subject to considered democratic debate and lawful procedure. They should be proportionate, i.e., adapted in a nuanced way, to the interests of the military, which would be compromised by the full exercise of human rights. Any restrictions on the rights of armed forces personnel that operate in a discriminatory fashion on the basis of race, ethnicity, religion, sex, or sexual orientation must be carefully scrutinised, given their suspect nature and the requirement for clear justification. The onus to show that it is necessary to restrict the rights of armed forces personnel should firmly lie with the military itself.

Human rights are not merely a matter of high-sounding aspirations on paper: they must also be fully implemented in daily practice in the armed forces. Human rights violations resulting from illegal practices (e.g., mistreatment of soldiers) are some of the most common violations occurring in the armed forces. Although laws and regulations prohibiting such practices often exist, it is their practical implementation that proves most difficult. The question of effective implementation of human rights is, therefore, crucial.

The South Asian countries must demonstrate that their military personnel receive effective operational training designed to uphold international human rights standards and international humanitarian law.[42] Human rights education is crucial in raising awareness and creating a professional culture within the military that includes respect for human rights as part of a commitment to democratic values. When this is achieved, the armed forces are not just defenders of a state's territorial integrity; they would also defend and embody its democratic commitments. Members of the armed forces are the only category of citizens, who are not only subject to the common laws of the land, but to the additional jurisdiction of military law. The members of the armed forces cannot be expected to respect human rights in their operations without their own rights being protected: these are two sides of the same coin. Any limitations on human rights must be provided for by law and should be consistent with international treaty obligations. They should be applied in an exceptional manner and strictly proportionate to the intended aim.

By virtue of being citizens, members of the armed forces need to enjoy the same human rights and fundamental freedoms as other citizens. Respect for the human rights of members of the armed forces contributes to a military that is firmly integrated in society. Respect for human rights in the barracks prevents the military from being misused by the government and turned against the civilian population. It also protects members of the armed forces against misuse and oppression by army commanders. Modern-day peacekeeping operations require armed forces personnel to integrate human rights work into their day-to-day operations. They will be better prepared for such activities if they themselves operate in an environment that respects and protects those rights, and requires them to internalise the values that underlie them. Contrary to the perceived conflict between human rights and combat effectiveness, respect for human rights actually serves to increase combat effectiveness.

Notes

1. According to Mann (1988), the four types of activities characteristic of modern states are: (i) the maintenance of internal order; (ii) military defence/aggression directed against foreign foes; (iii) maintenance of communications infrastructures: roads, rivers, message system, etc., and (iv) economic redistribution: the authoritative distribution of scarce material resources among different ecological niches, age-groups, sexes, classes, etc. Mann, Michael. 1988. *States, War and Capitalism: Studies in Political Sociology*. Oxford: Basil Blackwell Ltd.
2. The international humanitarian law (IHL) has been drawn up for application in times of armed conflict. IHL distinguishes two types of armed conflicts: (i) international armed conflicts, opposing two or more States, and (ii) non-international armed conflicts, between governmental forces and non-governmental armed groups, or between such groups only. Where IHL is not respected, human suffering increases and the consequences of the conflict become more difficult to repair. IHL has been defined as: International rules, established by treaties and customs, which are specifically intended to solve humanitarian problems directly arising from international or non-international armed conflicts and which, for humanitarian reasons, limit the rights of the parties to a conflict to use the methods and means of warfare of their choice or protect persons and property that are, or may be, affected by conflict. Y Sandoz, *Commentary on the Additional Protocols of 8 June 1977 to the Geneva Conventions of 12 August 1949*, Geneva: ICRC.
3. These are the right to life, the right against torture and other inhuman treatment, the right against slavery and servitude, and retroactive criminal legislation or punishment. Article 4 (2), International Covenant on Civil and Political Rights, 1966.
4. For example, Article 27 of the Fourth Geneva Convention of 1949 states: "....all protected persons shall be treated with same consideration by the Party to the conflict in whose power they are, without any adverse distinction based, in particular, on race, religion or political opinion."
5. International law recognises at least four different types of conflict situations, each of which is governed by a different set of legal norms: (i.) situations of tensions and disturbances; (ii.) international armed conflicts; (iii.) wars of national liberation; and (iv.) internal armed conflicts. The term "internal tensions and disturbances" refers to situations that fall short of armed conflict, but involve the use of force and other repressive measures by a government to maintain or restore public order or public safety. Only international human rights law (IHRL) applies in such situations and the governments are permitted to derogate from or limit a restricted set of obligations under IHRL in the context of tensions and disturbances. The term "international armed conflict" refers to situations that involve two or more states engaged in armed conflict. In such situations, the central provisions of IHL become operative, particularly those contained in the four Geneva Conventions and Protocol I to the Geneva Conventions. In addition, most human rights guarantees remain applicable in such situations, albeit subject to the same types of derogations and limitations permitted to governments in situations of internal tensions and disturbances. The term "wars of national liberation" refers to armed conflicts in which "peoples are fighting against colonial domination and alien occupation and against racist regimes in the exercise of their right to self-determination." Generally speaking, the same provisions of IHL and IHRL that apply

in the context of international armed conflict apply equally in Pthe context of wars of national liberation. The term "internal armed conflict" refers to all armed conflicts that can not be characterized as either international armed conflicts or wars of national liberation. Protocol II of 1977, provides that internal armed conflicts "must take place in the territory of a High Contracting Party between its armed forces and dissident armed forces or other organized armed groups which, under responsible command, exercise such control over a part of its territory as to enable them to carry out sustained and concerted military operations and to implement (Protocol II)." Freeman Mark, International Law and Internal Armed Conflicts: Clarifying the Interplay between Human Rights and Humanitarian Protections, available at: http://www.jha.ac/articles/a059.htm

6. Preamble and Articles 1.3, 55, and 56. The United Nations (UN) has human rights as one of its central ideals. The Preamble of the UN Charter seeks 'to reaffirm faith in fundamental human rights, in the dignity and worth of the human person, in the equal rights of men and women and of nations large and small'. In pursuing this goal UN member states have concluded seven major human rights treaties which establish human rights standards in a variety of different areas.
7. 1. Universal Declaration of Human Rights (UDHR), adopted by the UNGA in 1948; 2. International Covenant on Civil and Political Rights (ICPPR), 1966; 3. The International Covenant on Economic, Social and Cultural Rights (ICESCR), 1966; 4. The UN Convention on the Elimination of All Forms of Discrimination against Women (CEDAW), 1981; 5. The Convention against Torture and Other Cruel, Inhuman or Degrading Punishment, 1984; and 6. The UN Basic Principles and guidelines on the right to a remedy and reparation for victims of gross violations of international human rights laws and serious violations of international humanitarian law. UN Doc. E/CN.4/2005/L.10/Add.11 (19 April 2005).
8. For example Article 33 of the Constitution of India states that the Parliament can make a law abrogating or restricting the fundamental rights of members of the armed forces for ensuring the proper discharge of their duties and for the maintenance of discipline among them. Similar restrictions on the fundamental rights of the armed forces personnel have been made in the Constitutions of Bangladesh (Article 45), Pakistan (Article 8), and Sri Lanka (Article 15).
9. The Government of Pakistan has signed the ICCPR on 17 April 2008. Upon signature, the Government has made reservation: "The Government of the Islamic Republic of Pakistan reserves its right to attach appropriate reservations, make declarations and state its understanding in respect of various provisions of the Covenant at the time of ratification." Though it has not ratified the ICCPR till date, many of its provisions are reflected in Pakistan's Constitution. For instance, Article 9 of the ICCPR dealing with protection against arbitrary arrest, detention or exile corresponds to Article 10 of the Pakistan Constitution. Hassan Tariq, Supreme Court of Pakistan: The Case of Missing Person, *Criterion*, Vol. 4, No. 3. July/September 2009, p. 7-27.
10. India signed the United Nations Convention against Torture and other Cruel, Inhuman or Degrading Treatment or Punishment (UNCAT) in 1997, but was shy to ratify it. In a belated move the Government has introduced the Prevention of Torture Bill in the Parliament on 22 April 2010. The Bill is aimed at harmonizing Indian law with UNCAT, a condition that is necessary for its ratification. Under the prevention of Torture Bill, public servant who obtains a confession by causing grievous physical or mental hurt

or danger to life of any person are guilty of torture and liable for imprisonment up to 10 years. There have been a few criticisms about the Bill. According to Ferreira, 'The proposed legislation is not only a climb-down from the standards set by the UNCAT, but, in many ways, is in direct opposition to the basic norm of non-derogability of the right of freedom from torture'. Ferreira Arun, A Critical Appraisal of the Prevention of Torture Bill, 2010, *Economic & Political Weekly*, May 22, 2010, Vol. XLV, No. 21, p. 10-12. Also see: Tarunabh Khaitan, A Bill designed to fail, *THE HINDU*, May 19, 2010, available at http://www.hindu.com/2010/05/19/stories/2010051957251300.htm.

11. For more details see: Jha U.C. 2009. *The Military Justice System in India: An Analysis*, New Delhi: LexisNexis.
12. The Pakistan Army Act was amended in November 2007. It has expanded the jurisdiction of the military courts to try civilians on charges of terrorism, anti-national activities, sedition, attacks on army personnel and attacks on the President.
13. In 1971, East Pakistan became Bangladesh as a result of an ethnic revolt supported by the Indian armed forces. The existing laws of Pakistan were adapted by the Bangladesh (Adaptation of Existing Laws) Order 1972.
14. Recently the military law professionals from the US Pacific Command hosted a military law exchange programme with the Sri Lankan Defence Ministry to exchange ideas on ways to improve transparency, accountability and human rights in military justice system. http://www.dailynews.lk/2007/08/25/sec10.asp.
15. Section 22 of the Nepalese Army Act, 2006 has been considered as objectionable provision. The International Commission of Jurists, a Geneva based NGO has urged for amendment to Section 22 of the Act, as it provides for amnesty (statutory bar, or blanket immunity, from legal proceedings in any court, for acts carried out by a member of the Nepal Army in the "course of discharging his duties" that result in the death of, or loss to any person), for crimes under international law such as crimes against humanity, war crimes, and gross human rights violations in general such as extrajudicial killings, enforced disappearances and torture. http://www.icj.org/news.php3?id_article=4201&lang=en
16. These are: (i) The right to a fair and public hearing; (ii) Equal access to, and equality before, the courts; (iii) The right to a competent, independent and impartial tribunal established by law; (iv) The right to a presumption of innocence until proved guilty according to law; (v) The right to prompt notice of the nature and cause of criminal charges; (vi) The right to adequate time and facilities for the preparation of a defence to the defendant and to his counsel; (vii) The right to a trial without undue delay; (viii) The right to defend through legal counsel of one's own choice and to free legal assistance; (ix) The right to an interpreter and the right to examine witnesses; (x) Prohibition of self-incrimination; (xi) Prohibition of double jeopardy; (xii) The right to appeal against conviction and sentence to a higher tribunal established according to law; and (xiii) The right to compensation for miscarriage of justice.
17. Rowe Peter. 2006. The *Impact of Human Rights on Armed Forces*, Cambridge: Cambridge University Press, p.72.
18. Rowlinson, Simon P, 'The British Military Justice System', 52 *AFL Rev*, (2002), p. 17-52.
19. For details on 'field punishment' see Chapter IV on 'Offences and Punishment'.
20. The highest ad hoc military tribunal which could be constituted under the South Asian

military legal systems is a General Court Martial (GCM). It can award sentence up to the death, except in case of Nepal, where a GCM is empowered to award 'life imprisonment along with confiscation of entire property'.

21. He is responsible for: (i) making the decision to prosecute or not to prosecute; (ii) deciding the charges against the accused; (iii) appointing the military prosecutor or counsel for prosecution; (iv) appointing the court-members of his choice; (v) appointing a defending officer, (he can also deny a counsel on the grounds of expediency); (vi) detailing a judge advocate for trial--the judge advocate, the prosecutor, judge advocate and the court members come under his authority in the chain of command; (vii) reviewing the sentence awarded by the court-martial and referring the proceedings back to the court for reconsideration (enhancing the punishment), even if an accused is acquitted by the court (except under the Indian Navy Act, 1957); (viii) considering the pre-confirmation petition of the accused; (ix) confirming or not confirming the sentence awarded by the court-martial; and (x) considering the post-confirmation petition of the convicted person.
22. The provisions relating to the SCM were introduced only to discipline the Indian troops and were envisaged to facilitate the trial of native troops by British commanding officers. They were suitable for British military commanders who wanted to take swift action against Indian soldiers and were most frequently utilised for the trial of military offenders. They could award the punishment of one year's imprisonment and dismissal from service after a summary trial. Page 101 of the Manual of (British) Indian Military Law (1935 Edition), states: "The discipline of the Indian Army depends in a great measure on the summary court-martial. When a soldier or other person amenable to the act has committed an offence which is ordinarily triable by court-martial, a commanding officer, when determining by what court the accused is to be tried must bear in mind that the legislature, in conferring upon him the power of a summary court-martial, intends that he shall exercise these powers.....It should, however, be remembered that even a comparatively slight punishment promptly inflicted is often more deterrent than a heavier one which follows long after the offence, and this is especially so with Indian troops."
23. In a recent case the Delhi High court, while comparing the powers of the SCM in India with that in the USA, commented that the picture in India is a sad one, the law being a vestige of the colonial era. The Court further held: "Mindful of the fact that Article 33 of the Constitution of India confers unbridled powers on Parliament to bring into place a situation which severely abridges the Fundamental Rights of a citizen, it becomes the bounden duty of the Courts to ensure that the equality doctrine is not needlessly nullified. It also becomes essential that the Courts should interpret the law in a manner which will reduce to the minimum the inroads into the infringible rights contained in Chapter III of the Constitution......A SCM must be an exception and not the rule. It can only be convened where the exigencies demand an immediate and swift decision....The decision to convene an SCM must be preceded by a reasoned order which itself will be amenable to judicial review." *Lance Naik V.P. Singh v. Union of India,* WP (C) 2511/1992 decided on 25 January 2008.
24. Section 133 of the Army Acts: Bar of appeals - No remedy shall lie against any decision of a court-martial save as provided in this Act, and for the removal of doubt it is hereby declared that no appeal or application shall lie in respect of any proceeding or decision

of a court martial to any court exercising any jurisdiction whatever.

25. Lahore High Court's Rawalpindi Bench has issued a judgement setting aside the conviction of a lieutenant colonel by the Field General Court Martial (FGCM). Lt-Col Munir Ahmed Gil, had invoked the jurisdiction of the court in the year 2000 against his 1999 conviction by the FGCM on charges of concealing his property which enabled him to claim financial benefits from the army. The decision is being considered important by the analysts because it could open a flood of pleas to the civilian courts against the decisions of military courts.http://letusbuildpakistan.blogspot.com/2009/01/lahorehigh-court-makes-history-by.html.
26. Jha U C. 2010. *Armed Forces Tribunal*, New Delhi: Mana[illegible]cations.
27. Constitution of Sri Lanka, Article 140 and 141; and Section [illegible] Sri Lankan Army Act.
28. *Nallaratnam Singarasa v. The Hon. Attorney General, Colombo*, S.C. Spl (LA) No. 182/99, decided on 15.09.2006. The Supreme Court held: "the accession to the Optional Protocol in 1997 by the then President and Declaration made under Article 1 is inconsistent with the provisions of the Constitution......and is in excess of the power of the President as contained in Article 33(f) of the Constitution. The accession and declaration does not bind the Republic qua state and has no legal effect within the Republic...... In these circumstances the Petitioner cannot plead a legitimate expectation to have the findings of the Human Rights Committee enforced or given effect to by an order of this Court."
29. Section 21 of the Indian Army Act, 1950, states that army personnel cannot (i) be associated in any way with any trade union, or any society, institution or association, or any class of societies, institutions or associations; (ii) attend or address any meeting or to take part in any demonstration organised by any body of persons for any political or other purposes; and (iii) communicate with the press or to publish or cause to be published any book, letter or document. Similar provisions exist in all the South Asian countries.
30. Sweden's first association for military personnel was established almost a hundred years ago. The Swedish Association of Military Officers (SAMO) has a membership of 9,500 officers of all ranks. The association promotes the interests of military officers by taking part in the process of decision-making, which influences the working conditions for officers. Strikes or other offensive actions are allowed only during the negotiation period and not while an agreement is still valid. SAMO also cooperates at the governmental level on general defence issues (however, not on political matters such as foreign policy or the national budget). The advantage of the Swedish model is that officers feel more satisfied with their work because of the knowledge that their concerns are being addressed.
31. German soldiers have had the right to be members of trade unions and professional associations since the re-establishment of the armed forces in 1955. With 210,000 members representing all ranks and status groups, the Association represents the general, ideological, social and career interests of its members, as well as their families. The union is represented at the level of barracks, battalions, regional executive boards and at the federal level. It is politically and financially independent of any authority and of any political party and is financed solely by members' fees. Being the authoritative organisation for service personnel, it is consulted by parliament and elected governments

when preparing any legislation affecting the interests of servicemen, their families and their surviving dependents. The Association also maintains close contact with the political parties, parliament, parliamentary groups and committees as well as the Minister of Defence. Its main focus is to take care of the interests of armed forces personnel sent on international missions.

32. In 2008, the Government of India has made certain policy changes which would allow permanent commission to women officers in selected branches of the army. The Delhi High Court's recent verdict has struck down gender discrimination in the Army and the Air Forces. It has allowed permanent commission to women officers, which has gone against the recommendations of military brass. *Babita Puniya v. Union of India*, WP (C) 1597/2003 decided on 12 March 2010. The Delhi High Court disposed of a bunch of ten petitions by its order of 12 March 2010. Also see: The Delhi High Court grants women in the armed forces the right to permanent commission, so far denied on flimsy grounds. Women's Battle, FRONTLINE, Volume 27 - Issue 07, Mar. 27- Apr 09, 2010. http://www.frontline.in/stories/20100409270703600.htm.

33. The Government of India has denied induction of women officers into combat duties. 'Government says no induction of women into combat duties now', *THE HINDU*, New Delhi, 15 December 2009, p.18.

34. In India, the Armed Forces Tribunal Act, 2007 has created special Tribunal. The Tribunal and its Benches have become functional since August 2009. The armed forces personnel who are not satisfied with the relief in the 'service matters' may approach the tribunal for redress of their grievances.

35. For instance the civil liberties organisations have dubbed the Indian Armed Forces (Special Powers) Act [AFSPA] and have accused the Indian Government of violating the international standards of human rights, defined by the Constitution and the international covenants. The United Nations Human Rights Committee, in 1991, found Section 4 of the AFSPA to be incompatible with Articles 6, 9 and 14 of the International Covenant on Civil and Political Rights (ICCPR), 1966, which was ratified by the India on 10 April 1979. Indian law permits members of the armed forces accused of crimes to be prosecuted by either the military or civilian justice systems. However, AFSPA requires prior approval of the central government for civilian prosecutions of military personnel. The armed forces may take over case from the civil authorities for trial of soldiers by a court-martial under the Army Act.

36. In 1993, the UN Human Rights Committee, the body of experts monitoring the implementation of the ICCPR, adopted General Comment No. 22 on the right to freedom of thought, conscience and religion, and affirmed that the right to conscientious objection to military service can be derived from Article 18 of the ICCPR. The Committee was of the view that the ICCPR does not explicitly refer to a right to conscientious objection, but such right can be derived from Article, inasmuch as the obligation to use lethal force may seriously conflict with the freedom of conscience and the right to manifest one's religion or belief.

37. The Australian Defence Act grants a total exemption from military service on the grounds of conscientious belief for those who could prove that the doctrine of their religion forbade them to bear arms or perform military service. Conscientious objection and selective conscientious objection are available to persons conscripted to serve in the Australian Defence Forces. In the US, under the Military Selective Act, section 456 (j), no person is required to be subjected to combatant training and service in

the armed forces, 'who by reason of religious training and belief, is conscientiously opposed to participate in war in any form'. A member of the armed forces may seek either separation or assignment to non-combatant duties for reasons of conscientious objection. This is achieved by administrative discharge and is discretionary within the military service concerned. In the US, during the Vietnam War, over 170,000 officers and men were classified as 'conscientious objectors' between 1965 and 1970.

38. It requires all Israeli citizens and residents to perform military service---three years for men and two years for women. Section 36 (1) of the Defence Service Law gives the Minister of Defence a general discretion to exempt anyone from military service. The law also provides for various types of exemption from military service, discriminating between men and women. Women are exempted on reasons of conscience, in which case the women requesting the exemption will have to present her case to a Committee composed of civilians. In December 2002, the Israeli Supreme Court [Judgement in David Zonschein's case, HCJ 7622/02, *Israeli Law Review*, Vol. 36, No. 2 Fall 2002, p.1-17] affirmed the possibility of granting exemption from military service for reasons of conscientious objection.
39. In a recent case in the UK, a general court-martial in Hampshire convicted Flight Lieutenant (Dr.) Malcolm Kendall-Smith on five charges, including refusing to serve in Basra. He was dismissed from the air force. As an additional punitive measure Kendall-Smith was ordered to pay £20,000 from his personal savings towards the costs of his defence. Dr. Kendall-Smith told the military hearing that he had refused to serve in Basra because he believed that the invasion of Iraq was illegal and did not want to be complicit in an "act of aggression" contrary to international law. The doctor told the court, "I have evidence that the Americans were on a par with Nazi Germany with [their] actions in the Persian Gulf, and that ongoing acts of aggression in Iraq and systematically applied war crimes provide a moral equivalent between the US and Nazi Germany."
40. *OKA Nair v. Union of India* AIR 1976 SC 1179.
41. Rowe Peter. 2006. The *Impact of Human Rights on Armed Forces*, Cambridge: Cambridge University Press.
42. Section 20 of the Nepal Army Act, 2006, provides that individuals inducted in the army shall be trained in human rights and international humanitarian law.

10

Implementation of International Humanitarian Law

International humanitarian law (IHL) is a branch of the international law and is also known as 'law of war' or 'law of armed conflict'. It has been defined as international rules, established by treaties and customs, which are specifically intended to solve humanitarian problems directly arising from international or non-international armed conflicts and which, for humanitarian reasons, limit the rights of the parties to a conflict to use the methods and means of warfare of their choice or protect persons and property that are, or may be, affected by conflict.[1] The term IHL is of relative recent origin and does not appear in the Geneva Conventions of 1949. The IHL seeks to mitigate the effects of war, first in that it limits the choice of means and methods of conducting military operations, and secondly it obliges the belligerents to spare persons who do not or no longer participate in hostilities.

IHL Treaties

The IHL comprises all those rules of international law which are designed to regulate the treatment of the individuals--- civilians or armed forces, wounded or active in an armed conflict. The most important instruments of IHL are the four Geneva Conventions of 1949 and their Additional Protocols of 1977. They are supplemented by treaties on particular matters including prohibitions of certain weapons and the protection of certain categories of people and objects, such as children and cultural property, and include a number of rules of customary international law. Main treaties of international humanitarian law are following.

- Convention (I) for the Amelioration of the Condition of the Wounded and Sick in Armed Forces in the Field. Geneva, 12 August 1949.
- Convention (II) for the Amelioration of the Condition of Wounded, Sick and Shipwrecked Members of Armed Forces at Sea. Geneva, 12 August 1949.

- Convention (III) relative to the Treatment of Prisoners of War. Geneva, 12 August 1949.
- Convention (IV) relative to the Protection of Civilian Persons in Time of War, Geneva, 12 August 1949.
- Protocol (I) Additional to the Geneva Conventions of 12 August 1949, and relating to the Protection of Victims of International Armed Conflicts. Geneva, 8 June 1977.
- Declaration provided for under article 90 of Additional Protocol I: Acceptance of the Competence of the International Fact-Finding Commission.
- Protocol (II) Additional to the Geneva Conventions of 12 August 1949, and relating to the Protection of Victims of Non-International Armed Conflicts. Geneva, 8 June 1977.
- Convention on the Rights of the Child, New York, 20 November 1989.
- Optional Protocol to the Convention on the Rights of the Child on the Involvement of Children in Armed Conflict, New York, 25 May 2000.
- Rome Statute of the International Criminal Court, 17 July 1998.
- Convention for the Protection of Cultural Property in the Event of Armed Conflict, The Hague, 14 May 1954.
- Protocol to the Convention for the Protection of Cultural Property in the Event of Armed conflict, The Hague, 14 May 1954.
- Second Protocol to the Hague Convention of 1954 for the Protection of Cultural Property in the Event of Armed Conflict, The Hague, 26 March 1999.
- Convention on the Prohibition of Military or any other Hostile Use of Environmental Modification Techniques, New York, 10 December 1976.
- Protocol for the Prohibition of the Use of Asphyxiating, Poisonous or Other Gases, and of Bacteriological Methods of Warfare, Geneva, 17 June 1925.
- Convention on the Prohibition of the Development, Production and Stockpiling of Bacteriological (Biological) and Toxin Weapons and on their Destruction, opened for signature in London, Moscow and Washington, 10 April 1972.
- Convention on Prohibitions or Restrictions on the Use of Certain Conventional Weapons Which May be Deemed to be Excessively Injurious or to Have Indiscriminate Effects. Geneva, 10 October 1980.
  - Protocol on Non-Detectable Fragments, 10 October 1980 (Protocol I to the 1980 Convention).
  - Protocol on Prohibitions or Restrictions on the Use of Mines, Booby-traps and Other Devices, 10 October 1980 (Protocol II to the 1980 Convention).
  - Protocol on Prohibitions or Restrictions on the Use of Incendiary Weapons, 10 October 1980 (Protocol III to the 1980 Convention).

  - Protocol on Blinding Laser Weapons, 13 October 1995. (Protocol IV to the 1980 Convention).
  - Protocol on Prohibitions or Restrictions on the Use of Mines, Booby-Traps and Other Devices as amended on 3 May 1996 (Protocol II as amended to the 1980 Convention).
  - Amendment to the Convention on Prohibitions or Restrictions on the Use of Certain Conventional Weapons Which May be Deemed to be Excessively Injurious or to Have Indiscriminate Effects, 21 December 2001.
  - Protocol on Explosive Remnants of War, 28 November 2003 (Protocol V to the 1980 Convention).
- Convention on the Prohibition of the Development, Production, Stockpiling and Use of Chemical Weapons and on their Destruction, Paris, 13 January 1993.
- Convention on the Prohibition of the Use, Stockpiling, Production and Transfer of Anti-Personnel Mines and on their Destruction, Oslo, 18 September 1997.
- Protocol (III) Additional to the Geneva Conventions of 12 August 1949, and relating to the Adoption of an Additional Distinctive Emblem (Red Crystal). Geneva, 2005.
- Convention on Prohibition of the Use, Development and Destruction of Cluster Munitions, 2008.

Many of the rules of IHL are also considered part of customary international law based on widespread, representative and virtually uniform practice of States accepted as legal obligation and therefore mandatory for all parties to an armed conflict.[2]

Implementation of the IHL

The Geneva Conventions of 1949 and their Additional Protocols of 1977 are the principal treaties governing aid to and protection of the victims of armed conflict. In order to secure the guarantees provided by these instruments, it is essential that the States implement their provisions to the fullest possible extent. Implementation mechanism can be divided into three categories, (i) the preventive measures to be taken in peacetime, (ii) ensuring respect during conflicts, and (iii) repressing violations.[3] For effective implementation of the IHL, it is necessary that it is placed within the framework of national legislation.

The four Geneva Conventions of 1949 in identical language stipulate[4] that the High Contracting Parties have an obligation to "undertake, in time of peace as in time of war, to disseminate the text of the present Convention as widely as possible in their respective countries, and, in particular, to include the study thereof in their programmes of military and, if possible, civil instructions, so that the principles thereof may become known to the entire population, in particular to the armed fighting forces, medical personnel and the chaplains." Under the Geneva Conventions and their Additional Protocols a range of measures are expected on the part of states parties to these instruments. The important ones are:

- To have the Conventions and Protocols translated into the national language(s).
- To spread knowledge of their provisions as widely as possible both within the armed forces and the general population.
- To repress all violations listed as such in the above-mentioned instruments and, in particular, to adopt criminal legislation that punishes war crimes.
- To adopt measures to prevent the misuse of the Red Cross and other recognised emblems.
- To ensure that protected persons enjoy judicial and other fundamental guarantees during armed conflict.
- To appoint and train persons qualified in IHL, in particular legal advisers within the armed forces.
- To provide for the establishment of National Red Cross/Red Crescent Societies, civil defence organisations, and National Information Bureaux.
- To take account of IHL when selecting military sites and in developing and adopting military tactics.
- To ensure that protected sites (cultural) are properly situated and marked.

It is quite obvious that some of these measures will require adoption of legislation or regulations. Others may require development of educational and training programmes, recruitment and training of personnel, production of identity cards and other documents, setting up of special structures, and introduction of planning and administrative procedures. All these measures are essential to ensuring effective implementation of IHL. The ratification status of South Asian countries as regard to IHL treaties is as follows.[5]

	Bangladesh	**India**	**Nepal**	**Pakistan**	**Sri Lanka**
GC I to IV 1949	YES	YES	YES	YES	YES
AP I 1977	YES	NO	NO	NO	NO
AP II 1977	YES	NO	NO	NO	NO
AP III 2005	NO	NO	NO	NO	NO
ICC Statute 1998	YES	NO	NO	NO	NO
Hague Conv. 1954	YES	YES	NO	YES	YES
Hague Prot. 1954	YES	YES	NO	YES	NO

Hague Prot. 1999	NO	NO	NO	NO	NO
ENMOD Conv. 1976	NO	YES	NO	YES	YES
Gas Protocol 1925	YES	YES	YES	YES	YES
BWC 1972	YES	YES	NO	YES	YES
CCW 1980	YES	YES	NO	YES	YES
CCW Prot. I 1980	YES	YES	NO	YES	YES
CCW Prot. II 1980	YES	YES	NO	YES	YES
CCW Prot. III 1980	YES	YES	NO	YES	YES
CCW Prot. IV 1995	YES	YES	NO	YES	YES
CCW Prot. II a 1996	YES	YES	NO	YES	YES
CCW Amdt 2001	NO	YES	NO	NO	YES
CCW Prot. V 2003	NO	YES	NO	NO	NO
CWC 1993	YES	YES	YES	YES	YES
Ottawa Treaty 1997	YES	NO	NO	NO	NO
Cluster Munition Convention, 2008	NO	NO	NO	NO	NO

Although South Asia has a proud humanitarian traditions and rule protecting civilians and combatants dating back to thousands of years, IHL treaty accession and implementation rates are low in the region as compared to other parts of the world. Some highlights are:

- While the South Asian countries may have various political or tactical reasons for not signing a weapon convention treaty, the main IHL treaty---the four Geneva Conventions of 1949--- have been signed and ratified by all the five countries.[6]
- Apart from India and Sri Lanka no country has taken measures to make Geneva Conventions a part of domestic law, a fact which is crucial for their enforceability.[7]
- Other than Bangladesh and Maldives, no country in South Asian has ratified the two Additional Protocols of the 1949 Geneva Conventions.[8]
- Bangladesh is the only country which has ratified the Rome Statute of the International Criminal Court,[9] while Ottawa Treaty relating to Anti-Personnel Landmines has been signed and ratified by Bangladesh, Bhutan and Maldives.
- Bangladesh has also legislated "Act No XIX of 1973" which creates the crimes of crimes against humanity, crimes against peace, genocide and war crimes at the domestic level and creates a Tribunal in order to prosecute such crimes.[10]

Nepal and Sri Lanka[11] are the only countries in the South Asian region, which have constituted the National Committee for the Implementation of International

Humanitarian Law. In Nepal the Committee was established on 26 February 2007. Its mandate is to support the development of national legislation in implementation of IHL treaties to which Nepal is party and to review existing law. The Committee conducts activities aimed at promoting knowledge in the field of IHL. The posts of chairman and secretary are held by the Ministry for Law, Justice and Parliamentary Affairs. The Committee is composed of representatives of the Office of the Prime Minister and of the Council of Ministers, as well as of the ministries for Law, Justice and Parliamentary Affairs, Foreign Affairs, Defence, Home affairs, Health and Population, Education and Sports, Culture, Tourism and Civilian Aviation, and Women, Children and Social Welfare.

The South Asian countries have witnessed a number of deadly conflicts,[12] and their armed forces are also involved in internal armed conflicts.[13] While employed in armed conflicts,[14] the armed forces of the Bangladesh, India, Nepal, Pakistan and Sri Lanka have been accused of violations of IHL.[15]

This chapter will analyse the effectiveness of the South Asian military legal systems and the extent to which it can prosecute a military person for violations of grave breaches of Geneva Conventions[16] and other crimes contained in the Rome Statute. It will also examine the concept of command responsibility, the right to a fair trial available to a military accused and compensation to victims towards gross violations of IHL in the context of the South Asian countries. In addition, it will explore the need for a systematic review of the military legal systems in the region—not merely from the point of view of the offences it could try; but also the systems and procedures followed in a trial and the appellate forums available to an accused—to make it compatible with the demands of IHL.

Rome Statute of the International Criminal Court

The Rome Statute of the International Criminal Court (ICC) was adopted on 17 July 1998. The Rome Statute is unique in many ways. First, it has created a permanent tribunal, the ICC, to deal with all crimes of serious concern to the international community as a whole. Its jurisdiction and mandate are not limited to specific events in specific places, or to any specified time-frame. Second, the Rome Statute provides that the ICC shall exercise jurisdiction over individuals,[17] unlike the other permanent international tribunals, such as the International Court of Justice. The ICC's powers and functions include holding individuals accountable, and subjecting the accused to investigation, arrest, detention, prosecution and if found guilty, incarceration. The Rome Statute creates obligations on the part of state parties to provide the means to enforce these powers. The Statute limits the ICC's focus to genocide, crimes against humanity, war crimes and aggression.

As regards, personal jurisdiction, once as a country ratifies the Rome Statute, it becomes subject to the ICC's jurisdiction.

The Rights of Soldiers

The world over, armed forces are governed by a special code of conduct designed to ensure the highest standard of discipline among the members. An independent legal system for the armed forces has been provided by almost all the democracies. Speedy trials and predictable decisions aid the military in its effort to maintain order and uniformity. In addition to enhancing discipline, order, uniformity, efficiency and obedience, the military court addresses certain offences unique to the military.[18]

Post-1857 British codification is the progenitor of the South Asian military legal systems. Only a few minor changes were made before the British laws were adopted by independent India, Sri Lanka, Pakistan and Nepal.[19] Bangladesh has not carried out any significant change in the Pakistan Army Act, 1952, adapted after Independence in 1972. Nepalese Army Act, 2006 adopted by the democratic country has also been criticised for certain lacunas.[20] These legal systems regulate the rights of military personnel in the South Asian countries.

In the past, a soldier remained at the mercy of his military superiors. They were given certain rights to complain about unfair treatment to their superiors. This right to make a complaint, however, cannot be compared to challenging a breach of human rights. There was no one standard of fair treatment for a military soldier, as they functioned under system that operated differently in different parts of the world. Military punishments varied and generally exceeded the degree of severity of criminal sanctions available in the civil courts. Corporal punishments or the death penalty were not uncommon.

Today, there are a large number of rights contained in these international human instruments which have a bearing on the human rights of soldiers. Some of these rights relate to the right to life; the right to liberty--detention under military justice systems; the right to equality--differences in treatment of women and minorities; the right to a fair trial and hearing during courts-martial; the right to freedom of thought, conscience, religion or belief subject to military requirements; the right not to be subjected to cruel, inhuman, or degrading treatment in military service; the right to freedom of opinion and expression—with a limit on public statements by members of the armed forces; and the right to peaceful assembly or protest by service personnel. A very obvious feature of human rights instruments is that they recognise, at least implicitly, that some human rights are deserving of a higher degree of protection than others and that they may not be abrogated.

Principle of Complementarity

An important element of the principles guiding the ICC is that the national criminal justice processes should be used if they are adequate to ensure the investigation, prosecution and punishment related to a crime. This principle, called 'complementarity', is dealt with in the Preamble and in Articles 1 and 17 of the Rome Statute. For example, paragraph 4 of the Preamble affirms, 'that the most serious crimes of concern to the international community as a whole must not go unpunished and that their effective prosecution must be ensured by taking measures at the national level and by enhancing international cooperation,' and emphasizes, 'that it is the duty of every State to exercise its criminal jurisdiction over those responsible for international crimes.' Preamble paragraph 11 plainly states that the ICC shall be complementary to national criminal jurisdictions.

In contrast to the 'primacy over national courts' of the two *ad hoc* Tribunals for Yugoslavia (ICTY) and Rwanda (ICTR)[21] as well as the Special Court for Sierra Leon (SCSL),[22] the complimentarity entails that the States can bar the ICC investigation and prosecuting cases, by adequately adjusting them in their domestic jurisdiction. To that end the Rome Statute sets forth the substance of complimentarity[23] and procedure for its application [24] in the form of a regime of admissibility.[25]

The Statute is clear that national courts have the first right and duty to prosecute perpetrators of international crimes. However, the ICC is empowered to intervene not only where the existing national judicial machinery is insufficient to allow a successful prosecution, but also where national governments are unwilling or unable[26] to fulfil their responsibility to prosecute. Thus, though the principle of complementarity preserves national criminal jurisdiction as primary, it allows the ICC to step in when States fail to act and allow a person accused of genocide, war crimes or crimes against humanity from escaping justice altogether.

The complementarity principle is the fulcrum that prioritises the authority of domestic forums to prosecute the crimes defined in Article 5 of the Rome Statute. Phrased another way, the complementarity principle is intended to preserve the power of the ICC over irresponsible states that refuse to prosecute nationals who commit heinous international crimes, but balances that supranational power against the sovereign right of states to prosecute their own nationals without external interference. [27] Arsanjani explains the basic descriptive meaning of complimetarity: 'the ICC is not intended to replace national courts, but operates only when they don't.'[28]

Another reason for this is that criminal law is traditionally seen as central aspect of sovereignty, over which States have an interest in retaining control. The theme of complimentarity runs through the Statute, coming in many places, but it is clear from very start that it is a major aspect of the ICC. Together with Article 19, which provides complimentarity challenges by States or persons, these provisions make clear that States can, by investigating or prosecuting the matter themselves, remove the matter from ICC, even if it wants the case. Through the principle of complimentarity, the system of international criminal justice established by the Rome Statute creates a presumption in favour of repression of ICC crimes at the national level. Article 18 provides a frankly exaggerated protection to the primacy of national jurisdiction. [29]

Crimes under the Rome Statute

The ICC has jurisdiction over four categories of crimes: genocide, crimes against humanity, war crimes and aggression.[30] These crimes[31] have been described as "the most serious crimes of concern to the international community as a whole", and as "unimaginable atrocities that deeply shock the conscience of humanity". Articles 6, 7 and 8 of the Rome Statute define the crimes of genocide, crimes against humanity, and war crimes. These definitions also contain a list of acts that can amount to the said crimes when the threshold test for each crime is met. These crimes are somewhat more recent in origin than many of the so called 'treaty crimes', in that their recognition and subsequent development is closely associated with the human rights movements that arose subsequent to World War II.[32]

Genocide

Article I of the Genocide Convention confirms that "genocide", whether committed in time of peace or in time of war, is a crime under international law. Article 6 of the Rome Statute reproduces the definition of genocide provided in Article II of the UN Convention on the Prevention and Punishment of the Crime of Genocide (1948).[33] The Rome Statute and the Genocide Convention identify five specific acts committed with the intent to destroy, in whole or part, a national, ethical, racial or religious group. The five acts are: killing members of the group, causing serious bodily or mental harm to members of the group, imposing conditions on the group calculated to destroy it, preventing births within the group and forcibly transferring children of the group to another.[34]

Crimes against Humanity

The definition of crimes against humanity contained in Article 7 of the Rome Statute is broader than that contained in the statutes of the Yugoslavia[35] and Rwanda[36] tribunals. The list includes rape, sexual slavery, enforced prostitution, forced pregnancy, enforced sterilisation, and any other form of sexual violence.

It also includes the forced transfer of a population, enforced disappearance of persons and apartheid. Such acts, however, must be committed as part of a "widespread or systematic attack directed against any civilian population, with knowledge of the attack" and there must be "multiple commissions of [the specified act]... pursuant to or in furtherance of a State or organisational policy to commit such attack." These last requirements limit the scope of the ICC's jurisdiction over crimes against humanity, notwithstanding the comparatively broad list of offences.

War Crimes

War crimes do not have the heavy evidentiary requirements of crimes against humanity. The Rome Statute divides war crimes into four categories: (a) grave breaches of the Geneva Conventions of 12 August 1949; [37] (b) other serious violations of the laws and customs applicable in international armed conflict, within the established framework of international law; (c) in the case of an armed conflict not of an international character, serious violations of Article 3 common to the four Geneva Conventions; and (d) other serious violations of the laws and customs applicable to armed conflicts that are not of an international character, within the established framework of international law.

The definition of war crimes is of relevance to South Asian countries, as their armed forces[38] are deployed in humanitarian missions of the UN, and also internally, to aid civil power. Personnel of the armed forces could be held responsible for war crimes in "armed conflicts not of an international character" [39] and also in "international conflicts". Article 8, Paragraph 2 (b) of the Rome Statute is similar to Article 75 of the First Additional Protocol of 1977 to the Geneva Conventions, to which SA countries are not a party. The provisions contained in the said paragraph severely restrict a state's discretion to choose the means and methods of warfare it considers appropriate to the military situation on the ground by enforcing a particularly high duty of care towards civilians. While many of the rules derived from the First Protocol could be considered binding under customary international law, the Rome Statute still contains innovations -- including a provision prohibiting "attacks against buildings dedicated to religion, education, art, science or charitable purposes..." are outlawed.[40] Article 8, para 2 (c) and (d) apply to non-international conflict, serious violations of article 3 common to the four Geneva Conventions.

The crimes listed under Article 8 (2) (a) of the Rome Statute correspond exactly to the relevant provisions of the Geneva Convention and are subject to the same limitations, i.e. they shall be qualified as crimes only when committed in an international armed conflict, and against persons protected under the relevant

Geneva Convention. Rape, sexual slavery, enforced prostitution, forced pregnancy and enforced sterilisation occurring during international armed conflicts shall also be qualified as war crimes, provided they constitute a grave breach according to the Geneva Convention.

The Rome Statute states that "the Court shall have jurisdiction in respect of war crimes, in particular when committed as part of a plan or policy or as part of a large-scale commission of such crimes." While the ICC is guided to take cognizance of a suspected war crime only when it is a part of large-scale policy, the words "in particular" make it clear that this is not a requirement. The language does not preclude jurisdiction over a *single* act defined in Article 8, para 2, and says nothing about the rank or status of the person committing that single act.

Offences against Administration of Justice

The ICC is also given jurisdiction over 'offences against the administration of justice', where these relates to proceedings before the Court.[41] The Statute specifies that these must be committed intentionally. These are perjury or the presentation of evidence known to be false, or forged; influencing or interfering with witnesses; corrupting or bribing officials of the Court or retaliating against them; and; in case of the officials of the Court, soliciting or accepting bribes. The Court can impose a term of imprisonment of up to five years or fine upon conviction.

Offences and Punishments under the South Asian Military Legal Systems

The offences listed in the Army Acts of Bangladesh, India, Pakistan, Nepal and Sri Lanka resemble each other closely, therefore, for the sake of brevity, only the Indian Army Act, 1950 has been referred to henceforth. Chapter VI of the said Act creates three categories of offences triable by the court martial:

- Offences which are specifically military in nature such as offences of misconduct in the face of the enemy, mutiny, desertion, absence without leave, disobedience of orders, sleeping on the post, violation of good order and discipline.
- Civil offences committed at any place in or beyond India, but deemed to be offences committed under the Army Act.[42]
- Offences of murder, culpable homicide not amounting to murder, or rape committed by a person subject to the Act against any person, if these offences are committed (i) while on active service, or (ii) at any place outside India, or (iii) at a frontier post specified by the central government.[43]

The Indian Army Act defines some war crimes as crimes under national law, and provides for universal jurisdiction over such crimes. Military personnel accused of breaches in the nature of torture, inhuman and degrading treatment, destruction of property etc. can be tried under different provisions of the Army Act.[44] Some offences under the Army Act that can be equated with breaches of IHL, are listed in the following table. [45]

Breach of IHL	**Offence under the Army Act, 1950**	**Punishment under the Army Act, 1950**
Appropriation of property	Section 36 (b): Breaking into house in search of plunder	14 years of rigorous imprisonment (RI)
Disobedience	Section 41: Disobedience of lawful command	14 years of RI
Making perfidious use of protective emblem	Section 45: Unbecoming conduct	Dishonourable dismissal (cashiering) for officers
Destruction of historic monuments, works of art, property	Section 64: Offences against property	7 years of RI
Inhuman treatment, wilfully causing great suffering	Section 46: Disgraceful conduct of a cruel kind	7 years of RI
Torture, inhuman treatment.	Section 63: Act prejudicial to good order and discipline.	7 years of RI
Destruction of place of worship	Section 64 (b): Defiling of place of worship, wounding religious feelings	7 years of RI
Murder, rape on active service	Section 69, 70: Civil offences	Death

For serious offences, a military accused [46] could be tried under the Indian Penal Code (IPC). The IPC criminalises certain acts that can amount to torture. The following criminal offences could be used to prosecute those responsible for torture:

- Voluntarily causing hurt to extort confession is punishable by up to one year of imprisonment and a fine (Section 323 IPC). If the hurt caused is grievous, the maximum punishment is ten years of imprisonment and a fine (Section 326 IPC).
- Wrongful confinement to extort confession or compel restoration of property, which carries a maximum punishment of three years of imprisonment and liability to pay a fine (Section 348 IPC).
- A public servant[47] disobeying the law, with intent to cause injury[48] to any

person, is liable to a punishment of up to one year of imprisonment and/or a fine (Section 166 IPC).

- A public servant concealing the design to commit an offence that it is his/her duty to prevent is liable to punishment which depends on the imprisonment or fine provided for the concerned offence (Section 199 IPC).

Nothing in the Rome Statute obliges States to strengthen their capacity to prosecute genocide, crime against humanity, or war crimes. However, States that do not strengthen their national criminal legislation may run a risk of being held 'unwilling or unable' to genuinely carry out proceedings. Most States will want to be certain that they can meet the complementarity test and retain the choice of prosecuting persons domestically, particularly where the person is national or where the crime was committed on the territory of the State.

Another area that needs consideration is that the punishments authorised under the South Asian military legal systems are more severe than those under the prevailing civil-criminal justice system or the Rome Statute. The maximum punishment that can be awarded by the ICC under the Rome Statute is life imprisonment in addition to a fine.[49] The table of punishments contained in the Army Act, on the other hand, includes the death penalty. The other punishments listed are transportation for life; rigorous or simple imprisonment up to 14 years; cashiering (in case of officers); dismissal from service; reduction to the ranks; forfeiture of seniority or service; reprimand; and forfeiture or stoppage of pay and allowances. [50]

Command Responsibility

The highly peculiar features of the armed forces are (1) centralised command, (2) hierarchy, (3) discipline, (4) *esprit de corps*. The centralised command structure ensures that a continuous chain of command links the very lowest echelon with the supreme headquarter. The forces are arranged in a pyramid of authority, each echelon owing explicit and peremptory obedience to the orders of its superior. The responsibility of military leaders originates from the law of war and was codified in the Hague Convention No. IV of 1907 and its Regulations respecting the laws and customs of war on land.[51]

The commanders at various hierarchical levels are responsible for ensuring that while participating in an armed conflict, the forces under their command follow the IHL. Command and leadership are not necessarily the same. The former is a legal status, an authoritative position recognised under the law. The latter comprises the skills and techniques necessary to influence soldiers to submit to the orders issued by those in authority or those holding the lawful status of command. The responsibility for the success or failure of a military mission falls squarely on the commander's shoulders. However, the commander's responsibility extends to more than just mission success. In the U.S. Army doctrine, for example, commanders are "responsible for everything their command does or fails to do."

In an armed conflict, each belligerent party bears the State responsibility for the conduct of members of its armed forces. The modern doctrine of command responsibility can be defined as the responsibility of commanders for war crimes committed by subordinate members of their armed forces or other persons subject to their control. This doctrine holds commanders responsible for failure to prevent or punish subordinates for their unlawful actions. The concept of 'command responsibility' in armed conflicts has two aspects. In the first place, it concerns the responsibility of a commander who has given an order to a subordinate to commit an act which is in breach of the law of armed conflict or whose conduct implies that he is not averse to such a breach being committed. Second, it covers the plea of the subordinate that he is not responsible for any breach because he was acting in accordance with the orders of or what he presumed to be the wishes of his commander, a plea that is more commonly described as that of 'compliance with superior orders'. The subordinate putting forward such a plea contends that the superior alone is responsible.

The trial of General Yamashita is perhaps the most frequently cited World War II command responsibility case. It was the first international trial to find a commanding officer criminally liable for the crimes committed by his subordinates.[52] *Yamashita* was charged with unlawfully disregarding and failing to discharge his duty as a commander to control the acts of members of his command by permitting them to commit war crimes. Although it was not alleged that Yamashita had actually issued illegal orders, in finding him guilty, the US military commission found that the public notoriety of the crimes was such that the accused *must have known* of them and failed to take action to prevent them or punish those responsible.

In appeal, the US Supreme Court ruled that: *the law of war presupposes that its violation is to be avoided through the control of the operations of war by commanders who are to some extent responsible for their subordinates.* The Court held that there was an affirmative duty to take such measures as were within the commander's power and appropriate to protect prisoners of war and the civilian population. The standard applied by the court was that the atrocities were so widespread that Yamashita *must have known* of them despite the fact that there was no evidence that the accused had knowledge of the acts or was directly connected to them.

After World War II, the principle of a superior's indirect command responsibility was affirmed by the war crimes tribunals, and notably by the trials held by the United States, France, the United Kingdom and the Soviet Union under

Control Council Law No. 10 in the *Medical*, the *Hostage* and the *High Command* cases.[53] The Nuremberg Tribunal and the subsequent trials held under Control Council Law No. 10 imposed criminal responsibility on military commanders for failure to act and prevent crimes from being committed. It was held in the *Medical* case that there is an 'affirmative duty' on superiors to take the appropriate steps when facing crimes committed by subordinates: "The law of war imposes on a military officer in a position of command an affirmative duty to take such steps as are within his power and appropriate to the circumstances to control those under his command for the prevention of acts which are violations of the law of war."

The Geneva Convention of 1949 lays down that each belligerent Party bears responsibility under international law for the conduct of all members of its armed forces, and the State is obliged to maintain discipline, law and order at all times.[54] All members of armed forces are subject to the military and criminal code of the States they serve, and in case of infraction they are liable to be prosecuted before military or civil courts of that State.[55]

Article 3 of the Geneva Conventions (Common Article 3) states that in cases of armed conflict not of an international character occurring in the territory of one of the High Contracting Parties, each Party to the conflict shall be bound to apply as a minimum the provisions to protected persons: those not taking active part in hostilities; members of armed forces who have laid their arms; members of armed forces who are *horse de cambat* by sickness, wounds, detention etc.[56]

The Additional Protocol I to the Geneva Conventions, adopted in 1977, was the first international treaty to codify the doctrine of command responsibility, creating an affirmative duty to repress grave breaches of international law. The provisions relating to command responsibility are contained in Articles 86 and 87 of the Protocol. A commander is liable for grave breaches committed by a subordinate "if he knew, or had information which should have enabled him" to conclude in the circumstances at the time, that his subordinate was committing or was going to commit such a breach and did not take all feasible measures within his power to prevent or repress the breach. Apart from being liable to be considered a party to war crimes committed by his subordinates, a commander has a general duty to maintain discipline and this includes a duty to take action in respect of war crimes committed, or about to be committed by his subordinates or by other persons under his control. Protocol I places the responsibility on the high contracting Parties to ensure that commanders prevent breaches, train their subordinates not to commit breaches and take action against offenders.

The commanders are to prevent and, where necessary, suppress and report to the competent authorities breaches of the Geneva Conventions and Protocol I. This applies in relation to members of the armed forces and other persons under their command. The commanders are also responsible for making members of the armed forces under their command aware of their obligations under the Conventions and the Protocol.

The doctrine of command responsibility has been codified in Article 28 of the Rome Statute. Article 28(a) imposes individual responsibility on military commanders for crimes committed by forces under their effective command and control if they "either knew or, owing to the circumstances at the time, should have known" that the forces were committing or were about to commit such crimes. Interpreted literally, Article 28(a) adopts the stricter "should have known" standard. It is felt that this provision will serve as a deterrent, and impel a commander to be aware of what his subordinates are doing. Paragraph (a) of Article 28 delineates the individual criminal responsibility of the military commanders, while paragraph (b) provides for the responsibility of non-military superiors. Individuals in positions of authority, whether civilians or within the military hierarchy, may incur criminal responsibility under the doctrine of command responsibility on the basis if their *de facto* as well as *de jure* positions as superiors.[57] The doctrine of command responsibility plays a fundamental role in regulating the behaviour of superiors and their subordinates in times of war.[58]

The armed forces of the South Asian countries have been deployed in UN multinational missions as part of the UN peacekeeping operations. The main purpose of deploying armed forces in peace missions is not to engage in military operations but to protect the lives of civilians from opposing militia groups and to ensure the safe delivery of humanitarian assistance as a part of the agreement with the UN. There is no unified disciplinary system for all the military contingents in multi-force operations. The normal practice is to allow each visiting force to exercise its disciplinary process over its own personnel in the territory of the host State. Any possibility of the UN taking disciplinary action against its peacekeepers is not visible in example, though misconduct has been reported in many operations. [59]

A common senior officer is placed in command of the multi-national force for passing orders to the national commanders, who in turn, command their own national contingents. The normal military structure operates within each national contingent in terms of superior–subordinate relationship. The national commanders have orders from their national superiors to obey the orders of the overall commander. The rules of engagement issued to a national contingent may impose some limitations on the soldiers of visiting forces.[60]

A person who attacks a UN force or its property during an armed conflict will commit a war crime and can be tried by the ICC for violation of the Rome Statute. However, the liability of a commander for a breach of IHL or human rights by members of a multinational force is not well defined.[61] Since none of the South Asian countries, other than Bangladesh, are party to the Rome Statute, and they have also not ratified the Additional Protocols to Geneva Conventions, it is imperative that the concept (of responsibility of the commander) be analysed, keeping in view the existing realities of armed conflict and developments in international law.

Command Responsibility in South Asian Countries

The military law of the South Asian countries does not contain any provision relating to command responsibility in armed conflict (international or internal) as specified under Article 28 of the Rome Statute.[62] A military commander is responsible for the conduct of those under his command or authority and over whom he has effective control.[63] For a military commander, responsibility by failure to act requires that a superior-subordinate relationship exists, that the superior knew, had reasons to know or, as the case may be, should have known that the act had been or was going to be committed, and that he negligently failed to take the necessary and reasonable measures to prevent that and punish the perpetrators. It has been ruled by the ICTR that superiors who plan or incite or order their subordinates to commit an unlawful act are subject to an aggravating circumstance and it should result in longer sentences. [64]

We ought to examine the options available to incorporate this standard of superior responsibility into the military manuals of the South Asian countries. If we are to project ourselves as an armed force that supports the rule of law, the internationally accepted "knew or should have known" standard of command responsibility should be followed domestically. This is more likely to prevent international crimes because it places a greater burden on commanders to pay attention to the acts of subordinates, an affirmative duty to stay informed.

The Right to Fair Trial

Under the Rome Statute, the accused is protected to a great extent from arbitrary and summary trials, which is contrary to the view the world had during the trials of WW II criminals.[65] The Rome Statute provides a detailed codification of procedural guarantees to an accused. Articles 66 and 67 of the ICC Statute, deal respectively with the presumption of innocence and with all other guarantees of a fair trial.[66] Article 67 of the Rome Statute, entitled 'Rights of the Accused', is modelled on Article 14 (3) of the ICCPR, one of the principle human rights treaties.[67] The right to a fair trial is also enshrined in the UDHR,[68] the regional human rights conventions,[69] as well as in humanitarian law instruments.[70]

Article 67 of the Rome Statute states that in the determination of any charge, the accused shall be entitled to a public hearing conducted fairly and impartially. The accused shall have the following minimum guarantees:

- To be informed promptly of the cause and content of the charge, in a language which the accused fully understands and speaks;
- To have adequate time and facilities for the preparation of the defence and to communicate freely with a counsel of the accused's choosing in confidence;
- To be tried without undue delay;
- To be present at the trial, to conduct the defence in person or through legal assistance of the accused's choosing;
- To be informed, if the accused does not have legal assistance, of this right and to have legal assistance assigned by the Court in any case where the interests of justice so require, and without payment if the accused lacks sufficient means to pay for it;
- To examine the witnesses against him and to obtain the attendance and examination of witnesses on his behalf under the same conditions as witnesses against him. The accused shall also be entitled to raise defences and to present other evidence admissible under this Statute;
- To have, free of any cost, the assistance of a competent interpreter and translations to meet the requirements of fairness;
- Not to be compelled to testify or to confess guilt and to remain silent, without such silence being a consideration in the determination of guilt or innocence;
- To make an unsworn oral or written statement in his defence; and
- Not to have imposed on him or her any reversal of the burden of proof or any onus of rebuttal.

Judicial guarantees to a prisoner of war (POW) under IHL are as follows.

- The right to be tried by an independent and impartial military/civil court (Article 84 (2), GC III).
- The right not be tried more than once for the same act or on the same charge (Article 86 GCIII).
- The right to be informed of the nature of the charge brought against them (Article 104 (2) GC III).
- The right to present a defence: assistance by one of his prisoner comrade as well as an interpreter, to be defended by a qualified advocate or counsel of choice (Article 99 and 105, GC III).
- The principle of legality *nullum crimen sine lage* (Article 99 (1), GC III).
- The prohibition of passing of sentence and the carrying out of execution without previous judgement pronounced by a regularly constituted court affording all the judicial guarantees which are recognised as indispensable by civilized people (Common Article 3 of four GC's of 1949).
- The right to be informed of their right to appeal, and the time limit within which he may do so. (Article 106 GC III).

- The non-renounceable nature and character of the rights conferred by IHL (Common Article 7 of four GC's of 1949).
- Sentence announced on POW must be served in the same establishment and under same conditions as in the case of members of the armed forces of the detaining power (Article 108, GC III).

Article 63 (2) of the Rome Statute, however, provides that if the accused, being present before the Court, continues to disrupt the trial, the Trial Chamber may remove the accused and shall make provision for him or her to observe the trial and instruct the counsel from outside the courtroom, through the use of communications technology, if required. Such measures are to be taken only in exceptional circumstances after other reasonable alternatives have proved inadequate, and only for such duration as are strictly required.

Penalty

According to the Rome Statute, the basic penalty to be imposed by the Court is one of imprisonment, up to and including life imprisonment in extreme cases. Article 77 of the Rome Statute declares that the Court may impose imprisonment for a specified number of years, which may not exceed 30 years.[71] Article 77 further states the Court may impose "a term of life imprisonment when justified by the extreme gravity of the crime and the individual circumstances of the convicted person." In addition to imprisonment, the Court may order fine and forfeiture of proceeds, property and assets derived directly or indirectly from that crime, without prejudice to the rights of bona fide third parties. In imposing a sentence of imprisonment, the Court is to deduct the time previously spent in detention in accordance with an order of the Court. The Court may also deduct any time otherwise spent in detention in conduct underlying the crime. [72]

Compensations to Victim

The Statutes of the ICTY and ICTR clearly deny victims any right to reparation. The ICTY statute for example, states that "the penalty imposed by the Trial Chamber shall be limited to imprisonment....in addition to imprisonment, the Trial Chamber may order the return of any property and proceeds acquired during criminal conduct, including by means of duress, to their rightful owners". On the other hand, the Rome Statute of the ICC explicitly allows for civil damages to be awarded in international cases, and states in Article 75:

Reparations to victims

1. The Court shall establish principles relating to reparations to, or in respect of, victims, including restitution, compensation and rehabilitation. On this

basis, in its decision the Court may, either upon request or on its own motion in exceptional circumstances, determine the scope and extent of any damage, loss and injury to, or in respect of, victims and will state the principles on which it is acting.

2. The Court may make an order directly against a convicted person specifying appropriate reparations to, or in respect of, victims, including restitution, compensation and rehabilitation. Where appropriate, the Court may order that the award for reparations be made through the Trust Fund provided for in article 79.
3. Before making an order under this article, the Court may invite and shall take account of representations from or on behalf of the convicted person, victims, other interested persons or interested States.
4. ...
5. ...
6. Nothing in this article shall be interpreted as prejudicing the rights of victims under national or international law.

This is for the first time; the international community has recognised the legal right of a victim to seek reparations.[73] The UN General Assembly resolution of 2005, "Basic Principles and Guidelines on the Right to a Remedy and Reparation for Victims of Gross Violations of International Human Rights Law and Serious Violations of International Humanitarian Law"[74] makes it obligatory upon the States to respect and ensure respect for and implement international human rights law and international humanitarian law. This obligation to respect and ensure respect emanates from (a) treaties to which a State is a party; (b) customary international law; and (c) the domestic law of each State. The States must ensure that their domestic law is consistent with their international legal obligations by:

- Incorporating norms of international human rights law and international humanitarian law into their domestic law, or otherwise implementing them in their domestic legal system;
- Adopting appropriate and effective legislative and administrative procedures and other appropriate measures that provide fair, effective and prompt access to justice;
- Making available adequate, effective, prompt and appropriate remedies, including reparation, as defined below;
- Ensuring that their domestic law provides at least the same level of protection for victims as that required by their international obligations.

The South Asian states are to ensure that a victim of a gross violation of international human rights law or of a serious violation of international humanitarian law has equal access to an effective judicial remedy as provided for under international law. Obligations arising under international law to secure the right to access justice and fair and impartial proceedings are required to be reflected in domestic laws. To that end, States are required to disseminate, through public and private mechanisms, information about all available remedies for gross violations of international human rights law and serious violations of international humanitarian law.

As regard reparation for harm suffered, adequate, effective and prompt reparation is intended to promote justice by redressing gross violations of international human rights law or serious violations of international humanitarian law. Reparation should be proportional to the gravity of the violations and the harm suffered. *Compensation* should be provided for any economically assessable damage, as appropriate and proportional to the gravity of the violation and the circumstances of each case, resulting from gross violations of international human rights law and serious violations of international humanitarian law, such as (a) physical or mental harm; (b) lost opportunities, including employment, education and social benefits; (c) material damages and loss of earnings, including loss of earning potential; (d) moral damage; and (e) costs required for legal or expert assistance, medicine and medical services, and psychological and social services.

Appeal and Revision

The judgements of the Trial Chamber are subject to appeal. The prosecutor may appeal on grounds of procedural error, error of fact or error of law. The defendant may appeal a conviction on grounds of procedural error, error of fact, error of law or any ground that affects the fairness or reliability of the proceedings or decision. The prosecutor is also entitled to appeal a conviction on behalf of the defendant. [75] Sentences may be appealed by both prosecutor and the convicted person on grounds of disproportion between the crime and the sentence. If, during an appeal against sentence, the Court considers that there are grounds to set aside a conviction, it may intervene to quash the judgement. The Court may also intervene on sentence during an appeal taken against the conviction only.

Where the Appeals Chamber grants the appeal on a point of law or fact that materially influenced the decision, or because of unfairness at the trial proceedings affecting the reliability of the decision or sentence, it may reverse or amend the decision or sentence, or order a new trial before a different Trial Chamber. It may vary a sentence if it finds it disproportionate to the crime. In a defence appeal, the Appeal Chamber cannot modify a decision to the detriment of the convicted person, for example, by increasing a sentence beyond that imposed at trial or by adding convictions under additional counts. In order to determine an issue, the Appeal Chamber can also call evidence. An appeal is decided by a majority of the judges.

On the discovery of new evidence, it is also possible to seek revision of a conviction or sentence. Revision involves intervention at the appellate level that does not call into question findings of the Trial Chamber. The discovered piece of evidence may relate to false evidence or forged or falsified document on which conviction was based or to a serious misconduct or breach of duty on the part of a judge of the Trial Chamber.[76] While granting the review, the Trial Chamber may reconvene the original Trial Chamber, constitute a new Trial Chamber or dispose of the matter itself. In the event of discovery of a miscarriage of justice as a result of new facts where a person has already suffered punishment, that person is entitled to compensation, unless he was responsible for the non-disclosure of the fact in question.[77]

Trial under the South Asian Military Legal Systems

Under the military legal system, the rationale for dispensing justice through military tribunals vested with varying powers is that military discipline requires the quick disposal of offences relating to armed forces personnel. The tribunals are constituted depending upon the nature and gravity of the offence and the rank of the accused. Under the South Asian military legal systems, the court martial[78] is the single most important institution for disciplining military forces, preventing atrocities and punishing military personnel for offences committed during peace, war or on active service.

Ad hoc Tribunals

Military tribunals (general court martial, district court martial, summary general court martial and summary court martial) constituted under the Army Act (or Air Force Act or the Navy Act) are *ad hoc* with an aim to secure obedience to the commander. The general court martial and summary general court martial are competent to try any offence listed in the Army Act and award a penalty up to the death sentence. Other courts-martial [79] have limitations of jurisdiction with regard to the offence and the categories of personnel they can try. The court martial is a criminal court and has no civil jurisdiction. [80] Only a court martial that is properly convened and composed is authorised to render valid judgements.

Role of Convening Authority

Under the military legal system prevalent in South Asian, the convening authority, who is a senior military commander, plays a decisive role in the administration of military justice. He appoints investigating officers, decides the charges, selects the court members,[81] controls their future service career, provides legal aid to the accused and reviews the findings of the court martial. He can set aside the findings of the court martial or send back the proceedings for review by the same court. He also has the right to reduce or mitigate sentences imposed on the convicted person. He can deny the service of a defence counsel on the ground of expediency. In short, the convening authority plays a dominant role in the military legal system and controls every aspect of disciplinary proceedings. Naturally, there are problems inherent in a system that gives the commander such absolute control over judicial matters. The rights of the individual soldier are rarely accorded much weight or consideration and commanders with such sweeping powers can easily abuse the system to the point where the rule of law is replaced by the commander who operates as a law unto himself. Besides, the rights available to an accused during a trial by a court martial do not conform to the international standards.

Other nations, such as the US, the UK, Australia, Canada, Israel and South Africa have restricted the role of the commander in their military justice systems in order to limit actual bias as well as accusations and perceptions of unlawful command influence in judicial proceedings.

Military Judiciary

In the South Asian countries, the Judge Advocate General (JAG) is the superintendent of the administration of military justice. The Army, Air Force and Navy have their own JAGs who head the judiciary of their respective services. The judicial department has a selected cadre of officers qualified in law. The judge advocate does not perform any of the functions either of an advocate or of a judge. He does not preside at a court martial trial, but sits besides the presiding officer in the capacity of the legal adviser to the court, prosecution and defence, and as the representative of the Judge Advocate General.[82] Unlike the military justice systems of other democracies,[83] the JAGs in the South Asian countries are organisationally and operationally subordinate to the convening authority, who controls their service career. The officers of the JAG department, therefore, may not be independent and thus in a position to give a fair and just opinion.

Sentencing

Another shortcoming in a trial by court martial, as compared to the Rome Statute of the ICC is that decisions regarding 'guilt' as well as 'sentencing' are taken by military officers untrained in law. An enlightened sentencing decision requires a sophisticated and informed judicial officer. And only a trained and experienced judge can truly evaluate any additional factors necessary for determining an appropriate sentence.[84]

International standards mandate that all persons shall be entitled to **equality before the courts** (including equal access to courts). Every individual is entitled to a **fair and public hearing** held by a competent, independent and impartial tribunal established by law.[85] The establishment of special courts for certain categories of persons, such as military personnel is, however, not prohibited as long as the procedural guarantees are observed.

The Right to Appeal [86]

The general right to a fair hearing established in Article 67 of the Rome Statute provides defendants with a powerful tool to go beyond the text of the Statute, and to require that the Court's respect for the rights of an accused keep pace with the progressive development of human rights law. [87] **In the context of post-trial rights,** international standards mandate that anyone convicted of a crime shall have the **right to appeal to a higher authority,** i.e., the right to have the conviction reviewed by a higher tribunal, to ensure at least two levels of judicial scrutiny of the case. The guarantees of fair trial must be observed throughout the review proceedings.

In contrast, the military legal systems of the South Asian countries do not provide for any right to appeal[88] against the decision of a military court, a legacy of the British administration.[89] They also fall short of the international legal standards in that they do not provide free legal aid, are not free from command pressure and are prone to being applied with discretion. As a result, neither the persons tried by these systems nor outsiders perceive of them as just and fair. To a military accused, such a system does not provide the necessary safeguards required in a fair trial.[90] To an outsider, courts-martial seem readily subject to manipulation by commanding officers. While these problems affect all military trials, whether for routine indiscipline or serious abuses, they are invariably exacerbated when the victim is an alleged militant. In such cases, the military justice system is seen as being unjust by both the accused who feel that they are being treated unfairly, and the victims of abuse and their families who feel that justice has not been done.

The international consensus that perpetrators of international crime should not go unpunished is being advanced by a flexible strategy, in which newly established international tribunals, treaty obligations and national courts all have their role to play.[91] In countries like the US, the UK, Australia, Canada, China, Israel, Switzerland, and the Republic of South Africa the military legal system has been amended to make it compatible with the international norms.[92]

Military Legal Training

The IHL, encompassing the Geneva and Hague Conventions, set out the duties and responsibilities of commanders and soldiers and the legal parameters within which the military profession must operate. The conduct of training in the armed forces must be a command responsibility. Para 87 of Additional Protocol I requires a military commander to (i) prevent, suppress and report to higher authorities breaches of IHL; and (ii) ensure that members of the armed forces under his command are aware of their obligations under IHL. In cases where a commander is aware that his subordinates have either committed or are about to commit a breach of IHL, he must take necessary steps to prevent such violations and initiate disciplinary or penal action against violators. Many of the world's militaries have put these obligations into practice by disseminating IHL as widely as possible to the rank and files. The governments in the South Asian countries must ensure that IHL is integrated into all relevant aspects of military doctrine, education, training manuals and justice system.

Challenges Ahead

In the last 20 years, the national legal systems in the SA countries have made qualitative advances. This is due, in large part, to the impact of international human rights norms on national legislation. The international legal system now includes the concept of international criminal accountability for the commission of certain international crimes, and the emerging concept of the duty to protect the human rights of innocents. In March 2006, the UN General Assembly adopted the "Basic Principles and Guidelines on the Right to a Remedy and Reparation for Victims of Gross Violations of International Human Rights Law and Serious Violations of International Humanitarian Law". [93] This UN document states that in cases of gross violations of international human rights law and serious violations of international humanitarian law constituting crimes under international law, States have the duty to investigate and prosecute the person allegedly responsible for the violations.

The international standard relating to "superior responsibility" should be incorporated so that it does not appear that South Asian military commanders have a greater degree of immunity in military operations than those from the rest of the world. Moreover, adopting such a standard will bring the military justice system of the South Asian countries in line with the customary international law of war.

At present, the South Asian military legal systems do not have any provision to deal with crimes against humanity per se, meaning that such crimes are not defined and codified in accordance with international standards. While there are some war crimes that can be prosecuted under these systems, there are many for which there is no jurisdiction in military criminal law. There is a need to include certain crimes pertaining to internal or international armed conflicts in the military manuals. For example, (i) attacking civilians, (ii) attacking civilian objects, (iii) attacking personnel or objects involved in humanitarian assistance, (iv) employing prohibited bullets, (v) using protected persons as human shields, (vi) starvation as a method of warfare, and (vii) destroying or seizing the enemy's property.

Crimes against humanity and war crimes have been defined and incorporated in the criminal codes of Australia, Canada, Germany, The Netherlands, New Zealand, South Africa, Spain, Argentina, and the United Kingdom. This has enabled them to prosecute the same crimes as are within the subject matter jurisdiction of the ICC. Even as non-parties to the Rome Statute, the South Asian countries must modernise their military codes to fully incorporate genocide, crimes against humanity, and war crimes to enable them investigate and prosecute alleged civilian and military perpetrators of such crimes. This would shield their nationals from the scrutiny of the ICC under the principle of complementarity, which is based on a nation's ability and willingness to prosecute the same crimes as are found in the ICC's jurisdiction.

Article 67 of the Rome Statute guarantees the highest standards of protection for the rights of the accused in all trials before the ICC. The right to a fair trial and the other due process protections in the Rome Statute were derived principally from the ICCPR[94] and partly from the UDHR. These rights need to be guaranteed by all the South Asian countries in every trial conducted at the national level, including trials of international crimes.

Global cooperation in the context of UN peacekeeping missions makes it necessary for these countries to take a broader, international approach while evaluating their military legal systems. Not only would an international perspective furnish ways of improving these systems, but it would also alter the manner in which these systems are perceived. Implementation of the Rome Statute provides an excellent opportunity for any State to affirm its abhorrence of the crimes mentioned in the Statute and establish universal jurisdiction over them. The term 'implementation' encompasses measures that must be taken both in wartime and peacetime. In this discussion, we would like to focus on peacetime implementation measures that are necessary to ensure that (a) both civilian and the military personnel are familiar with the rules of IHL; (b) the structures, administrative arrangements and personnel required for compliance with the law are in place; and (c) legal mechanisms for punishing violations of this law exist. [95]

National Committees for the Implementation of IHL

National implementation of humanitarian law is an on-going process requiring the cooperation of a range of government ministries and national organisations. A number of States[96] have established national committees or working groups on IHL bringing together national authorities, experts, and in some cases organisations such as the National Red Cross or Red Crescent Society. The role and composition of these committees vary from country to country, in some cases covering both human rights and humanitarian law. While there is no legal obligation to establish such committees, they have been found to be a valuable means of promoting national implementation of IHL.[97] Only Nepal and Sri Lanka have so far constituted the National Implementation Committee. All the South Asian countries must make attempt to establish national committee for implementation of IHL.

The organisation and objectives of a national committee must be determined by the State at the time of the committee's formation. However, since its purpose is to further the implementation and promote knowledge of IHL at the national level, the committee should have the following characteristics:

- It should be able to evaluate existing national law in the light of the obligations created by the Conventions, Protocols, and other instruments of IHL.
- It should be in a position to make recommendations for further implementation, to monitor the law and ensure it is applied. This may involve proposing new legislation or amendments to existing law, coordinating the adoption and content of administrative regulations, or providing guidance on the interpretation and application of humanitarian rules.
- The committee should play an important role in promoting activities to spread knowledge of IHL. It should have the authority to conduct studies, propose activities, and assist in making IHL more widely known. The committee should therefore be involved in instructing the armed forces in this domain, teaching it at various levels of the public education system and promoting the basic principles of IHL among the general population.

Given its functions, a national humanitarian law committee requires a wide range of expertise. The committee must include representatives of the government ministries concerned with implementing IHL. Precisely which ministries are relevant will depend on the committee's mandate, but they are likely to include Defence, Foreign Affairs, Internal Affairs, Justice, Finance, Education and Culture. It may also be useful to have representatives of legislative committees, members of the judiciary and personnel from the headquarters of the armed forces.

Perhaps the best way to resolve the issue would be for the South Asian governments to amend their military legal systems to comport with the international standard.[98] The South Asian countries would have to ensure that an arrested military person must be informed of the date, time and location of arrest, and should have the right to be informed about the offence for which he is arrested. He must be allowed to contact one person of his choice at public expense and make at least one telephone call to a legal advisor at public expense. In all trials before military tribunals the accused should be entitled to the services of a qualified lawyer of his own choice as defence counsel.[99] The counsel should be made available at a sufficiently early stage of the proceedings so that he can fully advise the accused and continue to do so through all the stages up to appeal. This would ensure undivided loyalty of the defence counsel to the accused.

The South Asian countries need to incorporate provisions of Article 14 of the ICCPR into the military manuals to ensure that the accused is provided the basic guarantees of fair trial. These countries should also incorporate the concept of "command responsibility" and Article 6, 7 and 8 (2) of the Rome Statute into their military Acts.[100] The penalties applied to a particular crime under military law need not be the same as those in the Rome Statute, but they must be commensurate with the seriousness of crimes. The death penalty existing in the SA military legal systems is more severe than those provided in the Rome Statute. However, the SA countries must ensure prohibition of cruel, inhuman or degrading punishments.[101] There should be no immunity for armed forces personnel from prosecution for crimes under international law.[102] There is also a need to create a mechanism so that a victim of a miscarriage of justice is suitably compensated by the government.[103]

The judicial branches (Judge Advocate General) of the armed forces need to be alienated from the military chain of command. Military judges must be from the JAG branch as they would have necessary independence to withstand pressure from the senior military commanders. The decisions of the military tribunals should be made appealable to higher civilian courts and finally to the Supreme Court of the country.[104]

For dissemination of the IHL, it is necessary to publish a military manual on IHL and to distribute them to military and paramilitary circles. The training on IHL needs to be incorporated in the doctrines of military and paramilitary forces in all the South Asian countries.[105]

Being members of the United Nations, the South Asian countries need to foster respect for international law and treaty obligations. A significant advantage of such a course would be that the international standard would be clearly codified as domestic law and allow the armed forces to continue with their policy of trying service members alleged to have violated the law by a court martial.

The principle of 'complementarity' built into the Rome Statute ensures that the ICC does not displace the responsibility of States to prosecute the most serious crimes of international concern. However, to reserve the right to do so, a State must conform to the international standard. Seen in this context, it would be advisable for the South Asian countries to amend their military Acts to create a basis of culpability for commanders equal to the international standard. It would be beneficial from a policy standpoint for the armed forces to try those who violate the law of war as criminals under domestic law rather than as war criminals. Moreover, asserting that domestic jurisdiction exists to cover alleged violations of the law of war may prevent jurisdiction from being asserted by another country or an international tribunal.

At the heart of the international criminal justice system are the measures that must be taken by individual States under their own legal systems to prosecute international criminals on behalf of the international community. These national procedures and mechanisms need to be clearly prescribed, comply with international human rights law, and be of sufficient quality so that in dealing with the worst criminals, international justice is not brought into disrepute. It is hoped that the SAARC forum will continue to strive for the enforcement of humanitarian norms throughout the region.

Notes

1. Sandoz Y, Swinarski Christophe and Zimmermann Bruno (eds.). 1987. *Commentary on the Additional Protocols of 8 June 1977 to the Geneva Conventions of 12 August 1949*, Geneva: ICRC.
2. The International Committee of the Red Cross (ICRC), has uncovered a large body of customary rules the majority of which are claimed to apply to both international and non-international armed conflicts. Henckaerts Jean-Marie and Louise Doswald-Beck. 2005. *Customary International Humanitarian Law Rules: Volume I Rules*, Cambridge: Cambridge University Press.
3. Sassoli Marco, The Implementation of International Humanitarian Law: Current and Inherent Challenges, *Yearbook of International Humanitarian Law*, Vol. 10, 2007, p.45-73.
4. Article 47, 48, 127 and 144 of the respective four Geneva Conventions of 1949.
5. Information as of 7 June 2010, available at http://www.icrc.org/IHL.nsf/(SPF)/party_main_treaties/$File/IHL_and_other_related_Treaties.pdf
6. Bangladesh (4 April 1972), India (9 November 1950), Nepal (7 February 64), Pakistan (12 June 1951) and Sri Lanka (26 February 2006).
7. A. The Geneva Conventions Act, 1960, does not seem to have been an adequate piece of legislation incorporating India's international humanitarian law obligations into domestic law. The Supreme Court of India has noted some of the limitations of the Act in *Rev. Mons. Sebastiao Francisco Xavier dos Remedios Monteiro* v. *The State of Goa,* AIR 1970 SC 329, as follows: "To begin with, the Geneva Conventions Act gives no specific right to any one to approach the court. The Act was passed under Art. 253 of the Indian Constitution read with entries 13 and 14 of the Union List in the Seventh Schedule to implement the agreement signed and merely provide for certain matters based on Geneva Conventions. What method an aggrieved party must adopt to move the Municipal Court is not very clear. The Act by itself does not give any special remedy. It does give indirect protection by providing for penalties for breaches

of Conventions."

B. Sri Lankan Government adopted the Geneva Conventions Act, No. 4 of 2006, 26 February 2006 and published in the Official Gazette on 3 March 2006. The Act gives effect to the Geneva Conventions of 1949. It contains provisions on the punishment of grave breaches of the four Geneva Conventions and establishes universal jurisdiction over these crimes. The Act sets out the obligation to serve notice of trial of protected prisoners of war and internees on the protecting power or on the prisoner's representative. It contains provisions on the legal representation of persons brought for trial for a breach of the Act, on appeals by protected prisoners of war and internees, on reduction of sentence and on custody. The Act also establishes the jurisdiction of the High Court of Sri Lanka for the purpose of determining whether persons who have taken part in hostilities should be granted prisoner-of war status in accordance with Article 5 of the Third Geneva Convention. The Act provides for the prevention and sanction of misuse of the Red Cross emblem and other distinctive emblems.

8. Additional Protocol I pertains to protection for civilians and military and civilian medical personnel during international armed conflicts, while Protocol II deals with protection during non-international conflicts. Protocol I also deals with methods and means of warfare and combatants and prisoner-of-war status; protection of civilians against effects of hostilities; precautionary measures in attack; and the duty of commanders towards repressing grave breaches of Geneva Conventions and Protocol. One of the controversial aspects of Additional Protocol is that it relates to wars of national liberation. Article 1 (4) of AP I includes as 'international those 'armed conflicts in which people are fighting against colonial domination .....in exercise of their right of self-determination.' It is felt by India and Pakistan that the expanded definition could give cover to the 'terrorists' as 'irregular' fighters. Bangladesh has signed and ratified AP I and AP II on 8 September 1980.

9. On 23 March, 2010, the government of Bangladesh ratified the Rome Statute of the International Criminal Court. The Statute will enter into force for Bangladesh on 1 June, 2010, bringing the total number of States Parties to the Rome Statute to 111. By ratifying the Rome Statute, Bangladesh became the first State Party in South Asia.

10. Act No. XIX of 1973, An Act to provide for the detention, prosecution and punishment of persons for genocide, crimes against humanity, war crimes and other crimes under international law. In force since 20 July 1973. The Bangladesh Gazette, Extra, 20 July 1973.

11. Sri Lanka established its National IHL Committee in early 2000, under the chairmanship of the Legal Advisor to the Ministry of Foreign Affairs. The members of the Committee included representatives of the relevant line Ministries and departments such as the Legal draftsman's Department, the Attorney-General's Department, the Ministry of Defence and also included representatives from the Army, Navy, Air Force and the Police. The priority issues before the Sri Lankan National Committee have been the framing of enabling legislation to give effect to the 1949 Geneva Conventions. Accordingly, the Geneva Conventions Act, No. 4 of 2006 was enacted within a relatively short period of time. The Act also provides for the prevention and sanction of misuse of the Red Cross emblem and other distinctive emblems. The Committee has also recommended Sri Lanka's accession to the 1954 Convention of the Protection of Cultural Property in the times of Armed Conflict. Accordingly, Sri Lanka has acceded to the 1954 Convention.

The Committee has also discussed the work of the Directorate of Humanitarian Law and Human Rights in the Sri Lanka Army and the Human Rights Cell in the Navy and the Air Force.

12. For detail discussion see Chandran D. Suba & Chari P.R. (ed), 2010. *Armed Conflicts in South Asia 2009: Continuing Violence, Failing Peace Process*, New Delhi: Routledge.
13. In addition to Kashmir, these include India's counterinsurgency in the far northeast of the country, Pakistan's anti-terrorist operations and struggle to contain Taliban in Swat valley, Bangladesh's paramilitary 'Bangladesh Rifles' coup and killing of more than 70 military officers, Sri Lanka's attempt to end 25-years civil war--a military solution to political problem, and Nepal's Maoist in the government having problem with induction of armed Maoist in the national Army and simmering ethnic protest in the Terai plains.
14. An armed conflict has been defined as a contested incompatibility that concerns government or territory or both where the use of armed forces between two parties results in at least 25 battle related deaths in a year. Of these two parties, at least one has to be the government of a state. Harbom Lotta (ed), 2008, '*States in Armed Conflict 2007*,' Sweden: Uppasala University; Department of Peace and Conflict Research, p. 25.
15. A. Some of the accusations are deliberate attacks against civilians, forced displacement of civilian populations, the destruction of infrastructure vital to the civilian population and of civilian property are just some examples of prohibited acts that have been perpetrated on a regular basis. Individual civilians have also been the victims of violations of the law such as murder, torture, cruel treatment and outrages upon personal dignity, and rape and other forms of sexual violence. There are also allegations that have been used as human shields by the armed forces as well as non-state actors. Persons detained in relation to armed conflicts have been deprived of their basic rights, including adequate conditions and treatment while in detention, procedural safeguards aimed at preventing arbitrary detention and the right to a fair trial. Human rights workers have also been made targets at many instances.

    B. UN High Commissioner of Human Rights has alleged that in the recent conflict in Sri Lanka more than 2,800 civilians may have been killed and 7,000 others wounded since January 2009. Certain actions being undertaken by the Sri Lankan military and by the LTTE may constitute violations of international human rights and humanitarian law. http://news.bbc.co.uk/1/hi/world/south_asia/7942051.stm

    Also see Amnesty International Report 2008; Human Rights Watch Report; Waiting for Justice: Unpunished Crimes from Nepal's Armed Conflict, September 2008. Reports available at: <http://www.hrw.org/doc/?t=asia&document_limit=80,20> <http://hrw.org/english/docs/2008/04/11/global18516_txt.htm>

    C. The Pakistan army has been involved in internal conflicts since the last five decades. There were allegations that the army personnel tortured suspected Taliban militants and sympathizers in Swat where the army recently carried out anti-Taliban operations. The 10.17 minute video, showing uniformed soldiers beating, kicking and whipping civilians was put on the BBC website. There were also reports of hundreds of mutilated bodies of suspected Taliban militants at various places in Swat and other parts of the Malakand region. The bodies have given rise to allegations of extra-judicial killings by the military; but Pakistan army strongly denied the allegation. THE HINDU, New Delhi, Saturday, October 3, 2009, p. 15.

16. Grave breaches of four Geneva Conventions of 1949 are:
    Willful killing; torture or inhuman treatment, including biological experiments; willfully causing great suffering or serious injury to body or health (Art. 50/ 51/130/147 of GC 1-IV respectively).
    Extensive destruction and appropriation of property, not justified by military necessity and carried out unlawfully and wantonly (Art. 50/ 51/147 of GC I, II and IV respectively).
    Compelling a prisoner of war [or a protected person] to serve in the forces of the hostile Power (Art. 130 and 147 of GC III and GC IV respectively).
    Willfully depriving a prisoner of war [or a protected person] of the rights of fair and regular trial prescribed in this Convention (Art. 130 and 147 of GC III and GC IV respectively).
    Unlawful deportation or transfer or unlawful confinement Art (147 GC IV).
    Taking of hostages (Art. 147 GC IV).
17. The concept of individual criminal responsibility for international crimes was, for a prolonged period, a very innovative concept. It is a popularly held belief that the concept was first firmly established in international law as a result of the IMT and IMTFE judgements. Damgaard Ciara, 2008, *Individual Criminal responsibility for Core International Crimes*, Springer-Verlag Berlin, p. 86.
18. Besides offences at the time of war, other military offences triable by courts-martial are mutiny, desertion, absence without leave, use of insubordinate language, disobedience, insubordination, ill-treatment of a subordinate and violation of good order and discipline.
19. The respective armies in the South Asian countries is governed by the Indian Army Act, 1950, the Nepalese Army Act, 2006, the Pakistan Army Act 1952, and the Sri Lankan Army Act, 1949. Their Navies and Air Forces have similar Acts for governance. The amendment of the Pakistani Army Act in November 2007 awards powers to military courts to try civilians on charges of terrorism, anti-national activities, sedition, attacks on Army personnel and attacks on the President.
20. Section 22 of the Nepalese Army Act, 2006 has been considered as objectionable provision. The International Commission of Jurists, a Geneva based NGO has urged for amendment to Section 22 of the Act, as it provides for amnesty (statutory bar, or blanket immunity, from legal proceedings in any court, for acts carried out by a member of the Nepal Army in the "course of discharging his duties" that result in the death of, or loss to any person), for crimes under international law such as crimes against humanity, war crimes, and gross human rights violations in general such as extrajudicial killings, enforced disappearances and torture. http://www.icj.org/news.php3?id_article=4201&lang=en
21. Article 9 of the Statute, International Criminal Tribunal for Former Yugoslavia and Article 8 of the Statute, International Criminal Tribunal for Rwanda.
22. Article 8 of the Statute, Special Court for Sierra Leon.
23. Articles 17 and 20 (3) Rome Statute.
24. Articles 18, 19 and 53(1)(b), Rome Statute.
25. Article 17 --- *Issues of Admissibility*
    1. Having regard to paragraph 10 of the Preamble and Article 1, the Court shall

determine that the case is inadmissible where:

(a) The case is being investigated or prosecuted by a State which has jurisdiction over it, unless the State is unwilling or unable genuinely to carry out the investigation or prosecution;

(b) The case has been investigated by a State which has jurisdiction over it and the State has decided not to prosecute the person concerned, unless the decision resulted from the unwillingness or inability of the State genuinely to prosecute;

(c) The person concerned has already been tried for conduct which is the subject of the complaint, and a trial by the Court is not permitted under Article 20, paragraph 3;

(d) The case is not of sufficient gravity to justify further action by the Court.

26. The inability may refer to the lack of substantive law or the existing legislation that does not meet the standards of the recognised international human rights. Lijun Yang, 'On the Principle of Complementarity in the Rome Statute of the International Criminal Court', 4 *Chinese Journal of International Law* (2005), p. 123.
27. Newton, Michale A. Lt Col, Comparative Complementarity: Domestic Jurisdiction Consistent with the Rome Statute of the ICC, 167 *Military Law Review*, p. 20.
28. Mahnoush H. Arsanjani, 'The Rome Statute for an International Criminal Court,' (1993) 93 *AJIL* 22-25.
29. Cryer Robert, 2005. *Prosecuting International Crimes*, Cambridge University Press, p. 148.
30. The Rome Statute provides the first treaty-based statement of the criminality of violations in internal armed conflicts. There are two strands to this position. Firstly, serious violations of Article 3 and of Protocol II are international crimes, over and above the criminality of the acts that they proscribe under national law. Secondly, the body of law applicable to internal armed conflict includes not just these provisions but also laws and customs of war that were traditionally regarded as confined to international armed conflicts. Griffin Mary, Ending the impunity of perpetrators of human rights atrocities: A major challenge for international law in the 21st century, *International Review of the Red Cross*, No. 838, 30 June 2000, p. 369-389.
31. In both the preamble to the Rome Statute and in Article 5.
32. Schabas William. 2004. *An Introduction to the International Criminal Court*, UK: Cambridge University Press, p. 27.
33. Since the Nuremberg Tribunal, and the passing of the Genocide Convention in 1948, the potential criminal responsibility of individuals for acts of genocide have been generally recognised. Schmitt Paul, 'The Future of Genocide suits at the ICJ: France's Role in Rwanda and Implication of the Bosnia v. Serbia Decision', *Georgetown Journal of International Law*, Vol. 40 No. 2, Winter 2009, p. 586.
34. All the South Asian countries are signatory to the UN Convention on the Prevention and Punishment of the Crime of Genocide, and have also ratified it.
35. 1993 Statute of International Criminal Tribunal for the former Yugoslavia.
36. 1994 Statute of International Criminal Tribunal for Rwanda.
37. The four Geneva Conventions of 12 August 1949: Convention (I) for the Amelioration of the Condition of the Wounded and Sick in Armed Forces in the Field, Convention (II) for the Amelioration of the Condition of Wounded, Sick and Shipwrecked Members of Armed Forces at Sea, Convention (III) Relative to the Treatment of Prisoners of

War, Convention (IV) relative to the Protection of Civilian Persons in Time of War.

38. In the South Asian context, the operational activities of the armed forces can be summed up as follows: 1. Combat Activities: Attacks, raids and direct action, 2. Non-Combat: National assistance (A) Security assistance like (i) Combating terrorism, (ii) Counter-insurgency, (iii) Special reconnaissance, (iv) Psychological operations, and (v) Show of force. (B) International assistance and peacekeeping operations.
39. For example, the Indian armed forces have been involved in counter-insurgency operations in Jammu and Kashmir and the North-East since 1950s. The excessive use of the armed forces in counter-insurgency operations has raised the question of violation of common article 3 of the Geneva Conventions of 1949. Various human rights organisation in the country and abroad and foreign and local media have criticised the effectiveness of Indian laws dealing with violation of human rights by armed forces personnel. They have also criticised the special laws--The Armed Forces (Special Powers) Act (AFSPA), giving enhanced power to the armed forces for dealing effectively with disruptive activities in specific areas. See: Amnesty International Report 2007, p.134.
40. Article 75, Protocol Additional to the Geneva Conventions of 12 August 1949, and Relating to the Protection of Victims of International Armed Conflicts (Protocol I), 8 June 1977; and Article 8, para 2 (b) (ix) of the Rome Statute.
41. Rome Statute, Article 70; Rules of Procedure and Evidence, Rules 162-169 and 172.
42. If charged under Section 69 of the Indian Army Act, 1950. Under the Sri Lankan Army Act, a person subject to military law can be tried by a civil court for any civil offence. If such person was convicted of a civil offence and sentenced to punishment by a court martial and is afterwards tried for the same offence and convicted by a civil court, then the civil court shall, in awarding punishment, have due regard to such punishment imposed by the court martial as that person may have already undergone (Section 77).
43. Section 69 and 70 Army Act, 1950.
44. The Nepal Army Act, 2006 has special provisions (section 62) related to crime of 'Torture and Disappearance'. It provides that an investigation committee will be formed and will be chaired by Deputy Attorney General, Chief Legal officer of Defence Ministry and an officer of the rank of major of Judge Advocate General department to investigate and refer these cases to Military Special Court (MSC). The MSC has first jurisdiction to try for the crime of 'Torture and Disappearance of civilian' and its appeal can go to Supreme Court. The MSC will be chaired by Judge of Appellate court appointed by the Government, and members shall be Secretary of Defence Ministry and Judge Advocate General.
45. Kumar Brig Nilendra (2000), *Court Martial and Military Matters*, New Delhi: Manas Publication, p. 188.
46. a. Captain Harish Uppal of the Indian Army was tried by a Summary General Court martial under Section 69 of the Army Act, 1950, for committing a civil offence, that is, Robbery (under section 392 of the Indian Penal Code), at Hajiganj, Bangladesh on 11 December 1971. He was awarded punishment of cashiering. The confirming authority considered that the punishment awarded by the court martial was lenient and ordered for its revision by the court martial. In revision, the same court sentenced him "to be cashiered and to suffer two years imprisonment". His writ petition under Article 32

of the Constitution was dismissed by the Supreme Court. For details see: *Capt Harish Uppal v. Union of India* AIR 1973 SC 258.

b. Major (Substantive) Des Raj Shanwal was tried by a General Court martial under Section 63 of the Army Act, 1950 for An Act Prejudicial to Good Order and Military Discipline, and Section 69 for committing a Civil Offence (under section 403 of the Indian Penal Code) for dishonestly misappropriating weapons captured during operation in Bangladesh. He was awarded the punishment of six months rigorous imprisonment and was also dismissed from service. For details see: *Lt Col Des Raj Shanwal v. Union of India*, CWP No. 736 of 1979, 2003 (7) SLR, Delhi HC.

47. Section 21, Indian Penal Code (IPC): Every commissioned officer in the Military, Naval or Air Forces of India is a public servant.
48. The term injury denotes any harm whatsoever illegally caused to any person, in body, mind, reputation or property (Section 44, IPC).
49. Article 77 of the Rome Statute.
50. Army Act, 1950, section 71.
51. Regulations to Hague Convention No. IV of 1907, Article 1(1), according to which the members of the armed forces must be commanded by a person responsible for his subordinates.
52. *Yamashita* was Commanding General of 14th Army Group between 9 Oct 44 - 2 Sep 45 and Military Governor of Philippines. During this period his troops committed widespread, brutal atrocities including acts of violence, cruelty and homicide inflicted on the civilian population resulting in the death of over 25,000 non-combatant men, women and children.
53. *United States v. Karl Brandt and others* (the *Medical* case), Vol. II Law Reports of Trials of War Criminals 171; *United States v. Wilhelm List et al.* (the *Hostage* case), Vol. XI Law Reports of Trials of War Criminals 759; *United States v. Wilhelm von Leeb et al.* (the *High Command* case), Vol. XI Law Reports of Trials of War Criminals 1.
54. Although the Geneva Conventions do not contain specific provisions relating to individual criminal responsibility, they do contain a common article on the criminality of grave breaches of the Geneva Conventions, from which it can be implied that individual criminal responsibility attaches to such grave breaches. See Article 49/Geneva Convention I, Article 50/Geneva Convention II, Article 129/Geneva Convention III, and Article 146/Geneva Convention IV. Damgaard Ciara, 2008, *Individual Criminal Responsibility for Core International Crimes: Selected Pertinent Issues*, Berlin: Springer, p.72.
55. For example, the Third Geneva Convention (Article 129) states: "The High Contracting Parties undertake to enact any legislation necessary to provide effective penal sanctions for persons committing, or ordering to be committed, any of the 'grave breaches' of the present Convention." The 'grave breaches' to which Article 129 relates are further listed in Article 130 as (i) wilful killing, (ii) torture or inhuman treatment, including biological experiments, (iii) causing great suffering or serious injury to body or health, and (iv) compelling a prisoner of war to serve in the forces of the hostile Power, or depriving a POW of the rights of fair and regular trial.
56. The Common Article 3 of the four Geneva Conventions of 1949: The acts prohibited against these persons are: (1) violence to life and person, in particular murder of all

kinds, mutilation, cruel treatment and torture; (2) taking of hostages; (3) outrages upon personal dignity, in particular, humiliating and degrading treatment; and (4) the passing of sentences and the carrying out of executions without previous judgement pronounced by a regularly constituted court affording all the judicial guarantees which are recognised as indispensable by civilized peoples.

57. The doctrine of command or superior responsibility has since 1997 featured in more than 12 cases in ICTY and ICTR. In each of these cases, it served as a basis for establishing criminal responsibility, and in several of them, as the sole basis. There appears to have been no doubt in the minds of the judges of the Tribunal that this application of the doctrine is consistent with international law. For further details see Jia Bing Bing, 'The Doctrine of Command Responsibility: Current Problems', *Yearbook of International Humanitarian Law*, Vol. 3, 2000, p. 132.
58. In order to meet its international obligations, the UK has passed the International Criminal Court Act, 2001. The military manuals of the US, Canada and Australia have also been amended to incorporate provisions relating to command responsibility.
59. Rowe Peter. 2006. *The Impact of Human Rights Law on the Armed Forces,* UK: Cambridge University Press, p. 224-40.
60. The international laws applicable in such situations may include: (1) International humanitarian law set out in the UN Secretary General Bulletin of 1999; (2) The Fourth Geneva convention of 1949, relating to protection of civilians; (3) The Third Geneva Convention of 1949, relating to protection of prisoners of war—if there is some degree of armed conflict between two or more states; and (4) Additional Protocol I to the Geneva Conventions of 1949, if the States to which the multinational forces belong are signatories to it.
61. Every UN Peacekeeping operation consists of military personnel provided by different states. In theory, the UN force commander has general responsibility for good order and discipline of the operation. He may make investigations, conduct inquiries; however, responsibility for disciplinary action in national contingent rests with commander of the national contingent. In the case of an alleged crime, the most UN administration can do is send the peacekeeper back to his home country. Once there, the peacekeeper is subject to military laws of his country, it is in their discretion also of whether to prosecute the peacekeeper. McCoubrey H. & White ND. 1996. *The Blue Helmets: Legal regulation of UN Military Operations*, Dartmouth Publishing Co Ltd, Aldershot, p. 178.
62. The Rome Statute of the ICC represents a vital development in the laws of internal armed conflict. The adoption of the instrument by a large number of States affirms a broad view of customary status given to the international law relevant to internal conflict by the Yugoslav and Rwanda Tribunals. This is particularly important in the light of the guiding principle that those crimes within the jurisdiction of the Court should be limited to 'the most serious crimes of concern to the international community as a whole.' In addition, the Rome Statute confirms in the most authoritative manner possible that individual criminal responsibility for such violations is now beyond any measure of doubt. Moir Lindsay. 2002. *The Law of Internal Armed Conflict*, Cambridge University Press, 2002, p. 160.
63. The ICTY is of the view that effective control emerges from the superior's capacity to give orders to those under his command, there being no requirement for the order to be

given in writing or in any particular form; *Prosecutor v. Tihomir Blaskic* Case No. IT-95-14 –T, Judgement, 3 March 2000, para. 290; The Prosecutor v. Dario Kordic and Mario Cerkez, Case No. IT-95-14/2-T, Judgement, 26 February 2001, para. 388.

64. *The Prosecutor v. Zlatko Aleksovski* Case No. IT-95-14/1-A, Judgement 14 March 2000, para. 183.
65. During World War II, Churchill and other Allied leaders flirted with the idea of some form of summary justice for major war criminals. Arieh J. Kochavi. 1998. *Prelude to Nuremburg: Allied War Crimes Policy and the Question of Punishment*, Chapel Hill, NC, and London: University of North Carolina Press, p. 63-91.
66. The fair trial question can be approached in at least two ways. First, are the substantive rights accorded to the accused adequate? This approach focuses on the rights delineated in the tribunal' statute, rules of procedure and evidence, and case law—for example, the right to confront witnesses or the right to council. A second approach to the problem of fair trial asks instead, whether these international courts have the independence and coercive powers necessary to ensure fair trial regardless of the sufficiency of paper rights accorded to the accused in the tribunals' statute. For example, can these courts make certain that the accused is able to obtain the evidence and witness necessary for a serious defence. Or do the courts' judges have the independence necessary to withstand political pressure from the state on which they depend. Cogan Jacob Katz, 'International Criminal Court and Fair Trials: Difficulties and Prospects', 27 *Yale Journal of International Law* (2002), p.114-115.
67. Fundamental instruments as the UDHR and the ICCPR define basic minimum standards and include norms which must be respected by any judicial system aspiring to international legitimacy. Paulsson Jan. 2005. *Denial of Justice in International Law*, UK: Cambridge University Press, p. 6. International Covenant on Civil and Political Rights, (1966), Article 14 (3) reads: In the determination of any criminal charge against him, everyone shall be entitled to the following minimum guarantees, in full equality: (a) To be informed promptly and in detail in a language which he understands of the nature and cause of the charge against him; (b) To have adequate time and facilities for the preparation of his defence and to communicate with counsel of his own choosing; (c) To be tried without undue delay; (d) To be tried in his presence, and to defend himself in person or through legal assistance of his own choosing; to be informed, if he does not have legal assistance, of this right; and to have legal assistance assigned to him, in any case where the interests of justice so require, and without payment by him in any such case if he does not have sufficient means to pay for it; (e) To examine, or have examined, the witnesses against him and to obtain the attendance and examination of witnesses on his behalf under the same conditions as witnesses against him; (f) To have the free assistance of an interpreter if he cannot understand or speak the language used in court; (g) Not to be compelled to testify against himself or to confess guilt.
68. Article 10 and 11 Universal Declaration of Human Rights, 1948.
69. American Convention on Human Rights (1978), Article 8; European Convention on Human rights (1955), Article 6; African Charter on Human and Peoples' Rights, Article 7.
70. Geneva Convention (III) Relative to the Treatment of Prisoners of war (1950), Articles 84-87 and 99-108; Geneva Convention (IV) Relative to the Protection of Civilians (1950), Article 5, and 64-76; Protocol Additional I (1977) to the 1949 Geneva

Conventions and Relating to the Protection of the Victims of International Armed Conflicts, Article 75; Protocol Additional II (1977) and Relating to the Protection of the Victims of Non-International Armed Conflicts, Article 6.

71. Rome Statute Article 77: Applicable Penalties
    1. Subject to article 110, the Court may impose one of the following penalties on a person convicted of a crime referred to in article 5 of this Statute: (a) Imprisonment for a specified number of years, which may not exceed a maximum of 30 years; or (b) A term of life imprisonment when justified by the extreme gravity of the crime and the individual circumstances of the convicted person.
    2. In addition to imprisonment, the Court may order: (a) A fine under the criteria provided for in the Rules of Procedure and Evidence; (b) A forfeiture of proceeds, property and assets derived directly or indirectly from that crime, without prejudice to the rights of bona fide third parties.
72. Rome Statute Article 78 (2).
73. Haskell John D., The Complicity and Limits of International Law in Armed Conflict Rape, *Boston College Third World Law Journal,* Vol. XXIX, Winter 2009, No. 1, p. 78.
74. UN G.A. Res. 60/147, U.N. Doc. A/RES/60/147 (Dec. 16, 2005).
75. Rome Statute, Article 81.
76. Rome Statute, Article 84.
77. Rome Statute, Article 85. The applicable procedure for compensation in such circumstances is provided in rules of Procedure and Evidence, rules 173-175.
78. A court martial is an ad hoc military court, convened under military authority to try and punish those (particularly members of armed forces) who violate the military law. Plural: courts-martial. Black's Law Dictionary, 17th Edition, West Group St Paul, Minn. 1999.
79. Like district court martial, or summary court martial.
80. The court martial is a criminal court as per the definitions in the Indian Code of Criminal Procedure, 1973, Section 5. By virtue of Section 152 of the Army Act, 1950, trial by the court martial is a judicial proceeding and the court martial is itself deemed to be a court within the meaning of the Code of Criminal Procedure, 1973. It has been held by the Supreme Court of India that in a proceeding before court martial, rules of natural justice should be observed: *S C Patnaik v. Union of India*, 1969 Cri LJ 930 Orissa. A court martial cannot enforce a contract or award damages in favour of an individual.
81. The South Asian military legal systems do not ensure that military officers constituting the tribunal (Courts Martial) are legally qualified or have the necessary independence from the operational military hierarchy. They may also be subjected to external interference in their judicial functions. According to Zappala, Impartiality and independence of the judges in the system of the *ad hoc* tribunals are guaranteed both in general and in *concreto*. The judges are employed full time and shall not exercise activities in conflict with their judicial function. They are elected by the General assembly and their conditions of employment are the same as those of the judges of the International Court of Justice. Zappala Salvatore. 2002. 'The Rights of the Accused,' in Cassese Antonio (ed), *The Rome Statute of the International Criminal Court: A Commentary*, Vol II, p. 1333-34.
82. The Nepalese Army Act (section 81) is an exception and provides that an accused may

request for a judge advocate from JAG Department to defend him during the trial by a court martial.

83. The UK, the USA, Australia, Canada, South Africa and Israel. For further details see: Jha UC. 2009. *The Military Justice System in India: An Analysis*, LexisNexis, p. 210-219.
84. Tonry Michael. 'The Functions of Sentencing and Sentencing Reform,' 58 (1) *Stanford Law Review* (2005), p. 37-66.
85. Article 14 ICCPR contains a catalogue of "minimum [procedural] guarantees" for an individual undergoing a trial for criminal charges. See n. 65 supra.
86. For Rights of the accused in trail proceedings see, Zappala, Salvatore, 2008, *Human Rights in Criminal Proceedings*, New York: Oxford University Press, p. 83-179.
87. Schabas William A. 2004. *An Introduction to the International Criminal Court*, Cambridge University Press, p. 98.
88. Generally, appeals serve two purposes. First, they function as a mechanism whereby parties can obtain a more favourable outcome to the proceedings. Second, appeals promote ideals such as consistency and fairness and regulate uniform interpretation of the law. Trechsel Stefan. 2005. *Human Rights in Criminal Proceedings*, New York: Oxford University Press, p. 362.
89. 1. India has become an exception to this as the Armed Forces Tribunal Act and its Benches have started functioning since August 2009, to hear appeals from court martial. 2. The Nepal Army Act, 2006 provides that a military accused alleged to have committed offences of 'torture or forced disappearance of civilians' to be tried by a special military court and shall have the right to appeal to the Supreme Court (section 62). 3. Lahore High Court's Rawalpindi bench has recently issued a judgment setting aside the conviction of a lieutenant colonel by the Field General Court Martial (FGCM). This is hailed as a "revolutionary" decision that might "open the floodgates to appeals against the military justice system". The higher courts in Pakistan have generally not interfered in the decisions of the military courts. http://letusbuildpakistan.blogspot.com/2009/01/lahore-high-court-makes-history-by.html
90. For example: free legal aid, the right to be defended by a counsel of his choice or financial assistance to hire services of a counsel.
91. Jonathan Charney, 'International Criminal Law and the Role of Domestic Courts,' 95 *AJIL* (2001), 120.
92. Today, the US military justice system gives military members virtually all the rights and privileges afforded to citizens who face prosecution in civilian courts. In many areas, such as, the right to counsel, pre-trial investigations, plea-bargaining, sentence, post-trial process, and appeals, the military justice system offers benefits that are more favourable to the accused than those available in the civilian system. It provides a series of review and appellate forum to ensure that the military accused does not suffers injustice: 1. Staff Judge Advocate (SJA) Review; 2. Automatic Review and Article 69 Process; 3. Military Courts of Criminal Appeals; 4. United States Court of Appeals for the Armed Forces; and 5. United States Supreme Court. Jha UC. 2009. *The Military Justice System in India: An Analysis*, LexisNexis, p. 107-130.
93. Adopted and proclaimed by General Assembly resolution 60/147 of 16 December 2005. Article 1 states that the States have an obligation under international law to ensure that their domestic law is consistent with their international legal obligations by: (*a*)

Incorporating norms of international human rights law and international humanitarian law into their domestic law, or otherwise implementing them in their domestic legal system; (*b*) Adopting appropriate and effective legislative and administrative procedures and other appropriate measures that provide fair, effective and prompt access to justice; and (*c*) Making available adequate, effective, prompt and appropriate remedies, including reparation.

94. ICCPR Article 14 paragraph 1 is of general application to the administration of justice and sets out various requirements in this regard. First, all persons are to be equal before courts and tribunals. Second, any determination of such courts and tribunals must be through a fair and public hearing by a competent, independent and impartial tribunal established by law. The minimum requirements to ensure a 'fair hearing' are under paragraph 3 of the Article. Conte Alex. 2004. *Defining Civil and Political Rights: The Jurisprudence of the United Nations Human Rights Committee*, UK: Ashgate, p. 117.
95. Kadam Umesh, Implemetation of International Humanitarian Law in Japan: The ICRC Perspective. Available at: < http://wwwsoc.nii.ac.jp/jsil/annual_documents/2005/2005_autumn/Kadam.pdf > visited 7 March 2009.
96. For example, the South Africa's National Committee on IHL was established in April 2006 by a decision of the executive management committee of the Department of Foreign Affairs. The Committee will be chaired by the Department of Foreign Affairs and composed of two representatives from relevant government entities (such as the ministries of Foreign Affairs, Justice, Defence, Police, Health and Education). The Committee may co-opt members from outside the government (e.g. the ICRC and academic circles). The Committee is assigned a broad mandate and should act as a focal point, providing leadership on all issues related to the domestic implementation and dissemination of IHL.
97. The Intergovernmental Group of Experts for the Protection of War Victims recommended that States "be encouraged to create national committees, with the possible support of National Societies, to advise and assist governments in implementing and disseminating IHL" and "to facilitate cooperation between national committees and the ICRC".
98. A number of countries have adjusted their legislations to ensure that it is possible to prosecute international criminals especially in domestic courts. Joseph Rikhof, 'Fewer Places to hide? The Impact of Domestic War Crimes Prosecution on International Impunity', *Criminal Law Forum*, Vol. 20, March 2009, p. 1-51.
99. *Estrella v Uruguay* (1983) (74/180) 29 March 1983. The Human Rights Committee opined that the assignment of a counsel by the court contravenes the principles of fair trial if a qualified lawyer of the accused's own choice is available and willing to represent him.
100. Article 87 of the AP I states, "any commander who is aware that subordinates or other persons under his control are going to commit or have committed a breach of the Conventions or of this Protocol, to initiate such steps as are necessary to prevent such violations of the Conventions or this Protocol, and, where appropriate, to initiate disciplinary or penal action against violators thereof." [The US Army Field Manual 27-10]. Nonetheless, commanders who fail to discharge their duty are rarely prosecuted for their failure to punish. A military commander's failure to punish constitutes a separate offence from the underlying atrocity that his troops have committed. The

failure to punish is therefore a substantive offence, and it renders the commander criminally liable or the atrocity itself. Sepinwall Amy J. 2009. 'Failure to Punish: Command Responsibility in Domestic and International Law', *Michigan Journal of International Law*, Vol. 30, No. 2, p. 255-56.

101. Article 5 of the UDHR states that "no one shall be subjected to torture or to cruel, inhuman or degrading treatment or punishment". Similar words have been used in several other international and regional documents, such as Article 7 of the International Covenant on Civil and Political Rights and Article 5 of the African Charter on Human and Peoples' Rights. Article 3 of the European Convention on Human Rights is worded slightly differently, declaring that 'no one shall be subjected to torture or to inhuman or degrading treatment or punishment', but the omission of 'cruel' is not significant since the term 'inhuman' is apt to cover such cases.

102. 1. For instance section 22 of the Nepalese Army Act, 2006 states: **Defending the acts performed in the discharge of duties:** No case may be filed in any court against a person under the jurisdiction of this Act who commits any act in good faith, in the course of discharging his duties, resulting in the death of or loss suffered by any person. Explanation: For the purpose of this Section, the phrase "committing any act in good faith, in the course of discharging his duties," means acts performed during the performance of duties as well as any action taken for internal security or self-defence, including flag march, patrolling and sentry duty. [**Such provision would need deletion**].

2. It is also necessary that the governments in the South Asian countries have effective control over the armed forces. There must not be a fear that an exhortation to the armed forces to apply IHL or human rights during the conflict will result in, or the threat of military coup. A possible consequence of such fear could be that the State may tolerate what are clear breaches of IHL or human rights carried out by the armed forces and thereby create a feeling of impunity on the part of soldiers concerned.

103. ICCPR Art 14 para 6. This provision exists under section 276 of the UK Armed Forces Act, 2006; and mirrors the civilian equivalent in section 133 of the British Criminal Justice Act, 1988.

104. The right to access to courts is fundamental and uncontroversial; its refusal the most obvious form of denial of justice. Paulsson Jan. 2005. *Denial of Justice in International Law*, UK: Cambridge University Press, p. 134.

105. For instance, the Indian Army, in 2000, has released its 'Doctrine', containing various aspects of military functioning. Section 20 of this 'Doctrine' focuses on operational and logistics training, professional progression and intellectual development at various levels. It states: "A dynamic, comprehensive and operationally-focused training philosophy is a mandatory requirement for producing combat- ready troops and units... Training must remain operationally-oriented, need-based, contemporary and structured towards practical applications." However, this document is silent upon the training in the IHL.

11

Conclusion and Recommendations

The South Asian region—India, Pakistan, Sri Lanka, Bangladesh, Nepal, Bhutan and Maldives—was the seat of one of the oldest civilizations which flourished over 4000 years ago. More than a thousand years after the decline of this civilization in the Indus region, much of it was unified under the able administration of the Mauryas. Agriculture thrived and so did crafts. Towns grew around markets, and ports established trade links with the outside world. The glorious past of this region is not the subject of this book. Yet it does seem ironical that today, it is known for poverty, internal disturbances and human rights challenges.

Most of the countries of the region were under colonial rule and gained independence after the Second World War. Since then, border conflicts have escalated and security concerns have often overshadowed regional cooperation. The nuclear tests conducted by India and Pakistan in 1998 have pushed the security competition to a new level. Today, the strength of active military and paramilitary forces in the region exceeds four million.

In the South Asian countries, excluding Nepal, the services are divided into the army, navy, and air force and each service has an independent code for its governance. In theory, the three service chiefs are coequals in the national command structure. However, in practice, the army dominates the defence establishment because of its imposing size. In the case of Pakistan and Bangladesh, the army chiefs have played a historical role in monitoring or commandeering the political process. In Bangladesh and Pakistan, coup leaders consolidated control over the country by assuming the powers of the army chief of staff, the president, and the extra-constitutional position of chief martial law administrator. During periods of direct military rule, the navy and air force chiefs of staff served as deputy chief martial law administrators, subordinate to the army chief of staff.

Though the militaries in South Asia have been modernising their arsenals, they are still governed by archaic legislations drafted by colonial rulers for the governance of mercenary forces. The statement of the French statesman Georges Clemenceau that "military justice is to justice what military music is to music" aptly describes the military justice systems of the South Asian countries. By and large, the military courts in these countries do not adhere to the general principles and international standards of justice and their procedures violate the rule of law. In all the countries, military justice is organisationally and operationally dependent on the military executive. Military judges are military personnel on active service who are subordinate to their respective commanders and subject to command influence.

Defenders of the military legal system have traditionally brushed off criticisms by claiming that reforms would be against military or national interests. Such defenders forget that the issue is not whether armed forces are necessary or whether they need a separate legal system, but whether that system satisfies the requirements of (i) the general principles of law and the international standards of justice, (ii) independence and impartiality, and (iii) international obligations with regard to human rights.

In all the South Asian countries, except Nepal, military courts are empowered to award the death sentence after a summary trial, where no law-trained officer is required to be present. The sentence awarded by a summary court cannot even be challenged in a civil court, except in India, where appellate tribunals were established only in August 2009. Military courts in Bangladesh and Pakistan have been used to try civilians. Commenting on this, the United Nations Special Rapporteur on the independence of judges and lawyers concluded that "international law is developing a consensus as to the need to restrict drastically, or even prohibit, that practice".[1]

In the South Asian countries, issues related to the functioning of the military legal systems remain shrouded in secrecy. In Western democracies such as the UK, the USA, Australia and Canada, reports of the military's judicial branch are open to public scrutiny and debate. In South Asia, however, a researcher would find it extremely difficult to obtain any information about the military legal system and the trials held under it. In India, though courts-martial have been declared public courts, their proceedings are invariably classified as 'confidential'. The mere possession of the records of these proceedings by a common man may lead to his prosecution under the Official Secrets Act.[2] Even the Defence Service Regulations of the Indian Army, which may be required to be examined in a military court or higher civilian courts by the defence counsel contains the warning: "The information given in this book is not to be communicated, either directly or indirectly, to the press or any person not holding an official position in the service of the Government of India".[3]

Evolving Military justice

The idea that "where there is an army, there is military justice" is not true and a large number of countries have abolished military jurisdiction either completely or at least in peacetime. Other countries have introduced safeguards into their constitutions or passed legislation in order to ensure against gross violations of human rights and to remove the trial of civilians from military jurisdiction. Several countries have amended their laws to ensure that members of the military who commit military offences enjoy the safeguards that are necessary for a fair trial. The European Court of Human Rights has held that "the armed forces of a country exist to protect the liberties valued by a democratic society, and so the armed forces should not be allowed themselves to march over, and cause substantial damage to such principles."[4]

According to Fidell (2002), "Military justice is going through a period of ferment that is both rare and broad."[5] In the past 30 years, the military organisation and its management have undergone a sea change in many parts of the world. Let us consider a few cases.

In Indonesia, the House of Representatives has placed on its list of priorities a proposal to amend the law on military courts, and formed a special committee to draft such a bill. The Indonesian president has stated that he would support the empowerment of civilian courts to try military personnel who commit ordinary crimes, and to limit the military court's authority to offences committed by military personnel in the context of their military duties.[6]

In the period 1974-85, Belgium saw the development of jurisdictional control of preventive detention, on the basis of the European Convention on Human Rights (ECHR). Since 1 January 2004, it has abolished military courts in times of peace. The old law of 1899 was found to be incompatible with the ECHR. The new law provides that in times of peace, members of the Belgian army shall be tried by civilian courts even for crimes committed outside Belgium. A new military court and a new procedure has been created for offences committed during war. The Office of the Military Judge Advocate General is a hierarchical body made up of professional military judges. It has three main functions: it is the representative of the Public Prosecutor's Office, it is responsible for the Judicial Police and it carries out military criminal investigations. On behalf of the Public Prosecutor's Office, the Office of the Military Judge Advocate General brings charges before the military courts and must ensure that all decisions and verdicts issued by the latter are properly enforced. Lastly, the victims and their successors can seek damages within the context of military criminal proceedings.[7]

In Canada, the Canadian Charter of Rights and Freedoms, an integral part of the Canadian Constitution, has been a remarkable catalyst for amending the military justice system and bringing it at par with the civilian justice system. In 1992, the Supreme Court of Canada affirmed the necessity for a separate military justice system. The latest changes to court martial system include:

(i) providing for non-commissioned members at or above the rank of warrant officer to sit as members of General and Disciplinary Court Martial panels when the accused is a non-commissioned member; (ii) reducing the period of detention that may be awarded at courts martial from two years to ninety days in keeping with the rehabilitative objectives of detention; and (iii) eliminating the death penalty from the scale of punishments in the Code of Service Discipline on the basis that it was no longer required as a punishment for service offences and its removal was consistent with other federal law. For the most serious offences, imprisonment for life with no eligibility for parole for twenty-five years has been substituted.[8]

In Finland, the military prosecution system was reformed in 2001. Prosecution tasks were shifted from military legal advisers to public prosecutors in order to prevent any possible influence of military authorities on court proceedings. In Ireland, a comprehensive review of the Irish military law system has been undertaken, with a view to adapt domestic law to the needs of European Convention on Human Rights (ECHR), including relevant decisions of the European Court of Human Rights (ECtHR). Israel too has in recent years re-evaluated its military legal system and carried out some reforms in consonance with the human rights norms laid down in the ECHR.

In the past, the military judiciary of the Netherlands decided whether a soldier was to be prosecuted for an alleged offence. If prosecution was decided upon, the soldier would be tried by a court martial. This meant that prosecution, sentence, punishment and execution were all in the hands of the military, with no civil exertion. In 1990, the system of military criminal law and military disciplinary law was modernised after a review of the existing legislation. Several new codes came into being and the jurisdiction over soldiers was transferred to civil courts. It is now concentrated at the Arnhem District Court and the Arnhem Court of Appeal. Disciplinary power and disciplinary measures are regulated in the *Wet Militair Tuchtrecht* (WMT). The public prosecutor, who is a civil servant, decides upon the prosecution of a soldier. Separate military chambers provide the necessary military element.[9]

The military justice system in the UK, to which South Asian military law owes its origin, has undergone a sea change. It has been extensively reformed since 1996 to ensure that it reflects the provisions of the ECHR more closely. In order to pre-empt the final decision of the ECtHR in *Findlay v UK*, [10] the country passed the Armed Forces Act, 1996, to revise the procedures and guarantee the objectivity and impartiality of courts-martial, largely by removing the conveners, court members and prosecutors at courts-martial from the normal military chain of command. The Human Rights Act, 1998, abolished the death penalty and replaced it with imprisonment.

In the year 2000, military persons in the UK were given the right to appeal to the ECtHR against the decisions of courts-martial. Next, the Armed Forces Act, 2001, made changes in the procedure for the trial and punishment of offenders under the Air Force and Army Acts. These include extending the eligibility for court martial membership to warrant officers, awarding costs for hiring a defence counsel, providing for the review of minor punishments awarded by the commanding officer by establishing a Summary Appeal Court, and for compensation for miscarriage of justice. The Armed Forces Act, 2006, consolidated service law into a single system. It abolished multiple systems of court martial and replaced these with a standing court martial. An accused now has an absolute right to elect trial by a court martial, and even where he does not so elect, he has the right to appeal to the Summary Appeal Court (SAC).

The Senate Committee constituted by the parliament of Australia, in its report on the "Effectiveness of Australia's Military Justice System" in 2005, made several recommendations for restructuring the country's military justice system. These resulted in the creation of the office of the Inspector General of the Australian Defence Force (IGADF). The role of the IGADF is to identify systematic causes of injustice within the military justice system and to provide a mechanism whereby the system can be reviewed and audited independently of the chain of command. The IGADF reports directly to the Chief of the Defence Force (CDF), and may investigate matters pertaining to discipline as well as administration. The Defence Legislation Amendment Act, 2006, has made several other changes in the Australian military justice system on the basis of the report of the Senate Committee. The Parliament replaced the court martial system with a standing court, the Australian Military Court (AMC). Recently, the High Court of Australia, in *Lane v. Morrison* (2009), has unanimously struck down the recently created AMC, declaring it unconstitutional.[11]

New Zealand's military justice system is based on the Armed Forces Discipline Act, which was enacted by Parliament in 1971 and came into force in 1983. In 1990 Parliament enacted the New Zealand Bill of Rights Act, which gave a range of international human rights protections the force of New Zealand law. In the decade which followed the Courts started to give increasing weight to human rights, including in the Armed Forces.

Taking note of these changes in 2002 the Chief of Defence Force commissioned a thorough review of the military justice system to ensure that it could operate properly in a changed legal landscape. At the same time, the opportunity was taken to design a system specifically for the needs of the defence force in the 21st century. From 1 July 2009, the new system has been introduced, aimed to modernise and provide a fairer justice system for all military personnel. The following five key changes have been introduced in the new system: (i) the summary trial system will operate across all three services; (ii) there will be a right of appeal from summary trials; (iii) summary trial will be available for senior officers; (iv) a permanent, independent court martial has replaced ad hoc courts martial;[12] and (v) two new offences of negligence: negligently failing to perform a duty and negligence performance of duty have been introduced. The right of the accused to elect trial by court martial instead of being tried summarily has been enhanced, as has the right to legal representation.

In France, since the abolition, in 1982, of military tribunals in peacetime, infractions of military laws, including common law offences committed by military personnel in the line of duty, fall within the competence of the ordinary criminal courts composed exclusively of civilian judges. Review of legality is ensured by the Court of Cassation, as in the case of the country's other jurisdictions. Military jurisdiction exists only for military personnel serving abroad and in time of war.[13] The same trend is to be noted in Germany, where persons who commit military offences are tried, in peacetime, by the ordinary criminal courts. Constitutional review is now carried out by the Federal Court of Justice instead of the Supreme Military Court. Thus, military penal tribunals exist only in times of war, and their decisions also remain subject to review by the Federal Court of Justice, which is composed of civilian judges.[14]

Prior to 1950, Americans in uniform were governed by legal procedures originally designed for mercenaries. So antiquated and unjust was the system that after World War II, there was a great protest by returning veterans, who demanded reforms which would guarantee to servicemen the basic principles of due process of law (Erwin, 1969).[15] This outcry resulted in the adoption of the Uniform Code of Military Justice Act (UCJM) in 1950.[16] Upon the enactment of the Military Justice Act of 1968, the military justice system attained virtual parity with the civilian justice system. In fact, under the military justice system, an accused has rights that are in many ways superior to those provided to a defendant in (civilian) criminal courts.

In the US, military courts, authorised by Article I of the Constitution, have jurisdiction over cases involving military members, including, in some cases, retired members. They have the power to convict for crimes defined in the UCMJ, including both uniquely military offences and crimes with equivalent definitions in civilian laws. The military court system includes courts-martial; a Criminal Court of Appeals for each branch of the armed services; and the US Court of Appeals for the Armed Forces (CAAF), which has discretionary appellate jurisdiction over all military cases. The US Supreme Court, the highest court in the USA, hears appeals from the CAAF. With the exception of potential final review by the US Supreme

Court, these Article I courts handle review of military cases in an appellate system that rarely interacts with Article III courts.[17]

Criminal defendants under the Article III judicial system have an automatic right to appeal to federal courts of appeal and then a right to petition the Supreme Court for final review. In contrast, defendants in military cases typically may not appeal to the US Supreme Court unless the highest military court, the CAAF, grants discretionary review.[18] In order to remove this disparity, two Bills have been introduced in the 111th Congress, the Equal Justice for Our Military Act of 2009 (H.R. 569) and the Equal Justice for Our Military Personnel Act of 2009 (S. 357). If passed, these Acts would authorise appeals to the US Supreme Court for all military cases, even if the CAAF declines review. They would amend the UCMJ to authorise appeals to the Supreme Court in military cases, regardless of the CAAF's acceptance or denial of an appeal. The UCMJ represents a masterful piece of legislation that balances the need for good order and discipline with the constitutional rights afforded to all United States citizens. It gives members virtually all rights and privileges that are afforded to citizens who face prosecution in civilian courts. In fact, in many areas---such as the right to counsel, the pre-trial investigation process, discovery, sentencing, post-trial processing, and appeals--the military system offers to an accused more safeguards than those available in the civilian system.[19]

The Chinese Army has traditionally held a privileged position within society and the State. In Imperial China, the Army was the main pillar of power on which the dynasties were built. In 1949, with the creation of the People's Republic of China, the beginnings of a military court system came into being. Chinese military courts were constantly active during the period of the Cultural Revolution. Under the 1954 Constitution of the People's Republic of China, military courts were set up as a form of special people's court as well as courts of appeal under the supervision of the Supreme People's Court.[20]

In 1982, a new Constitution of the People's Republic of China was adopted. With a few amendments made in 1988 and 1993, it remains in force. According to article 124 of the Constitution, the Chinese judicial system is made up of the Supreme People's Court, local people's courts, military courts and other special people's courts. Military courts are therefore special people's courts.[21] Like all people's courts, whether ordinary or special, military courts come under the judicial supervision of the Supreme People's Court. In all cases, 'military justice' is dispensed by the Military Court of the People's Liberation Army, the military courts of the regions, and the local military courts. The local military courts are attached to the units which make up the three branches of the People's Liberation Army. They try offences committed by military personnel below the rank of

Regiment or Battalion Commander as well as offences which do not carry the death penalty. In addition, as delegated by the military courts for the respective main military regions, they can try other cases that are assigned to them. The prosecutorial function in military courts is exercised by the Chief Prosecutor from the Military Prosecutors' Office, who is appointed by the Standing Committee of the National People's Congress.[22]

In South Africa, the need for a new military justice system was felt when the government conceded that the former system, dating back to the era of apartheid, was unconstitutional. The new military justice system has created permanent military courts under the Military Discipline Supplementary Measures Act 16 of 1999 (MDSMA) and the Military Discipline Code (MDC). It is applicable in peacetime as well as during war. The reforms have ensured greater conformity of the military justice system to the rule of law and human rights.

The principles of human rights have influenced the military justice systems of particularly those States that are party to the ECHR (for example, the UK) and those that are affiliated to such States, for example, Australia, Canada and New Zealand. The reason for this seems to be the access that offended individuals have to obtaining binding decisions by the ECtHR. In such decisions, the Convention is not only applied, but also interpreted in a way that entails a measure of progressive development. Highly relevant, in this context, is Article 5, paragraph 1 (a), which lays down that "Everyone has the right to liberty and security of person. No one shall be deprived of his liberty..." Equally relevant is Article 6, paragraph 1, which lays down:

> In the determination of his civil rights and obligations or of any criminal charge against him, everyone is entitled to a fair and public hearing within a reasonable time by an independent and impartial tribunal established by law.

These articles impose restrictions on the extent to which punishments can be awarded by summary procedures without due process. They also demand that military courts have to be independent. This means you cannot have a court composed of officers convened by a commander who may have an interest in the outcome, since justice must not only be done, but it must also be seen to be done.

We can grade the various military justice systems along an axis of 1–6, with the traditional, fully military courts-martial system at one end and the fully civilianised system at the other, as follows.

1 →	2	3	4	5	6
Court martial convened for individual cases. No right to appeal.	Court martial convened for individual cases. The right to appeal available.	Standing military courts, and standing appeal courts	Specialised civilian courts for military personnel	General civilian courts for military personnel in peacetime	General civilian court in peacetime and war

All changes in military justice systems have been from the left to the right in this table.[23] The military legal systems of Bangladesh, Nepal, Pakistan and Sri Lanka fall under the first category, where courts-martial are convened for individual cases. The Indian military justice system is in the process of shifting to the second category.

In general, the evolution of military justice across the world has enhanced the rights of the accused with reference to international human rights standards. The important elements of this evolution are greater independence of judges, establishment of standing courts, increased right to elect trial instead of summary procedures, and increased right to legal representation. There are, furthermore, trends with regard to shifting from military to civilian jurisdiction, particularly in peacetime, by reducing the competence of military courts, abolishing military courts and abolishing military prosecution. These trends are particularly visible in countries that are under the influence of the ECHR.

The concept that human rights are basic rights of all human beings, and that they are rights which must be guaranteed and which must be enforceable under the law derives from the idea of a society based on the rule of law. The establishment of independent courts not subject to executive control is a cardinal necessity of the rule of law (Barnett, 1998).[24] Military courts in the South Asian countries, with their arbitrary system of trial, thus cannot be said to adhere to the principles of the rule of law.

One of the main reasons for the persistence of an antiquated military legal system in the South Asian countries is the legal fraternity's lack of awareness about the system. To a great extent, the officers of the judge advocate branch may be held responsible for this. There is hardly any critical study of the system carried out by serving or retired officers of the branch. Even in cases where the civilian judiciary has criticised the system, the tendency amongst the military officers, including those of the judge advocate branch has been to defend the system, on the grounds that it is time-tested and indispensable for discipline. The military's legal branch in all the South Asian countries has remained indifferent to the changes in other democracies, and instead of recommending reforms, has tried to maintain the status-quo. Perhaps, the main reason for this is the military judiciary's subordination to the executive, and its dependence on the executive for career progression and perks. In a research study undertaken in India, on a question whether the judge advocates enjoy an independent status and are free to give their fair and just opinion in a trial, more than 50 per cent of respondents were of the view that they are not.[25] Since there is no legislative or administrative requirement, the armed forces as an institution have never undertaken any comprehensive study of their legal system.

Whether the courts or tribunals in any country are independent of the executive can be determined by seeing whether in cases of prosecution by the State, the outcome is never in doubt. Thus the civil courts in South Asia can be called independent, but military tribunals can certainly not be given this status because they remain under the command influence all the time. The accused is invariably found guilty and the only point in question is the severity of the sentence. The military courts are dependent on or subservient to the military executives and thus the whole concept of human rights is undermined in a military trial. The provisions are command-centered, commanders having extensive disciplinary powers. The sole purpose of a military trial is "to secure obedience to the commander". There are no independent civilian tribunals to review the 'administrative' decisions of the military commanders. The general and field general courts-martial can award death as the highest punishment. Very few changes have been made to military laws since their inception under imperial rule. It is the paramount duty of the government in each of these countries to bring about changes in the military justice system to ensure that the course of justice is not perverted. This change can be brought about only by making comprehensive changes in the military justice delivery system.

Judicial Intervention

The defence forces are so insulated from the rest of society that ignorance about military matters is not restricted to the uneducated. Even the judiciary in the South Asian countries is not fully equipped with knowledge about military matters. Since judges generally deal with civil cases, their understanding of military law is limited. It thus becomes tempting for them to choose the path of least resistance by supporting the military establishment in any controversial case. In the case of India and Sri Lanka, the few cases in which the courts have intervened have had little impact on military governance. The courts are generally of the opinion that any adverse comment on military authorities or any judgement against the military establishments may erode discipline in the armed forces. The judiciary perhaps in good faith believes that by supporting the organisation, it is affording an opportunity to the military hierarchy, as well as the government, to rectify the defects in the military justice delivery system.

In Bangladesh and Pakistan, the judiciary was assigned the subordinate role of giving its stamp of approval to every measure and every step taken by the military regime. The judiciary never dared to intervene in the military's internal affairs. It would be far-fetched to expect military commanders who abrogated the Constitution and violated the human rights of the masses to introduce human rights standards in the military justice system. Thus successive military governments have not taken any action to review the services Acts. The civil governments have been no better in this regard. And the soldier remains at the mercy of a legal system which was originally designed to enforce discipline in a mercenary force.

The Nepalese army has always been sovereign. When the Royal Army became a democratic army, the Army Act of 1959 was replaced by the Army Act, 2006. The new Act emphasizes the training of army personnel in human rights and international humanitarian laws. It also departs from the military laws of Bangladesh, India, Pakistan and Sri Lanka in that it makes specific provisions that offences related to torture and disappearance should be investigated and tried by a special court, and not by *ad hoc* military tribunals. It gives military personnel the right to move the Supreme Court against sentences awarded by the military tribunals.[26]

Recommendations

The existing system of military justice in the South Asian countries is an inheritance from imperialist rule. It is archaic, belonging to an age when the army was a band of mercenaries, and the system was regulated by the mere power of military command rather than the rule of law. Having undergone very little change in the last fifty years, the system remains under the control of the military commander, who exercises an almost unrestrained and unlimited discretion over it. The South Asian countries have modernised their military arsenals in the last twenty years, and two of them are nuclear powers. However, they have not made any reforms in their military justice systems on the basis of the emerging human rights norms or the prevailing civilian criminal justice system.

The recommendations are:

Military Legal System

- In the military statutes, most offences relating to the enemy, as well as mutiny, are punishable by the death penalty, while for other offences, imprisonment ranges from seven to 14 years. One may argue that these punishments are required for the effective functioning of the armed forces. However, the prescription of harsh punishment needs to be rationalised, keeping in view the changes made in other democracies. Since a large number of South Asian military personnel participate in peacekeeping missions with the armies of other countries, there is a need to maintain parity among the military legal systems.

- The jurisdiction of military courts should be limited to offences of a strictly military nature, which largely means internal disciplinary measures.
- The civil crimes, including those that amount to human rights violations, should be tried in ordinary civil courts, using established procedures in line with international standards. In particular, crimes involving serious violations of international human rights and humanitarian law, including rape and other forms of torture, extrajudicial executions and enforced disappearances, should be heard in the ordinary courts and not military tribunals.[27]
- An arrested military person must have the right to (i) be informed about the offence for which he is arrested; (ii) be informed of the date, time and location of arrest; (iii) contact one person of his choice at public expense; and (iv) make at least one telephone call to a legal advisor at public expense.
- In all trials before military tribunals, the accused should be entitled to the services of a qualified lawyer of his own choice as defence counsel.[28] The counsel should be made available at a sufficiently early stage of the proceedings so that he can fully advise the accused and continue to do so through all the stages up to appeal. This would ensure undivided loyalty of the defence counsel to the accused. The infrastructure required to meet the obligation to provide legal aid must be developed in the armed forces.[29]
- Military commanders the world over have been given statutory powers to dispose of minor offences committed by members of the military. The punishment awarded is not expected to have any adverse effect on the career of the accused.[30] The punishment awarded in a summary trial should also not be degrading and humiliating. It must not be such as to arouse in its victim feelings of fear, anguish and inferiority. The field punishment existing in the military statutes in Bangladesh, Nepal, Pakistan and Sri Lanka, needs to be abolished.
- There is no provision of bail for a military person arrested in connection with an offence. It is entirely at the discretion of the commanding officer or the superior military authority whether the person is released from arrest/ custody. The South Asian countries must provide a forum where cases for bail and appeals from summary trial can be taken up by an independent military judicial authority.
- Trial by SCM in the South Asian countries does not come up to the recognised standards of justice because there is no prosecutor and the court itself performs

some of the functions of the prosecutor. The accused is not entitled to defend himself with the help of a counsel or defending officer. Similarly, the SGCM is empowered to award the death sentence in a summary trial in which the accused is invariably denied the right to a fair trial. Both these *ad hoc* systems need to be abolished.

- The convening authority, by virtue of his position, has sweeping powers under the military legal system. Besides detailing a court of his choice, he virtually controls the entire judicial process. Even if he does not wish to influence the functionaries directly, they function under the command influence. The convening authority's power needs to be rationalised and divided among independent authorities to meet international standards.
- The officers of the JAG department are qualified in law, but do not function either as advocates or judges. The department of the JAG is placed under the administrative and functional control of the same executive who orders a trial by court martial and reviews the proceedings. Because of their position, the officers of the JAG department cannot be expected to give a fair and just opinion. They need to be insulated from the military chain of command.
- Though military tribunals in the South Asian countries have the jurisdiction to consider criminal offences, whether of a military nature or otherwise, they do not have the requisite characteristics of a judicial body, namely, competence, independence and impartiality. These shortcomings undermine the possibility of a fair trial in accordance with international standards. Military tribunals must, in all circumstances, apply internationally guaranteed fair trial procedures, as those required of ordinary courts.
- A court martial constituted under military law determines both the findings and sentence. Since the members of such a court are neither legally qualified, nor trained in the administration of justice, they must not be associated with the award of the sentence. This task must be allocated to the judge advocate.
- Unlike the military justice systems of the UK or the USA, the South Asian countries do not have an exclusive appellate forum where appeals against the decision of a court martial could be preferred. The "special court" in Nepal and the armed forces tribunals in India are not exclusive civilian appellate courts, as in the UK and the USA. Anyone convicted of a criminal offence has the right to a review of that decision by a higher judicial tribunal. An independent appellate forum consisting of judicial officers must be created in all the South Asian democracies.
- The protection against double jeopardy is enshrined in constitutions the world over.[31] In the countries under discussion, whilst this is available before a court martial, it is not available to prevent a second trial on the same offence before

a civil court. A person subject to military law in Bangladesh, Pakistan and Sri Lanka, and to the Air Force Act in India, who has once been tried and convicted or acquitted before a court martial can be tried again on the same charge by a civil court.[32] Armed forces personnel need to be protected against double jeopardy.

- The Nepal Army Act has been criticised because it provides impunity to the armed forces.[33] Section 22 of the Army Act, 2006, provides that no case can be filed against an army person who commits any act in good faith while discharging his duties, though it may result in the death of or loss to any person.[34] Provisions which give statutory immunity are problematic and need deletion.
- The issue of gender discrimination and inequality in the armed forces has been raised on a number of occasions. Since all the South Asian countries are signatories to CEDAW, an effort must be made to ensure that all members of the armed forces receive the same benefits and are treated equally.
- A military person, who is a victim of miscarriage of justice must be suitably compensated.[35]

International Human Rights

- International human rights law not only recognises the individual human rights of every human being, it also puts an obligation on states to ensure, secure or guarantee the effective enjoyment of human rights. These rights are enshrined in a number of international human rights treaties and international jurisprudence holds that they can be considered to be an obligation of customary international law. The duty to ensure effective enjoyment of human rights implies, amongst other things, that the state must adopt all necessary legislative and other measures to give effect to the rights guaranteed in international law,[36] an obligation confirmed many times by international human rights bodies.[37] In order to comply fully with their duty to give effect to human rights, South Asian states have to ensure human rights through their entire "legal, political and institutional system" and to organise "the governmental apparatus and, in general, all the structures through which public power is exercised, so that they are capable of legally ensuring the free and full enjoyment of human rights". They need to incorporate the provisions of Article 14 of the ICCPR into their military manuals to ensure that the accused is provided the basic guarantees of fair trial.
- The duty to ensure human rights also means that human rights impose a multidimensional obligation on states. In addition to the duty to adopt all necessary legislative and other measures, there are four main components

of the state's obligation. The state has a duty to prevent violations and to respect, protect, and promote human rights. The duty to respect entails the obligation to refrain from acts which would violate the rights; the duty to protect can be understood as the duty to protect persons from acts which would impede the enjoyment of their rights; and the duty to promote means the duty to take measures such as dissemination, training and education. Moreover, all human rights always have a procedural component, such as the obligation of states to provide adequate remedies and procedures for protection against human rights violations and investigation of these violations. The governments in the South Asian Countries have a duty to: (a) take legislative and other measures to give effect to rights, (b) investigate human rights violations, (c) provide effective remedies against violations, (d) bring perpetrators of certain violations to justice, and (e) provide reparation to victims.[38]

- The different obligations of the state are complementary and not alternative, and cannot be substituted for one another. The obligations of the state are also unconditional: they do not depend on one another, nor are they conditional on an individual complaint. They cannot be renounced by victims. While victims may, of course, renounce the individual reparation that is due to them, the state cannot, for instance, forego its obligation to investigate and make public the truth on gross human rights violations and to punish the perpetrators. This is a duty that the state has not only towards victims, but towards society as a whole.[39] The *UN Set of Principles for the Protection and Promotion of Human Rights through Action to Combat Impunity* [40] states: "The right to reparation shall cover all injuries suffered by the victim; it shall include individual measures concerning the right to restitution, compensation and rehabilitation, and general measures of satisfaction as provided by international law."[41] For victims of gross human rights violations, the South Asian countries must adopt all necessary legislative and other measures to give effect to rights, to investigate human rights violations, to provide effective remedies against violations, to bring perpetrators of gross human rights violations to justice, and to provide reparation to victims.
- The governments in the South Asian countries need to ensure that civilians are not subjected to the jurisdiction of ad hoc military tribunals as these put a veneer of legality on the impunity of the military members.[42]
- In times of state emergencies, recourse to martial law should not compromise the guarantees of a fair trial. Any derogation "strictly required by the exigencies of the situation" should be consistent and military tribunals should not be substituted for ordinary courts, in derogation from ordinary law.

International Humanitarian Law

- The South Asian countries should incorporate the concept of "command responsibility" and Articles 6, 7 and 8 (2) of the Rome Statute[43] into their military Acts.
- The penalties applied to a particular crime under military law need not be the same as those in the Rome Statute, but must be commensurate with the seriousness of crimes. The death penalty existing in South Asian military legal systems is more severe than any penalty provided in the Rome Statute. However, the South Asian countries must ensure prohibition of cruel, inhuman or degrading punishments.[44]
- The judge advocate branch of the respective services needs to be separated from the military hierarchy and placed under the ministry of either law or justice. This branch needs to be suitably augmented to impart military personnel with training in international humanitarian law (IHL) and provide advisors to commanders in the battlefield. This would ensure that military commanders give due consideration to humanitarian law while undertaking operations and choosing means and methods of warfare.
- The governments in India, Bangladesh, Nepal, Pakistan and Sri Lanka must ensure that effective remedy for serious violations of IHL[45] is available when a civilian has been allegedly tortured or killed by military personnel. The governments must ensure that their domestic laws provide at least the same level of protection for victims as that required by their international obligations.
- IHL also establishes minimum guarantees in judicial matters. In time of conflicts, the principles of humanitarian law, and in particular the provisions of the third Geneva Convention of 1949 and common Article 3 of the Geneva Conventions of 1949 or are fully applicable to military courts. An individual accused of having committed an offence related to the conflict is entitled to a fair trial. To ensure this, the judgement must be given by a court offering the essential guarantees of independence and impartiality.
- The decisions of military tribunals should be made appealable to higher civilian courts and finally, to the Supreme Court of the country.[46]
- There should be no immunity for armed forces personnel from prosecution for crimes under international law.[47]
- The armed forces must ensure that IHL, international human rights laws are integrated into the military's doctrine, training, operation and sanctions.
- The governments in Bangladesh, India, Pakistan and Sri Lanka must establish national committees to ensure implementation of IHL. It is important that such a committee include qualified persons. These may be individuals who

are not associated with government ministries, but who are appointed for their expertise in the fields of law, education, communications, and so on.

Armed forces personnel, like the other nationals of a country who are involved in criminal proceedings, whether as defendants, victims or witnesses, should have the assurance that they will receive an impartial hearing, that their rights will be respected and that, if they must stand trial, they may participate effectively in the critical examination of the evidence brought against them by the prosecution. The goal of the criminal law system should be to enforce respect for the rule of law, which will be impossible unless transgressions can be effectively submitted, publicly and in the presence of both parties, before independent and impartial tribunals devoted to upholding human rights.

This presupposes a specific and demanding role for those who, by whatever right, participate in judicial proceedings, as well as the existence of strict rules of procedure to ensure justice and equality for all parties to the case. Article 10 of the Universal Declaration of Human Rights requires the existence of an independent and impartial tribunal. This means that neither judges nor their courts should have any vested interest in the proceedings. There should be no corporatism and no interference from the hierarchy. Article 11 of the Universal Declaration of Human Rights requires guarantees of the right to defence and, in criminal cases, the presumption of innocence.

The South Asian countries have the right and the duty to protect the security of all those under their jurisdiction. This can be best ensured by security measures that respect human rights and the rule of law. Human rights law allows states to respond to security threats effectively, for example by giving them the right to limit and suspend certain rights in a state of emergency, but it also requires the maintenance of the rule of law. A state of emergency should be an extension of the rule of law in difficult circumstances, and not an abrogation of it. The military law system of the South Asian countries should adopt a procedure which is not only open and objective, but which also strives towards a liberal interpretation of the principles of natural justice.

The military justice must be "an integral part of the general judicial system". It is necessary to situate the development of military justice within the framework of the general principles for the proper administration of justice. Military tribunals must comply with the rules of international human rights law, not only in respect of civilians but also in respect of military personnel. The integrity of the judicial system, whether military or civil, should be observed at all times. To this end, the South Asian countries need to civilize their military justice system.

Notes

1. United Nations document E/CN.4/1998/39/Add.1, paragraph 78.
2. The Indian Official Secrets Act, 1889 was later replaced by the British Official Secrets Act, 1911. Since difficulty emerged in applying same in India, it was replaced by the Official Secrets Act, 1923. Other countries of the region have similar legislations.
3. .....the (Indian) defence ministry, among other security agencies, lacks a declassification procedure is beyond doubt. There are almost no official records available to scholars interested in this field. Even scholars at India's "official" and service-affiliated think tanks consisting of IDSA, CLAWS, CAPS, CENJOWS and NMF are denied access to data. As a consequence, they mostly churn out papers on every subject but that which analyses processes within the military.....Denial of access also prevents the creation of civilian expertise on these matters, weakening the quality of debate and ultimately India's democracy. As scholars and citizens are denied historical documents, there is little serious study or instruction on these institutions in civilian universities...... Rare is an enclave member who can challenge the institutional myths and official positions of his parent organisation. In the long run, this is harmful for democracy as different perspectives and counter-arguments are not adequately debated. Mukherjee Anit, Tell It Like It Is, The Times of India, New Delhi, June 9, 2010. http://timesofindia.indiatimes.com/Home/Opinion/Edit-Page/Tell-It-Like-It-Is/articleshow/6024645.cms
4. *Smith and Grady v. UK* (27 September 1999) at para.83.
5. Fiddel Eugene R. 'A worldwide Perspective on Change in Military Justice', in Fidell Eugene R. and Dwight H Sullivan (ed.), *Evolving Military Justice*, USA: Naval Institute Press, 2002, p. 209-217.
6. http://upiasia.com/Human_Rights/2009/09/23/bringing_justice_to_indonesias_military_court/6292/
7. Military Jurisdiction and International Law: Military Courts and gross Violations of Human Rights, Geneva: International Commission of Jurists, 2004, p. 181-185
8. Pitzul Brigadier-General Jerry ST and Commander John C Maguire, Canadian Code of Service Discipline, 52 *Air Force Law Review* (2002), p. 1-16.
9. Besselink Leonard FM. 2003. 'Military Law in the Netherlands', in Nolte Goerge (ed.), *European Military Law Systems*, Berlin: De Gruyter Recht, p. 624-645.
10. *Findlay v The United Kingdom* (1997) 24 EHRR 221.
11. In 2006, Australian Parliament passed sweeping reforms to Australia's military justice system in response to a 2005 Senate inquiry which found serious problems with the military justice system. Parliament replaced the court martial system with a standing court, the AMC, which was to display some features commonly associated with courts. The AMC commenced on 1 October 2007. But ex-Royal Australian Navy sailor Brian Lane brought a challenge to the new system after he was charged for a 2005 incident which alleged he had placed his genitals on a Royal Australian Army sergeant's forehead - - known as "teabagging". The High Court held that laws creating the Australian Military Court required it to use the exercise of judicial power of the Commonwealth conferred under Chapter III despite it being stated in the legislation it wasn't a court under the Constitution. Thus the High Court ordered a writ of prohibition barring the court from proceeding in cases. The Court ruled that the country's military justice system is unconstitutional because its judges are not independent of the military command — throwing into doubt 171 cases judged in the past two years. *Lane v.*

Morrison [2009] HCA 29.

12. Section 78, Armed Forces Discipline Act 1971, as amended, on 1 July 2009, by section 22 (1) and (2) of the Armed Forces Discipline Amendment Act (No 2) 2007 (2007 No 98), provides that the Court Martial has jurisdiction to try any charge against a person subject to this Act in respect of an offence against this Act, whether committed in New Zealand or elsewhere.
13. Disciplinary power and measures are regulated by three main texts: the General Statute of the Military from 1972, the Decree No. 75-675 of 28 July 1975—Regulation of General Discipline in the Armed Forces (RGDA) and the Code of Military Justice. The RGDA has been modified by Decree No. 2001-537 of 20 June 2001. Gerkrath Jorg, 'Military Law in France', in Nolte Goerge (ed.), *European Military Law Systems*, Berlin: De Gruyter Recht, p. 275-336..
14. Nolte George. 2003. 'Military Law in Germany', in Nolte Goerge (ed.), *European Military Law Systems*, Berlin: De Gruyter Recht, p. 337-425.
15. Ervin, Sam J. 1969. 'The Military Justice Act of 1968,' 45 *Military Law Review*, p.77-98. Edmund, M. Morgan. 1965. 'The Background of the Uniform Code of Military Justice,' 28 *Military Law Review*, p. 22.
16. The Uniform Code of Military Justice contained in Title 10 of the United States Code, Sections 801 through 946. It is the military's criminal code. The foundation of military law is the Constitution of the United States.
17. Schlueter, David A. 2004. *Military Criminal Justice: Practice and Procedure*. US: LexisNexis.
18. Roan, Lieutenant Colonel James B. 2002. 'The American Military Justice System,' 52 *The Air Force Law Review* 2002.
19. Rives, Major General Jack L. and Major Steven, J. Ehlenbeck. 2002. 'Civilian Versus Military Justice in the United States: A Comparative Analysis,' 52, *Air Force Law Review,* p.213-232.
20. Military Jurisdiction and International Law: Military Courts and gross Violations of Human Rights, Geneva: International Commission of Jurists, 2004, p. 217-220.
21. Report by the Working Group on Arbitrary Detention - Addition Visit to the People's Republic of China, United Nations document E/CN.4/1998/44/Add.2, 22 December 1997, paragraph 17.
22. Article 67 of the Constitution.
23. Dahl Arne Willy, '*International Trends in Military Justice*', Judge Advocate General for the Norwegian Armed Forces and the President of the International Society for Military Law and the Law of War.
24. Barnett, Randy E. 1998. *The Structure of Liberty, Justice and the Rule of Law*. Oxford: Clarendon Press.
25. The respondents (n=220) included serving and retired officers of three services, personnel below the officer rank and advocates with exposure in the military justice system. Jha U C. 2009. *The Military Justice System in India: An Analysis*, New Delhi: LexisNexis, p. 223.
26. Sections 20, 62 and 119, Nepal Army Act.
27. The same rules apply whether a soldier of the South Asia is accused of committing a human rights violation within the country or while serving overseas. When the Army operates overseas in peacekeeping or similar international operations, its military

personnel are subject to the laws of the country in which they serve and should be tried by the civilian courts in that country for crimes that are not internal military matters, including acts that amount to human rights violations. However, in most cases the jurisdiction of the local courts is excluded because of a Status of Forces Agreement (SOFA) setting up the peace-keeping operation, or under a similar agreement giving immunity to the foreign military personnel. If so, then the military personnel should be tried by the civilian courts in their country for such non-military crimes committed overseas, as they should be if the act was committed domestically.

Principle 29 of the Updated Set of Principles for the Protection and Promotion of Human Rights through Action to Combat Impunity (the "Impunity Principles") provides: "The jurisdiction of military courts must be restricted solely to specifically military offences committed by military personnel, to the exclusion of human rights violations, which shall come under the jurisdiction of the ordinary courts or, where appropriate, in the case of serious crimes under international law, of an international or internationalised criminal court." E/CN.4/2005/102/Add.1, 8 February 2005.

28. *Estrella v Uruguay* (1983) (74/180) 29 March 1983. The Human Rights Committee opined that the assignment of a counsel by the court contravenes the principles of fair trial if a qualified lawyer of the accused's own choice is available and willing to represent him.
29. The insufficiency of legal aid to the accused during a court martial is a serious defect of the present systems. The most significant is the absence of the services of an experienced legal officer as counsel for the accused. Except in Sir Lanka, where counsel is allowed, the other military systems do not give an exclusive right to the accused to engage a civilian lawyer at government expense. In reality, very few of the accused can engage a civilian lawyer at their own expense and service officers normally detailed for the duty are inexperienced and unwilling to undertake this commitment.
30. The human rights issues that might arise in these cases are whether (a) the punishments awarded could amount to torture, or degrading or inhuman treatment, and (b) if the cumulative effect of the punishment is serious, whether the accused had the right to refuse summary trial and face a court martial, where detailed procedural rights are available.
31. Indian Constitution, Article 20 (2); Pakistan Constitution, Article 13, Nepal Intérim Constitution Article 24 (6).
32. Pakistan and Bangladesh Army Acts, section 96; Sri Lanka Army Act, section 77; Indian Air Force Act, section 126. The provision of successive trial by a criminal court and a court martial contained in section 127 of the Indian Army Act were omitted in 1992, The Nepal Army Act, section 70 provide protection against double jeopardy.
33. International Commission of Jurists Report, September 2006.
34. Section 22. Defending the acts performed in the discharge of duties: No case may be filed in any court against a person under the jurisdiction of this Act who commits any act in good faith, in the course of discharging his duties, resulting in the death of or loss suffered by any person.
35. ICCPR Art 14 para 6. This provision exists under section 276 of the UK Armed Forces Act, 2006; and mirrors the civilian equivalent in section 133 of the British Criminal Justice Act, 1988.
36. Article 2 (2) ICCPR; Article 2 (c) & (d) CERD; Article 2 (a) CEDAW; Article 4 CRC;

and Article 2 (1) CAT.

37. Human Rights Committee: *General Comment No 31 on Article 2 of the Covenant: The Nature of the General Legal Obligation Imposed on States Parties to the Covenant*, 21 April 2004, CCPR/C/74/CRP.
38. *General Comment No 31 on Article 2 of the Covenant: The Nature of the General Legal Obligation Imposed on States Parties to the Covenant*, 21 April 2004, CCPR/C/74/CRP.4/Rev.6. Also see Case *X and Y v the Netherlands*, Judgement of 26 March 1985, Series A 91, para 27; Case *Aksoy v Turkey*, Judgement of 18 December 1996, Reports 1996-V I, para 98.
39. The *UN Principles and Guidelines on the Right to a Remedy and Reparation for Victims of Gross Violations of International Human Rights Law and Serious Violations of International Humanitarian Law* stipulate that reparation "includes the following forms: restitution, compensation, rehabilitation, satisfaction and guarantees of non-repetition". Adopted by Commission on Human Rights Re solution E/CN.4/RES/2005/35 of 20 April 2005 and by General Assembly resolution 60/147 of 16 December 2005.
40. Recommended by the Commission on Human Rights resolution 2005/81 of 21 April 2005. In its resolutions on impunity, the UN Commission on Human Rights has noted that these Principles have already been applied at regional and national levels: E/CN.4/RES/2004/72, 21 April 2004, para 16; E/CN.4/RES/2003/72, 25 April 2003, para 14; E/CN.4/RES/2005/81, para 21.
41. Principle 34. The International Court of Justice has also stated in its judgement in the case of *Avena and other Mexican Nationals*, 'what constitutes "reparation in an adequate form" clearly varies depending upon the concrete circumstances surrounding each case and the precise nature and scope of the injury, since the question has to be examined from the viewpoint of what is the "reparation in an adequate form" that corresponds to the injury.'
42. In the case of *Rodrigo Rojas De Negri and Carmen Gloria Quintana Arancibia v. Chile*, in which two young people were detained by a military patrol and then beaten, doused in petrol and set on fire and which had been dealt with by the Chilean military courts, the Inter-American Commission on Human Rights pointed to "the various irregularities pertaining to legal process inherent in the military justice system in Chile" and stated that "the actions of these military courts have served to provide a veneer of legality to cover up the impunity which the members of the Chilean Security Forces enjoy when they are found to be involved in flagrant violations of human rights".352 The Commission also stated that, "these irregularities pertaining to legal process inherent in Chilean military justice are reflected in the abusive recourse to secrecy in the conduct of the proceedings. The situation that has thereby arisen has made it virtually impossible to gain access to basic elements of the trial and allows the military authorities to control the evidence submitted. Annual Report of the Inter-American Commission on Human Rights, 1987-1988, OEA/Ser.L/V/II.74, Doc. 10 Rev. 1, 16 September 1988, Resolution N° 01a/88, Case 9,755 (Chile), Considerings 7(c).
43. War crimes, genocide and crimes against humanity have to be incorporated in the military legal systems of the South Asian countries. These crimes have been defined and incorporated in the criminal codes of Australia, Canada, Germany, The Netherlands, New Zealand, South Africa, Spain, Argentina and the United Kingdom. This has enabled them to prosecute the same crimes as are within the subject matter of jurisdiction of

the ICC. Under the principle of complementarity, a nation's ability and willingness to prosecute the same crimes as are within ICC jurisdiction essentially shields that nation's nationals from ICC scrutiny. Article 67 of the Rome Statute guarantees the highest standards of protection for the rights of the accused in all trials before the ICC. These rights need to be guaranteed by all States in every trial conducted at the national level, including trials of international crimes. The right to a fair trial and the other due process protections in the Rome Statute were derived principally from the ICCPR and partly from the Universal Declaration of Human Rights, 1948.

44. Article 5 of the UDHR states that "no one shall be subjected to torture or to cruel, inhuman or degrading treatment or punishment". Similar words have been used in several other international and regional documents, such as Article 7 of the International Covenant on Civil and Political Rights and Article 5 of the African Charter on Human and Peoples' Rights. Article 3 of the European Convention on Human Rights is worded slightly differently, declaring that 'no one shall be subjected to torture or to inhuman or degrading treatment or punishment', but the omission of 'cruel' is not significant since the term 'inhuman' is apt to cover such cases.
45. G.A. Res. 60/147, U.N. Doc. A/RES/60/147 (Dec. 16, 2005).
46. The right to access to courts is fundamental and uncontroversial; its refusal the most obvious form of denial of justice. Paulsson Jan. 2005. *Denial of Justice in International Law*, UK: Cambridge University Press, p. 134.
47. 1. For instance section 22 of the Nepalese Army Act, 2006 states: Defending the acts performed in the discharge of duties: No case may be filed in any court against a person under the jurisdiction of this Act who commits any act in good faith, in the course of discharging his duties, resulting in the death of or loss suffered by any person. Explanation: For the purpose of this Section, the phrase "committing any act in good faith, in the course of discharging his duties," means acts performed during the performance of duties as well as any action taken for internal security or self-defence, including flag march, patrolling and sentry duty.
    2. It is also necessary that the governments in the South Asian countries have effective control over the armed forces. There must not be a fear that an exhortation to the armed forces to apply IHL or human rights during the conflict will result in, or the threat of military coup. A possible consequence of such fear could be that the State may tolerate what are clear breaches of IHL or human rights carried out by the armed forces and thereby create a feeling of impunity on the part of soldiers concerned.

Bibliography

Administration of Justice, United Nations: Economic and Social Council, E/CN.4/Sub.2/2002/4 dated 9 July 2002.

A Guide to the Legal Revie250w of New Weapons, Means and Methods of Warfare; Measures to Implement Article 36 of Additional Protocol I of 1977, International Committee of the Red Cross, Geneva, January 2006.

Ahmed Samina. 2001. 'Pakistan: Professionalism of an Interventionist Military', in Alagappa Muthiah (ed) *Military Professionalism in Asia*, USA: East-West Centre.

Alagappa Muthiah. 2001. *Coercion and Governance: The Declining Political Role of the Military in Asia*, California: Stanford University Press.

Alley Roderic. 2004. *Internal Conflict and International Community: Wars Without End?* England: Ashgate.

Amos Perlmutter & Valerie Plave Bennett (eds.). 1980. *The Political Influence of the Military*, London: Yale University Press.

Andrews, J.A.1982. *Human Rights in Criminal Procedure: A Comparative Study*, The Hague: Nijhoff.

Arnold Roberta, Military Criminal Procedures and Judicial Guarantees: The Example of Switzerland, *Journal of International Criminal Justice*, 2005, Vol. 3, No. 3, p. 749-777.

Banerjee, Major General Dipankar. 2001. 'India: Military Professionalism of a First-World Army', in Alagappa Muthiah (ed) *Military Professionalism in Asia*, USA: East-West Centre.

Baxi Upendra. 2002. *The Future of Human Rights*, New Delhi: Oxford University Press.

Bekou Olympia and Robert Cryer, The International Criminal Court and Universal Jurisdiction: A Close Encounter, *International and Comparative Law Quarterly*, Vol. 56, January 2007, pp. 49-68.

Bonner David. 1985. *Emergency Powers in Peacetime*, London: Sweet & Maxwell.

Brownlie, Ian. & Guy, S Goodwin-Gill. 2000. *Basic Documents on Human Right.* New York: Oxford University Press.

Burke-White William W. 'Proactive Complementarity: The International Criminal Court and National Courts in the Rome System of International Justice',

Harvard International Law Journal, Vol. 49, No. 1, Winter 2008, p. 53-108.

Carnduff, H.W.C. 1904. *Military and Cantonment law in India.* Calcutta: Lahiri & Company.

Chandran D. Suba and P R Chari. 2010. *Armed Conflicts in South Asia 2009: Continuing Violence, Failing Peace Precess*, New Delhi: Routledge.

Chawla Shalini, 2009. *Pakistan's Military and Its Strategy*, New Delhi: KW Publishers.

Chibber Bharati, 'Political and Military Dimensions of Regional Security: A Study of ASEAN and SAARC', *World Affairs*, Vol. 13 No. 2, (Sep 09) p. 18-38.

Christian Walter, Silja Voneky, Volker Roben and Frank Schorkopf (eds.). 2004. *Terrorism as a Challenge for National and International Law: Security versus Liberty*, Berlin: Springer.

Clode Charles M. 1872. *Administration of Justice Under Military and Martial Law*, London: John Murray.

Cohen Stephen P. 1971. *The Indian Army: Its Contribution to the development of a Nation*, London: University of California Press.

Cohen, Stephen P. 2004. *The Idea of Pakistan*, Washington, DC: Brooking Institute.

Conte Alex. 2004. *Defining Civil and Political Rights: The Jurisprudence of the United Nations Human Rights Committee*, UK: Ashgate.

Damgaard Ciara. 2008. *Individual Criminal responsibility for Core International Crimes*, Berlin: Springer-Verlag.

David Saul. 2009. *The Bengal Army and the Outbreak of the India Mutiny*, New Delhi: Manohar.

Davidson Michael J. 1999. *A Guide to Military criminal Law*, USA: Naval Institute Press.

Detter, I. 2000. *The Law of War*, Cambridge: Cambridge University Press.

Dinstein Yoram. 2004. *The Conduct of Hostilities Under the Law of International Armed Conflict*, Cambridge: Cambridge University Press.

Downey JCT. 1987. *Management in the Armed Forces: An Anatomy of the Military Profession*, Dehradun: EBD Educational Private Limited.

Edmonds M. 1976, 'The Role of armed forces in the maintenance of law and order in Britain: A Discussion' in C.H. Enloe and U. Semin-Panzer (eds.), *The Military, the Police and Domestic Order: British and Third World Experiences*, London: Richardson Institute for Conflict and Peace Research.

Elias, Nobert. 1998. *On Civilization, Power and Knowledge*, Chicago: University of Chicago Press.

Fernandez-Sanchez Pablo Antonio, 2005. *The New Challenges of Humanitarian Law in Armed Conflict*, Martinus Nijhoff.

Finer S.E. 1988. *The Man on Horseback*, London: Printer Publishers.

Fleck Dieter (ed). 2008. *The Handbook of International Humanitarian Law*, Oxford: Oxford University Press.

Gabriel Rachard A. 1981. *Crisis in Command*, New Delhi: Himalayan Books.

Gane Christopher and Mark Mackarel (ed). 1997. *Human Rights and the Administration of Justice: International Instruments*, London: Kluwer Law International.

Gokhle Nitin A. 2009. *Sri Lanka: From War to Peace*, New Delhi: Har-Anand Publications.

Gray Christine. 2004. *International Law and the Use of Force*, 2004, New York: OUP.

Griffin Mary, Ending the impunity of perpetrators of human rights atrocities: A major challenge for international law in the 21st century, *International Review of the Red Cross*, No. 838, 30 June 2000, p. 369-389.

Gross Oren and Fionnuala Ni Aolain. 2006. *Law in Times of Crisis: Emergency Powers in Theory and Practice*, Cambridge University Press.

Handbook on Human Rights and Fundamental Freedoms of Armed Forces Personnel. 2008. Poland: OSCE Office for Democratic Institution and Human Rights (ODIHR).

Hargopal G. and Jagannatham B. 2009. 'Terrorism and Human Rights: Indian Experience with Repressive Laws', *Economic & Political Weekly*, Vol. XLIV No. 38, July 11, 2009, p. 76-85.

Hasan-Askari Rizvi. 2000. *Military, State, and Society in Pakistan*, London: Macmillan.

Haskell John D., The Complicity and Limits of International Law in Armed Conflict Rape, *Boston College Third World Law Journal,* Vol. XXIX, Winter 2009, No. 1, p. 78.

Hassan Tariq, 'Supreme Court of Pakistan: The Case of Missing Persons', *Criterion*, Vol. 4 No. 3, July/September 2009, p.7-27.

House John M. 2008. *Why War? Why an Army?* London: Praeger Security International.

Huntington Samuel P. 1956. "Civilian Control of the Military: A Theoretical Statement." In Heinz Eulau & others (ed.), *Political Behaviour: A Reader in Theory and Research*, Glencoe, Ill.: Free Press.

Hussain Nasser. 2003. *The Jurisprudence of Emergency: Colonialism and the Rule of Law*, The US: The University of Michigan Press.

Janowitz Morris. 1964. *The Military in the Political Development: An essay in Comparative Analysis*, Chicago: The University of Chicago Press.

Jha U. C. 2009. *The Military Justice System in India: An Analysis*, New Delhi: LexisNexis.

Joseph, Sarah. & Schultz, Jenny. 2000. *The International Covenant on Civil and Political Rights*. New York: Oxford University Press.

John Wilson (ed). 2009. *Pakistan: The Struggle Within*, Delhi: Pearson Longman.

Johnson Thomas A (ed.).2007. *National Security Issues in Science, Law and Technology*, London: CRC Press.

Lowther Adam B and Beverly Lindsay. 2009. *Terrorism's Unanswered Questions*, London: Praeger Security International.

Lynch Andrew, Edwina MacDonald and George Williams (eds.). 2007. *Law and Liberty in the War on Terror*, Australia; NSW: The Federal Press.

Mage John, The Nepali Revolution and International Relations, *Economic and Political Weekly*, May 19, 2007, p. 1834-39.

Marston Daniel P. and Chandar S Sundaram. (ed). 2007. *A Military History of India and South Asia, From the East India Company to the Nuclear Era*, London: Praeger Security International.

McCoubrey Hilaire and Nigel D White. 1996. *The Blue Helmets: Legal Regulation of United Nations Military Operations*, USA: Dartmouth.

Mel Neloufer De. 2007. *Militarising Sri Lanka*, New Delhi: Sage.

Mertus Julie A. 2009. *The United Nations and Human Rights: A Guide for a New Era*, UK: Routledge.

Moir Lindsay. 2002. *The Laws of Internal Armed Conflict*, UK: Cambridge University Press.

Mole, Nuala and Catharina Harby. 2006. '*The right to a fair trial, A guide to the implementation of Article 6 of the European Convention on Human Rights*', Published by the Directorate General of Human Rights Council of Europe F-67075, Strasbourg Cedex.

Moskos, C., J.A. Williams, and D. Segal (eds.). 2000. *The Post-modern Military: Armed Forces after the Cold War*, Oxford: Oxford University Press.

Nawaz Shuja. 2008. *Cross Swords: Pakistan, Its Army, and the Wars Within*, Karachi: Oxford University Press.

Nayak Nihar, 'PLA Integration into Nepal Army: Challenges and Prospects', *Strategic Analysis*, Vol. 33, No. 5, September 2009, p. 730-744.

Nesteroy V S and A.D. Pruefert. 2006. *Military Unionism: The Establishment of Professional Organisations/Trade Unions of Servicemen and their Present Position,* Moscow: Ves Mir.

Nolte, G. (ed.), 2003. *European Military Law Systems*, Berlin: De Gruyter Recht.

Noorani A G. 2009. 'Armed Forces (Special Powers) Act: Urgency of Review', *Economic & Political Weekly*, Vol. XLIV No. 34, August 22, 2009, p. 8-11.

Oije P.J.C. Schimmelpenninck van der, International Humanitarian Law from a Field Perspective—Case Study Nepal, *Yearbook of International Humanitarian Law*, Vol. 9, 2006, p. 394-417.

Omar Imtiaz. 2002. *Emergency Powers and the Courts in India and Pakistan*, The Hague: Kluwer Law International.

Perna Laura. 2006. *The Formation of the Treaty Law of Non-International Armed Conflicts*, Leiden: Martinus Nijhoff Publishers.

Rahman Taiabur. 2008. *Parliamentary Control and Government Accountability in South Asia: A Comparative Analysis of Bangladesh, India and Sri Lanka*, London: Routledge.

Rant Judge J.W., 2003, *Court martial, Discipline, and the Criminal Process in the Armed Services*, New York: Oxford University Press.

Renaut Celine, The impact of military disciplinary sanctions on compliance with international humanitarian law, *International Review of the Red Cross*, Vol. 90, No. 870, June 2008, p. 319-326.

Rohl Klaus F. and Stefan Machura (ed.). 1997. *Procedural Justice*. USA: Ashgate.

Rowe Peter. 1987. *Defence: The Legal Implications*, London: Brassey's Defence Publishers.

--------------.2006. *The Impact of Human Rights Law on Armed Forces*, Cambridge: Cambridge University Press 2006.

Roskill, Capt S.W. 1964. *The Art of Leadership*, London: Collins.

Russett Bruce (ed). 2008. *International Security and Conflict*, USA: Ashgate.

Sandoz Y, Swinarski Christophe and Zimmermann Bruno (eds.). 1987. *Commentary on the Additional Protocols of 8 June 1977 to the Geneva Conventions of 12 August 1949*, Geneva: ICRC.

Sano Hans-Otto and Gudmundur Alfredsson (ed). 2002. *Human Rights and Good Governance*. The Hague: Martinus Nijhoff Publishers.

Schiff Rebecca. 2009. *The Military and Domestic Politics: A Concordance Theory of Civil-military Relations*, London: Routledge.

Schlueter, D.A. 2004. *Military Criminal Justice: Practice and Procedure*, Virginia: LexisNexis.

Sepinwall Amy J. 'Failure to Punish: Command Responsibility in Domestic and International Law', *Michigan Journal of International Law*, Vol. 30, No. 2, (2009), p. 255-56.

Sherman Edward F., 'Military Justice Without Military Control', *The Yale Law Journal*, Vol. 82 (1973), p. 1398-1405.

Singh, Brig. K. Kuldip. 1998. *Overcoming Crisis in Leadership: Indian Army,* New Delhi: Manas Publications.

Singh Gopal and Ramesh Chauhan (eds.). 2005. *South Asia Today*, New Delhi: Anamika Publishers.

Singh Nagendra. 1969. *The Theory of Force and Organisation of Defence in Indian Constitutional History: From Earliest Times to 1947*, Bombay: Asia Publishing House.

Sinha Manoj Kumar. 2010. *International Criminal Law and Human Rights*, New Delhi: Manak Publications Pvt. Ltd.

South Asia Defence and Strategic Book, 2009, New Delhi: Pentagon Press.

Sun Tzu, *The Art of War*, London: Ducan Baird Publishers, 2005.

The Manual of Courts-Martial, United States, 2008 Edition.

The Military Balance, 2009, London: Routledge.

Trechsel Stefan. 2005. Human Rights in Criminal Proceedings, New York: Oxford University Press.

Wardlaw Grant. 1989. *Political Terrorism: Theory, Tactics and Counter-measures*, Cambridge: Cambridge University Press.

Wettberg Gregor. 2007. *The International Legality of Self-Defence Against Non-State Actors: State Practice from the UN Charter to the Present*, Berlin: Peter Lang.

What is a fair trial? A Basic Guide to Legal Standards and Practice. 2000. Lawyers Committee for Human Rights, USA: New York. Available at http://www.humanrightsfirst.org/pubs/descriptions/fair_trial.pdf

Wilson John (ed.). 2009. *Pakistan: The Struggle Within*, Delhi: Pearson Longman.

Y Sandoz, Commentary on the Additional Protocols of 8 June 1977 to the Geneva Conventions of 12 August 1949, Geneva: ICRC.

Zappala Salvatore. 2003. *Human Rights in International Criminal Proceedings*, New York: Oxford University Press.

INDEX